Flogging The Field

PHILIP MOSS

ISBN: 978-1-5272-5015-4

Also available from Amazon
as a Kindle eBook

Design, typesetting and cover illustration:
David Siddall Multimedia, Monmouth, UK
www.davidsiddall.com

ACKNOWLEDGMENTS

Jacqui Drakeford; David Siddall; Geraint Lewis; John Pattinson; Gwatkin's Cider; Norfolk Cider; Roger Wilkins Cider; Ray for delivering the same; Raglan Cider Mill; Gray's Cider; Weston's Cider; Thatcher's Cider; Organisers of game and country fairs and point-to-point meetings across the country ... with a few exceptions; The Bar at Living Heritage Shows; The Beer & Cider Tent at Devon County Show; Global Rifle; The French Army for their fabulous 24-hour ration packs; John & Debbie Byfleet, Pigeon Shooter, Starkie's Knife Sharpeners, Kemsdale Outdoors and Muntjac Trading for their generous hospitality over the years; The AA and the RAC without whom the LDV van would have had to have been abandoned on so many occasions; Laird's Sporting; Independent caterers at food vans too numerous to mention, especially those giving discounts to hard-pressed traders; Fortis Clothing; Countryman's Weekly; Margett Leather; Midland Clothing; Muckboots; Pat & Aly; Stolen Tool Company (a.k.a. Swollen Tool Company); Tidepool Wildfowling (or Tadpole Wild Flowers as couriers seem to prefer it); Ken Anderson; Woolsthorpe Wellies; The good folk at BASC, NOBS, Countryside Alliance and The Game & Conservancy Trust; Brian 'Bryn' Brinded for his advice and knowledge ... but not his jokes; Author, Marius Gabriel, for his advice & encouragement; The late Mackerel, the Patterdale Terrier, and finally, of course, the broadcaster and writer, Alan Titchmarsh.

Flogging the field – Dragging a rope between two men across an area of ground to scare rabbits and make them run into a net.

CONTENTS

This book is dedicated to my parents.

1. TIDY

PETER FIGGIS liked things 'tidy'. As a child, he kept his toys in their original wrappers and sorted them into different boxes. His bedroom was neat and orderly and even the bathroom benefitted from his cleansing presence. As Peter grew into adolescence, the trend persisted. His parents worried that, of all of their friends, they were the only ones with a tidy, teenage son. His room was immaculate. He insisted on doing his own washing and ironing. To the delight of his mother, he even took up housework.

To his accountant father's dismay, he carried this out wearing one of his mother's aprons. His father suspected for a time that his son might be turning 'homosexualist', as he termed it. But the apron thing was a one-off. There was no interest in musical theatre, flower-arranging or the poetry of Walt Whitman. Peter turned out to be straight, straighter than his father could possibly imagine.

At seventeen, Peter followed in his father's footsteps by applying his love of tidiness to language and behaviour. He and his father grew closer as they both railed at split infinitives, solecisms and shoddy syntax in newspapers, the inability of BBC presenters to pronounce any Welsh place-name correctly and, above all, numerical inaccuracy.

Maths was Peter's favourite subject at school. He loved its precision, its elegance and its utility. But what he really loved was when it involved money. Like the 'king in his counting house,' the young Peter was never happier than when he was sifting through bills and receipts or sorting out the mess that some lesser mortal had made of his financial affairs. His accountant father's heart swelled with pride and then with the congenital condition that was to take him off shortly after Peter's A Levels. Peter won a scholarship to a new university to study accountancy and financial management.

Removed from the security of his home, Peter, for the first time in his life, found himself alone. His conformist attitude had served him well until this point but, in the university environment, he was something of an innocent. He didn't seem to be 'tuned into the same station' as his peers when it came to language. He didn't seem to be 'a member of the same club' when it came to social activities. Not for Peter, the late-night partying, carousing and general bad behaviour that characterised most student 'nights out'. Not for him the burgling of college wine cellars or the sexual excesses of the accommodation hall. Peter just buckled down and worked.

Getting a first ensured his entrance onto the lower reaches of the greasy pole also known as Her Majesty's Department of Tax & Revenue Affairs. His lack of social skills ensured that the lower reaches were where he languished, incapable of understanding why his excellent work was never recognised or rewarded.

To take his mind off his lack of advancement, Peter started working on some of his own pet projects. It was against department rules to take official documents home with him so he scanned the important documents and worked from those. A trawl through the department's stationery expenses revealed that materials sufficient to run a substantial business were regularly being over-ordered and paid for by the taxpayer. His delighted seniors soon put a stop to the scam. Having saved the department many thousands of pounds, he felt that a level of gratitude or recognition might be in order. But if anything, things got worse. His immediate superior, Derek Erpinshaw, or 'Staples' as the rest of the office called him - for reasons

Peter was never quite able to fathom - became quite frosty. Still, this didn't last. Shortly after Peter's report, Derek was sent 'on a special mission' to the South Atlantic British Territory of Tristan da Cunha to investigate chicken smuggling.

Peter didn't share the general hilarity which greeted news of Erpinshaw's fate. But his colleagues found Peter's new pet project altogether less entertaining. The cost of sending civil servants to conferences in the UK had always fascinated Peter.

How could so much money be spent on a couple of evenings eating and drinking, he wondered. Why did everyone have to stay in hotels? Why couldn't they make do with B&B's or camper vans? Little did he suspect, but his new interest threatened that most sacred of bureaucratic totems: The Office Jolly.

Peter discovered that the issuing of departmental credit cards to those attending tax and revenue conferences had encouraged a level of expenditure which was, at best, lavish, and at worst, uncontrolled. As if the expensive canapés and free champagne at the launch party of Butterville's Purple Tax Handbook were not enough, Peter's colleagues had continued their bacchanal first at The Spreadeagle pub, then at Wheeler's for a lavish seafood supper before settling in the early hours of the following morning at a place called Spearmint Walrus for ... Peter knew not what.

He noted how quickly the room emptied when he asked Boswell from VAT Tribunals whether this place was a restaurant, a pub, or perhaps just a late night coffee bar.

There was a marked change in the way his colleagues treated him. He became even more isolated. Gone were the sniggering little groups which gathered to observe him from the safety of the water-cooler. Gone too were fellow workers from the communal table in the canteen. When Peter sat down, anyone else at the table bolted their food like a Labrador and left. Some were better at this than others. Administrative assistant, Neil Jenkins, tried to swallow a meatball whole and nearly died when it became wedged in his throat. Janice Twinge – from Admin – tried a rather clumsy version of the Heimlich Manoeuvre. This might have saved his life but his neck never the same again.

Isolation turned to enmity when he delivered his conference expense report to his superiors. Peter first realised that something was afoot when he came into the office early one morning to find Frank 'Cardman' Lampwick loitering disconsolately in the office kitchenette. Frank had been relocated to Belfast. Entirely missing the point that this had been as a direct result of his report and trying to be helpful, Peter said, 'you'll be able to organise office parties just like the ones you do here. Although I'm not sure they'll have any coffee bars with weird names like Spearmint Walrus.'

His face void of expression, Frank picked up his mug of coffee and emptied it over Peter's head.

Neil Jenkins, now sporting a shiny, hi-tech neck brace, was told he was to spend some time 'up North' looking into local retail VAT irregularities. Later that afternoon, he heard Jenkins's high-pitched, panicky outburst by the water-cooler: 'Do they even have physiotherapy in Tyneside?'

Dave Rosser, the evil genius behind so many taxpayer-funded office 'nights out', was found behind his desk at the close of the day, sobbing gently. He was to be 'let go' and was crying out of fear rather than regret. Everyone had heard stories about what 'they' do to ex-civil servants when they were let out into the general working population and it wasn't nice. God! They even had to contribute to their own pension!

Peter began to receive the attention he craved. He was even summoned to the Assistant Secretary's office.

'Actually, Figgis,' said Assistant Secretary Terence Dudley-Vaughan, 'we're pretty impressed with your work. It's rare to find someone in the civil service nowadays who gives so liberally of their own time.'

'Just a little recognition would be good, Sir,' responded Peter.

'Well, as I say, your humility has not gone unnoticed but, in the current circumstances, it would be quite difficult to advance you without pointing you out as some sort of 'Assistant Secretary's Pet'. I know it's easy to look at these situations as if it's simply a matter of *quid pro quo* but I'm afraid it's more complicated than that.'

'How is it more complicated?' asked Peter.

'Well, take the extra hours you are obviously putting in. If we paid for those, we would be riding a coach and horses through current overtime agreements and everyone would be jumping on the coach. It would be politically awkward and could risk undermining office morale.'

'Does that mean, then,' said Peter, 'that no matter how hard I work or how many investigations I carry out in my own time, I'll never get recognition for it?'

The Assistant Secretary switched to avuncular mode.

'We all value your input most highly and would hope that this short delay in sorting out your advancement wouldn't deter you from carrying on your excellent work. Do you have a new project in mind?'

'As it happens, I have,' said Peter. 'My investigation into office expenses within the UK was so productive that I thought I might do a similar job on departmental visits abroad.'

The blood drained from the Assistant Secretary's face. He leant forward and stared at Peter.

'You mean you're planning to look into departmental attendance at conferences and other events abroad?'

'Well, not so much planning as actually doing. I've already collated all the records and books I need, it's merely a matter of working through them and applying the same criteria that I used on the earlier report.'

'Good God!' said the Assistant Secretary, in a slightly strangled tone of voice and, after rather too long a pause, 'That's a brilliant idea!'

Peter could not help noticing that his superior had broken into a sweat.

'And your investigation would cover the activities of the senior grades in the department, would it? The number and type of events they attend abroad each year? The people they travel with? The means of travel? Board and lodging, as I believe it's called?'

'Yes,' said Peter. 'That's the sort of thing.'

'Hang on,' said the Assistant Secretary. 'I might have been a little hasty. Perhaps there is a way we could give you the recognition you deserve without all that delay nonsense. Why don't you give me twenty four hours to think things through and come and see me again.'

As soon as Peter had left the room, the Assistant Secretary was dialling a number on his mobile.

'Hello? Maurice is that you? Look, we need to talk... urgently.'

2. OUR BEST AND BRIGHTEST

NAMED after the Tudor statesman and axe-victim, The Cromwell Club had many senior civil servants amongst its members. They not only contributed to but encouraged the club's reputation for Machiavellian conspiracy and ruthless bureaucratic execution. Stalin would have fitted in nicely. The massed ranks of the club membership with civil service experience stretching back nearly three-quarters of a century were more than a match for any difficulty or disaster the tubercular political system of the United Kingdom could cough up.

Permanent Secretary, Maurice Grymm, eased himself into the fireside armchair and gazed across the mahogany expanse of the club's drawing room. Maurice was in his late sixties, a career civil servant, a mandarin at the height of his pin-striped power. He occupied a position of such potency in the administration, he even risked a few eccentricities. One of these was occasionally 'going commando'.

He found the friction of expensive cloth on his free-swinging member rather thrilling, especially when no one knew that he was without underwear. Fun in departmental meetings; immense fun in Cabinet committees surrounded by politicos. Their ignorance of his sartorial minimalism was almost a metaphor for their cluelessness regarding policy and its implementation.

He hadn't expected Terence Dudley-Vaughan's telephone call and was surprised by his insisting on an immediate meeting. No underpants on a rigid and upright office chair was one thing. On the unsupported, soft upholstery of the club armchair, it was entirely another. Now, squirming in discomfort, he risked serious injury at every turn.

Maurice knew that when another Cromwell Club member 'insisted,' he must take notice. Maurice saw Terence, or Terry as he had come to know him, not just as a valuable ally but also as a confidant. Together they were a formidable team.

'Let the little people worry about the politicians', Maurice once advised his subordinate, 'while we get on with the business of government.'

In any other walk of life, such hubris would be seen as eccentric. To senior grade civil servants who had mostly risen by trampling over the upturned faces of their less fortunate colleagues, it just seemed natural.

Maurice's discomfort increased with every second. After a furtive glance around the near empty drawing room, he eased his hand inside the waistband of his trousers to rearrange himself:

'Is everything in order, Sir?' asked a porter.

Maurice withdrew his hand catching a nail as he did so.

'Damn these club servants', he thought, examining his torn nail. 'They creep about like ghosts.'

'Mr. Dudley-Vaughan is here.'

'Thank you,' replied Maurice with a grimace.

'I'm sorry I've kept you waiting, M,' wheezed Terry breathlessly as he seated himself. 'I think we have a problem.'

'Oh really,' responded Maurice, feigning amusement. 'I'm sure it's not as serious as all that. Tell me everything. To know all is to understand all.'

Terry mopped his brow with a handkerchief.

'Good heavens,' said Maurice squirming round in his chair to face Terry, 'I haven't seen you this agitated since we had to hide the overspend on that infernal integrated tax and revenue computer database? If we can make a budget over-run of nine billion pounds disappear overnight without trace, I am sure we can solve whatever it is that's bothering you now.'

'It's about the expenses ...' began Terry.

'The expenses? Is that what all this nonsense is about? I've told you before. You don't have to reimburse the department. For goodness sake, how many times do I have to tell you. It's one of the perks of the job. First-class travel, five-star accommodation, dining of the finest; just accept it as one of the rewards of the weighty responsibility that we shoulder, Terry, my boy. Providing the paperwork has been mis-assigned and lodged in some basement filing cabinet marked 'Beware of the Leopard,' there is no evidence to tie you to any of it, is there?'

Terry looked down at the floor. 'Well, that's the thing.'

'What's the thing?' said Maurice.

'The thing is that someone has found the filing cabinet marked 'Beware of the Leopard' and has been busily drawing down the files.'

Maurice's glowing confidence dimmed a notch.

'Well, so what? No one's going to start an investigation, are they? We agreed. That sort of thing could be shot to bits in sub-committee. It'd never get off the ground.'

'The problem is that Peter Figgis – one of the drones from VAT tribunals – has been using ...'

At this point, Terry cast his eyes around the room to make sure that he would not be overheard. Maurice shifted forward in his chair and immediately regretted it as his left testicle was nearly crushed against the frame of the armchair.

'Using what?' he stage-whispered trying to control the pain, 'A hunting rifle, blackmail, a British Standard Utility Spanner? What has the man Figgis been using? Tell me!'

'He's been using his ... initiative.'

Maurice's shoulders slumped, receiving the news as Superman received a lump of Kryptonite. In the long, sad history of cock-ups, individual initiative was never far away from the root of the problem and Maurice and his peers hated it. 'Well,' said Maurice having considered the matter for a moment, 'I know it's a bit unorthodox but can't you do 'a banker'?'

'I don't think granting him a huge bonus is going to put him off,' replied Terry, surprised.

'Not a bonus, Terry,' drawled Maurice. 'You know, 'Fred the Shred'. Can't you just shred the evidence?'

'Not really, Maurice,' said Terry.

'Why not? You've done it before,' continued Maurice thinking aloud on Terry's past role in defence procurement. 'Don't you remember that assault rifle where none of the bullets would actually fit into the breach? There was mountains of paperwork on that and we made that disappear. The last I heard of it, it was clogging up the water intakes at one of our nuclear reactors. Dangerous? Yes. Legible? No.'

'You see, Maurice,' said Terry, his voice dropping to a barely audible whisper, 'He's already got the paperwork. No one knew what he was up to and he, well, got in beneath the radar.'

The dull ache in Maurice's left testicle was replaced with a tightness around the chest and a distinct feeling of queasiness. One man uses his initiative and civilisation starts to wobble.

'Do you know if he has looked at it yet?' muttered Maurice.

'No,' said Terry, remembering Peter's disarming frankness and openness, 'Actually, I don't think he has.'

'Good!' said Maurice decisively. 'Then what we need is a good old dose of evasive action. Find him something which will fully occupy his tiny mind to its fullest capacity. Something where he can persecute little people to his heart's content. There's nothing these people love more than sticking it to the *plebs sordida*. Give him a fancy, new title ... but no more money or he might get suspicious. Give him a budget which has to be accounted to the last penny. But above all, get him as far away from the records as possible. Out of London is good. Out of the country is even better! Come along now, Terry. There's not a moment to lose.'

Terry gazed in admiration at Maurice. What a bureaucrat! Nothing flustered him. He could play the game long or short and, when the chips were down, 'decisive' was his middle name. Maurice rose from his chair, turned to face the fireplace while his hand again disappeared inside his waistband for a second, and then limped towards the door.

He paused: 'On second thoughts. No, not out of the country. After all, we have to keep a curb on expenses.'

3. OPERATION WILD GOOSE

PETER knocked on the Assistant Secretary's glass office door. 'Enter, Figgis!' shouted Terry from behind his capacious, Bauhaus desk. 'Sit you down. With you in a moment.' He continued signing papers. The office was light and bright being on the top floor of the departmental building.

Terry was no privileged schoolboy. This Assistant Secretary had made his own path to the top. Grammar school in Kent and a double first in Social Sciences from a fashionable ex-Polytechnic, he was well-equipped for survival in the 'dog-eat-dog' world of senior grades.

No Victorian landscapes or Old Masters adorned these office walls. Far too 'establishment' for a man who carefully nurtured his maverick reputation. The fine art department had to dig deep in its vaults to meet his requests. Some near-pornographic sketches by Schiele above the drinks cabinet were in sharp contrast to Belgian artists from the twenties and thirties, most of whom appeared to be named after beers.

There were a couple of abstracts by Hoegaarden, a nude by Duvel, a screen print by Kwak and a dreary, brown landscape by Pemeke. But the office was dominated by a huge technochrome piece which appeared, to Peter at least, to be a portrayal of a man doing something unnatural to a sheep.

Terry flopped himself down opposite Peter on the sofa. He noted Peter's interest in the painting. 'Krapp-Innit.' he said.

Peter was taken aback by such a forthright criticism.

'I don't know, Assistant Secretary. There's no accounting for taste. I suppose that if you don't like it, you could always ask the department ...'

'No,' interjected Terry, 'The painter's name was Constance Krapp-Innit.'

'Oh! I see,' said Peter smiling.

'He was three times unlucky,' said Terry.

'Comedy name from Belgium, a comedy country. And as you see, he couldn't really paint either, so comedy painter.'

Peter felt uncomfortable. He remembered fondly his school trips to Ostend and Bruges and his discovery of the world of real chips, exotic foreign languages and rumours of prostitutes.

'I really don't like it that much,' said Terry, 'but it's colourful and a useful ice-breaker at meetings, as you've just seen. Can you tell what it is?'

'A shepherd with little or no social life?' ventured Peter.

'Oh yes. Very good, Figgis. I see what you're driving at. But no. It's Theseus overcoming the Minotaur. It portrays the triumph of man and reason over the realm of nature, myth and legend ... Still mustn't dawdle.'

Peter noticed his senior's slim-fit shirt buttons take the strain of a girth which had recently hit middle age at ramming speed as he leant forward on the sofa.

'Goodness,' said Terry with a knowing smile. 'You look like you've had a bit of a late night. You've got quite a set of luggage beneath those eyes.'

He continued, affably, 'Look, you don't mind if I call you 'Philip,' do you? It's a bit less formal.'

'But my name's Peter, Assistant Secretary,' replied Peter.

'Of course it is. Of course it is,' said Terry, recovering quickly.

'Just a slip of the old memory there. Peter it is, then. And when we are having these little meetings of ours to discuss matters – you know, just you and me, when there's no one else about – do feel free to call me Terry. It's a bit less of a mouthful than "Assistant Secretary," isn't it?'

Peter nodded and started to relax.

'I was wondering,' said Terry, almost as an afterthought, 'whether you'd made a start on that new project of yours yet?'

'Well, no,' said Peter. 'Not since yesterday. To be frank, Terry, I've spent all night thinking about today's meeting and that opportunity you mentioned.'

'Good, good,' said Terry. 'Of course you have. Promotion is, after all, a very serious matter. It's just that I hate to interrupt a man 'mid-investigation,' as it were. And if I'm perfectly honest here, Peter, you're going to need not just a clear desk but a clear head for this mission we've got lined up for you. Tell me, have you ever heard talk of the rank of Special Investigator in the department?'

Peter thought carefully before replying.

'No, Terry. I haven't.'

'Good, good. Hardly surprising, really, because, you see, it's a secret designation. It comforts me to think that there are still some departmental activities which remain confidential and have yet to be ridden through by the massed ranks of American software engineers, Australian deviants, investigative journalists, whistle-blowers and attractive blonde Russian research assistants ...'

Terry paused for a moment as if he was holding that final image in his mind's eye. For just a second, Peter could have sworn that he heard the Assistant Secretary emit a low, rumbling noise like a contented elephant before he went on.

'But that's all behind me ... us now,' continued Terry. 'This new mission would involve you becoming one of these special agents and operating for an extended period under-cover in the field.'

'So it'll be outdoors, then?' inquired Peter.

Terry stared at him. 'What will?'

'The mission. It'll be in a field? It'll be outdoors then, will it?' said Peter desperately seeking clarification.

Terry cast a sympathetic look in Peter's direction. 'Peter. When I say "in the field", I am referring to "the field of operations" or to make myself entirely clear, the operational parameters pertaining to the mission under discussion. Nod if you understand.'

'Oh,' said Peter, nodding. Once it had been translated into the 'bureaucratic,' there was no margin for misinterpretation.

Peter's mind raced. Was this really happening? Was he about to become some sort of departmental James Bond tracking down tax evaders and prosecuting them to the fullest extent of the law? Granted, 'licensed to fine' sounded less impressive than 'licensed to kill' but it was a start and, what's more, it really did sound like the recognition which he had longed for.

'Your mind is probably racing, isn't it, Peter?' continued Terry. 'You're probably asking yourself if this is really happening. You're probably thinking, "Am I about to embark upon a new career as a tax and revenue version of James Bond". Well, the mission I have in mind for you may not be as dangerous but it is every bit as important. I can tell you, Peter, that the James Bonds of this world would look pretty silly without the financial backing of Her Majesty's Government. And who makes sure that the flow of funds continues into the state coffers?'

His index finger jabbed the air.

'You know it, Peter. I know it. It's The Department.'

Terry adopted his finest Churchillian scowl to add a touch of gravitas to the moment before continuing.

'We don't have a Q department to kit you out with Aston Martins with contraceptive dispensers, watches that contain mints or briefcases which emit clouds of noxious gas and all that sort of rot. But we do have the next best thing. Nigel Grind from Stationery will be along to see you in about an hour armed with something which, since your recent report, has become quite a rarity; a departmental credit card. He will accompany you to the Victoria branch of CostCon where you will be able to purchase most of your requirements. Here's a list.'

Terry thrust a small file across the coffee table towards Peter before adding, 'We may not have a Q but I am pleased to tell you that we do have an M.'

Peter did a double-take. 'What? Like in the Bond films?'

'Well, no. Not really. It's just my little joke. I refer of course to our beloved Principal Secretary, Maurice Grymm; 'M' to his friends, who will be taking a close personal interest in your investigations.'

'How long will I be away for?' asked Peter. 'I have all of that material to get through for the new project.'

'Don't you worry your head about such things. I won't hear of it. Even as we speak, all that tiresome material is being collected from your office by my executive assistants. It'll be all filed away safely, ready for when you return from your mission.'

The office door opened and Mrs. Krasnagorsk, the top floor's tea lady, appeared pushing her trolley.

'Yes, that's no problem, Terry,' responded Peter.

Terry frowned slightly and nodded in the direction of the advancing tea lady.

'I mean. Yes, Assistant Secretary,' Peter corrected himself. Terry beamed his satisfaction.

Peter was surprised by a short but percussive dialogue in Russian which then took place between Terry and Mrs. Krasnagorsk before she set the table for tea.

'Tea and biscuits okay for you?' inquired Terry.

'Yes, that would be nice. Thank you, Assistant Secretary,' replied Peter.

'I'll be mother,' said Terry lifting the teapot.

'Sorry about that but I do like to keep up my Russian. You never know when it might come in handy. Mrs. Krasnagorsk has been with the department for years and speaks perfect English but she humours me with the occasional banter in Boris-speak.'

Peter sipped his tea and munched a mouthful of digestive wondering when Terry would get around to telling him about his new responsibilities.

'In fact,' continued Terry, 'Mrs. Krasnagorsk's daughter, the fragrant Irina, was a research assistant in this very department before she decided to move back to Russia, rather suddenly, actually ... to be closer to her family. She's done very well for herself.'

Terry made the low rumbling noise again. Looking into the middle distance, he lifted the tea cup to his lips but paused at the last moment.

'Mrs. Krasnagorsk tells me that she's now been appointed – or is it elected, I get so confused, nowadays – an MP in Moscow. You wouldn't think she was old enough. Such a lovely ... young ... flexible ... Anyway! Enough of me rambling on. I expect you're keen to hear about the details of your mission.'

'Well, yes. I am, rather.'

Terry leant forward and adopted a more formal manner.

'Peter, as a matter of procedure, I need to ask you a number of important questions. It would be helpful if you gave me clear and concise answers.'

Peter nodded.

'Peter, would you like another biscuit?'

'Yes, please. Is that one of the questions?' replied Peter.

'No, Peter. We haven't started yet.'

Terry was beginning to question the wisdom of unleashing this particular executive officer on an unsuspecting public. Still, the fact that he wasn't the sharpest pencil in the stationery cupboard might have its advantages. He would probably be easier to manipulate once he was in the field. About a year should do it, he thought. Yes, twelve months of living like a gypsy in all sorts of weather, mixing with some pretty uncouth rural types, eating road kill and drinking that infected horse urine which passes for cider 'in the sticks' should take the shine off his enthusiasm. God knows, having to use the portaloos at Cheltenham Festival was enough to make most people lose the will to live.

'Peter, are you a British citizen?'

'Yes, Terry. I am.'

'Peter, are you or have you ever been found guilty of any crime by a British Court?'

'No, Terry. I haven't.'

With each succeeding question, Peter's expectations soared until he felt like he would burst. Finally, Terry got the heart of the matter.

'Peter, do you know what I mean when I say, 'game fair'?

Peter's mind went blank. He had once heard Matthews from Pornography Investigations say that one of his snitches was 'on the game' but wasn't sure if that was the same thing.

'No, Terry. I don't.'

'Game Fairs,' began Terry, 'are outdoor events which take place all over the country. They are attended by people who take part in country sports. You know, hunting, shooting, fishing, the thing with birds and that other thing when they smear grease all over a pig ...'

Terry found himself quickly running out of examples as the closest he had ever got to a country sport was running after and trying to control his black flat-coated retriever, Fenton, when it ran amok in Richmond Deer Park.

He went on, 'They attend these events not just to see demonstrations of rural skills and country craft. They also attend so they can buy all the paraphernalia. This means that these shows have costermongers, traders, stallholders – call them what you will – in attendance. To put it bluntly, Peter – and I know this will come as a shock to you – it has long been the department's view that many of these vendors are trading at or above the VAT threshold. Furthermore, the department suspects that many of these traders are not paying their VAT, preferring to infest that shadowy realm of the commercially undead which we know as 'the cash economy'. Your mission, Peter, is to gather evidence which will enable us to prosecute these foul and ungodly tax-dodgers ...'

Terry paused here to consider whether the term was politically-correct civil service usage before concluding, '... to the fullest extent of the law.'

Peter gaped in disbelief. He knew that the criminal activity of tax evasion was as popular as football. That's why the investigations branch of the department was so big. But the prospect of his going out into the field, into that sort of field, the non-parameter type, filled him with dread.

He tried to interrupt with a question but Terry was on a roll. 'Do you have any idea about the sums we are talking about here, Peter?'

'Well no, Terry,' said Peter trying to recover his wits, 'but I would have thought many tens of thousands ...'

Terry leaned back in his armchair, raised a forefinger and jabbed it upwards, towards the ceiling.

'... hundreds of thousands?' hazarded Peter.

Terry's finger jabbed more urgently.

'Millions?' responded Peter. Terry let out a sigh of exasperation.

'Oh you poor, innocent executive officer. Peter, we are talking tens, possibly hundreds of millions. These people are like the bastard love spawn of Ray Mears and Charles Ponzi, … er ... if one of them were female. They are defrauding the Exchequer of huge amounts of revenue each and every year. It can't go on. Much as we would love to benefit from your investigative skills here at head office, we feel that the department and you, yourself, have a duty to perform. And that duty is to uncover evidence for successful prosecutions. In doing this, you will also receive your just reward of recognition and advancement for a job well done. Do you, Peter, accept your mission as Special Investigator in what we shall call: Operation Wild Goose?'

Terry again adopted his mock Churchillian gurn not so much to add gravitas but to give the whole exercise in the art of corporate arse-saving the look and feel of departmental policy. He needn't have tried so hard. With a fanatical glint in his eye and his voice trembling with emotion, Peter shouted, 'Yes, I do, Terry,' thereby swallowing the hook, the line and the sinker.

4. FIRSTS

FOR Special Investigator Figgis, the next seven days were a blur of activity. He would come to think of it as his 'week of firsts'. On Monday, it was the first time he'd heard of 'special investigators'; it was the first time he'd been called 'Philip'; it was the first time he'd called a senior grade by his first name; it was the first time he'd heard of 'game fairs'; it was the first time he'd ever shared a lift with someone quite as flatulent as Nigel Grind or made purchases at a branch of CostCon using someone else's credit card.

Yet this was only the beginning.

On Tuesday, Nigel Grind collected Peter from his Shepherds Bush flat and took him to another flat in West Ealing where, for the first time, Peter met a real countryman.

Absalom Grind was about the same age as Peter although it was difficult to tell beneath the unkempt hair, the full beard and the tweed hat. Abe, as he was called, was Nigel's cousin. He had been brought up to the city from deepest Somerset where he eked out an existence, so Cousin Nigel said, by 'living off the road'. He'd made one of his rare London appearances to teach Peter the basics of country living. Peter hoped, wrongly, that this experience would be similar to the cosy lifestyle portrayed in the magazine of the same name.

Abe had obviously made an effort to dress up for his city excursion but passing time and a diet of mostly road kill and cider was beginning to tell. He looked as if he'd been poured into his clothes but had forgotten to say 'when'. Bits of him appeared briefly through a bulging shirt-front, cuffs and the no-man's land between shirt and trouser as he moved. Luckily, when indoors, he didn't move much.

Mercifully, Abe's briefings on the theory and practice of country sports were mostly conducted outside during a series of short walks between pubs. Peter was carefully and comprehensively prepared for his rapidly approaching mission.

The 'firsts' continued.

It was the first time he had owned a sleeping bag let alone a 'five seasons' one. This at least ensured that he would not freeze to death sleeping outside in December. It was the first time he had owned a portable gas stove and a mess-tin.

That evening, another first. Peter shared an Indian take-away.

'You'd better go and wait for the delivery man outside,' Nigel told Peter. 'He only rings the doorbell once and, if nobody answers, he buggers off.'

'What happens to the curry?' asked Peter. From the expression on Nigel's face, it was clear that he had never wondered about this.

Peter kicked his heels on the West Ealing pavement as the drizzle turned to rain. Cars, lorries and buses all followed the day, moving slowly westward, their headlights reflected by the wet pavement.

Peter's reverie was disturbed by the arrival of a slight, scowling Chinese man on a noisy scooter wearing an old-fashioned pudding basin crash helmet. The scooter squealed to a halt and the rider hoisted two bags from the insulated box on the vehicle's luggage rack.

'Are you the Indian?' asked Peter. The delivery man stared at him incredulously before shouting back.

'What's wrong with you people? Why everyone asks me the same stupid damn question? Look at me! Do I look like Mahatma Gandhi? Can't you see? I'm Chinese! I'm fucking Chinese!'

His complaint tailed off into aggrieved Cantonese as he thrust the bags into Peter's grip with one hand and snatched the money offered by Peter with the other. He mounted his scooter and faded into the evening traffic.

It was the first time Peter had tasted take-away curry. He liked it and made a mental note to repeat the experience.

On Wednesday, the 'firsts' came thick and fast. It was the first time that Peter had learned how to prepare a rabbit carcass. At the appointed hour, Abe appeared in the kitchenette of the flat and dumped a bag of dead rabbits on the kitchen table saying, 'Before I get a lecture, these are farmed. You got to get 'em in months with no 'R' in them if you want good rabbit. If it'd been in May, I'd have shot them down the road in that field.'

'What field? You mean Ealing Common? I didn't know they had rabbits there,' said Peter.

'Just a few thousand,' replied Abe.

'What would have happened if someone had seen you with a gun on the common?' said Peter.

Abe smiled.

'No one would see me. Not unless I wanted to be seen. Now about these rabbits. First off, you have to press here to empty the bladder.'

Abe went through the motions. Then, without even the formality of a knife, he ripped open the underside of the rabbit carcass and with a practised thumb emptied the intestines, lights and lungs into the rubbish bin. Peter noticed that Abe set the kidneys and testicles to one side. He didn't inquire why but noticed Abe later that morning frying something.

'Be careful you don't nick the guts,' he warned Peter, waving a bloody forefinger. 'It don't smell nice and it spoils the meat.'

With his folding knife he removed the front legs and back feet, broke the neck and cut off the head before working the pelt over the back legs and then with a single effortless motion removed the grey-brown fur from the carcass. After he'd removed the bladder and anus, Abe looked up at Peter, held out the knife and smiled. 'Now it's your turn, boy.'

Peter's proficiency extended to numbers and nothing else. Handing him a knife was like handing a chimp an AK47. There was bound to be a mishap. Lacking the confidence to press his fingers into another animal's flesh, he decided to cut open the underside of the carcass. All went surprisingly well, until he failed to drop all the guts into the bin in one go. The end of the big gut stubbornly refused to separate itself from the carcass. Before Abe could stop him, Peter severed the gut just below the rabbit's appendix to allow the rest of the innards to fall into the plastic bag. The smell was vile.

It was the first time that Peter had ever been sick over a partially prepared rabbit carcass.

By eleven o'clock, Peter felt better and was now being subjected to Abe's explanation of the importance of drinking in game fair culture. Reaching beneath the table, he produced a three-litre plastic container with a hand-printed label which read:

Old Todger.

This year.

Mudgly, Soms.

'This is one of my favourites,' said Abe smacking his lips and producing two pint glasses. The liquid which he poured into each was a light straw colour and had the vaguely cloudy look of serum about it. Peter noticed that stringy structures resembling snot were suspended in the alleged apple-based beverage.

'You'll find this a lot better for you than that gassy piss they serve up in your London pubs.'

It was the first time Peter had ever tasted real cider. True, there were apples there but these were obscured by an alum-like dryness which gave his mouth the same pucker as a camel's arsehole, a chemical after-taste which reminded him of the boat varnish he had sampled at the age of four thinking it was golden syrup and, of course, the bits suspended in the solution which upon closer inspection not only looked like snot but felt like it as they slipped down his throat.

Abe got as far as telling Peter to persevere with cider – as he didn't stand a hope of keeping up with the beer drinkers on the shows – when Peter's breakfast made its second bid for freedom that morning.

Having recovered over a lunch of cheese sandwiches, Peter spent the afternoon being introduced to an astounding array of facts about country sports and activities which he had never suspected even existed. He tentatively tried another glass of cider whilst Abe was holding forth on cider production methods – a matter which was obviously close to his heart. This time, Peter managed to keep it down and, as the conversation progressed, he found that, providing he didn't study the liquid too closely, he quite liked the stuff after all.

Long-netting, falconry, lamping, ferreting, shotgun shooting, rifle shooting, airgun shooting, archery, slingshots were all given brief introductions before Abe turned his attention to dogs. It was about this time that Peter remembered the appearance of the second, or was it the third, plastic bottle of Old Todger. Abe was on a roll as he mapped out the basics about hounds, curre dogs, terriers and long dogs.

By teatime, the monologue turned to wild-fowling. Peter felt warm and relaxed but he had noticed Abe's words were becoming quite slurred. Whether this was the effect of the cider on those parts of Abe's brain responsible for speech or the parts of Peter's brain responsible for comprehension was not entirely clear. Peter, after considering that Abe had been on the Old Todger all day, decided it was the former.

Peter realised he needed to go to the loo. His brain sent out an order to the rest of his body that it should rise from his chair and move towards the bathroom in an orderly manner. Whether his legs were busy texting each other, conversing with other legs or just thinking about scantily clad legs, they didn't receive the message. As the rest of Peter's body launched itself in the direction of the bathroom, the legs were found wanting and, with an air of panic, Peter sank beneath the table landing in a heap on the floor.

'That'll be the cider n'all,' said Abe, sagely.

On Thursday morning, Peter woke up, for first time ever, on the floor. But that was the least of his problems. He was also experiencing his first cider hangover. He lay on his back with a sofa cushion over his face wondering where the pain was coming from. His mouth was unpleasantly dry and tasted like it had been used during the course of the night as an otter's latrine. His tongue wasn't coated; it was fully carpeted. When he felt strong enough to remove the cushion from his face, even the gloomy daylight seared his eyes. It took several minutes for him to regain focus. All the while, a dull throb kept up a regular beat at the back of his skull. He dragged himself into a chair and wondered if the flat was equipped with aspirin.

What on earth was that smell? Apparently, it was him. The foetid stale cider atmosphere confirmed that Old Todger had played its part in the previous evening's activities. Peter looked about him. He counted no less than five empty plastic containers five Old Todger around the room.

It was an overcast day and the curtains were drawn making the living room gloomier still. As Peter reached for a glass of water, he caught a movement out of the corner of his eye.

He froze, his pulse raced and he felt the hairs on his neck stand up. The shape and movement seemed entirely alien. It looked like a large plant had come to life in a corner of the living room and was now moving towards him. He let out a scream and bolted for the door. It was the first time he'd knocked himself out by running into the edge of a door. When he came to, he was lying on the sofa with a cold wet towel over one eye.

'Sorry about that,' said Abe still giggling. 'It was funny until you hit the door. I bought the ghillie suit to show you what camouflage was all about. I didn't realise you'd spook so easily.'

Before this week, Peter had been completely ignorant of the existence of camouflage clothing or its purpose. Now he saw that Abe was wearing a ghillie suit – a sort of huntsman's onesie – comprising long strands of green and brown mottled fabric which, when worn outside, helped the wearer blend in with the undergrowth. When it was worn inside a West London flat, it gave the impression of an aggressive plant-like, alien life-form. The hat had a mesh veil with similar bits of fabric all over it.

'Showing people this is much more effective than just talking about camouflage. People get the idea almost immediately ... well, obviously not you,' added Abe apologetically.

The rest of Peter's day was filled with guns. Starting with rifles and ending with shotguns. Peter had never realised that there were so many different types of and uses for guns. Abe explained the workings of a modern shotgun from the artillery-like splendour of the punt gun down to the rat-stopping .410.

Peter had never suspected that there were so many types of sports involving shotguns. Clay-shooting, skeet-shooting, driven shooting, rough shooting were all new to him. Abe stuffed Peter's mind with more facts and figures about country sports than it was healthy to contain. And all this was before Nigel returned to the flat with important information.

He had finally worked out the details of Peter's cover.

'You are an itinerant belt-maker moving from show to show and living in your van,' said Nigel in serious, hushed tones.

'We chose this because we found very few businesses selling belts at the shows and that belt-making is a relatively simple trade that even you can master in a short time. Abe, here, will show you everything you need to know and leave you with the tools. These are only for show. You won't have to make everything you sell, we'll get a box of stock made up for you every week and discretely delivered to the show ground.'

Before Peter could ask a question he was taken off to a delivery yard in Hammersmith to look at vans.

It was the first time he had been close to a van. It was the first time he had been in a van. It was the first time he had bought a van. The van in question was not a thing of beauty. The ten-year-old LDV Convoy 400 had obviously spent most of its life outside. A thick layer of green lichen covered much of the passenger side and rear doors. Into this, a passing illiterate had scrawled *Allso avalable in wite.* On the driver's side the same illiterate had inscribed:

I wish my gurlfrend woz this durty.

'Perfect!' said Nigel as he pressed nine hundred pounds into the waiting palm of the vendor.

'Couldn't you have got me something a bit better?' whined Peter.

'Absolutely not. A newer or cleaner van would arouse suspicion and probably envy from other traders. If we got you a new vehicle or at least one without as many dents, chances are it'd be nicked within the first month. This is just right. I mean, look at it. No self-respecting tea-leaf is going to risk prison for that, is he?'

'I don't know about that,' said Abe, 'she looks fine to me apart from the exhaust, the crack in the windscreen, the radiator leak, the oil leak and the dodgy brakes. Look 'ere,' he said sarcastically. 'This tyre's got some tread on it! Wouldn't 'ave paid a penny over five hundred if it'd been me.'

'Thank you, Abe. That'll do,' said Nigel, tartly.

With the paperwork completed for the new vehicle the three of them drove off towards Slough to find a market stall.

Turning into a yard, they were confronted by a pile of rusty metal market frame which was easily as tall as a double decker bus. Again, Nigel took the lead in the negotiation which was soon concluded.

'Load it up then,' he said looking at Peter and Abe.

'Well, aren't you going to lend a hand?' asked Peter.

'Certainly not,' replied Nigel tetchily. 'You've got to learn how to handle one of these by yourself. Anyway, I'm allergic to red oxide.'

Peter noticed the pieces that weren't rusty were covered in the matt red paint. He and Abe sorted through the pile selecting enough pieces to make up a ten-foot square market stall. As they loaded this, Peter noticed the red oxide for the rust had stained his palms.

'Couldn't I have a new stand, at least?' he asked Nigel.

'No point,' came the answer. 'They all rust up within a couple of weeks. Pre-rusted looks more authentic. Turn up with a new van and new market stall and you'll stand out like a sore thumb.'

It was getting dark by the time all the equipment had been procured. A box of well-used metal clips was shoved into the back of the van by Abe. Then another of plastic sheeting and canvases which looked like they had seen better days. Abe disappeared into a shed only to reappear a minute later with half a dozen long metal spikes, a sledge hammer and some ratchet straps.

'What are they for?' asked Peter.

'So you, your tent and everything in it doesn't get blown off the face of God's Earth,' replied Abe.

Peter laughed nervously. The others remained silent.

5. MACKEREL

THAT Friday, Peter found himself standing in a rainy, muddy field in The Great British Outdoors. The Funless Hall Country Weekend in deepest Warwickshire was already living up to its name.

It was pitch black and an hour before dawn. The mist had just moved up a gear to fine drizzle. As his eyes adjusted to the dark, he found himself standing in front of a row of trade stands. Through the eye holes of his balaclava, he surveyed the main ring off to the left surrounded by its post and wire fence. Underfoot, the liquid mud from two days of downpour rose through the seams of his shoes to soak his socks and freeze his toes.

Abe had obviously forgotten to mention that chronic trench foot was part of the trading lifestyle and that waterproof footwear would be an essential part of the survival kit.

'Typical,' thought Peter returning to his predicament.

'All my life I've been an indoors, bookworm type and now I'm expected to deal with all this just to get ahead.'

At times like this, he could almost hear his dear father's voice offering its words of advice and encouragement.

'Stop that bloody snivelling and get on wi' it!... and you can take that pinny off 'n all. You look like a right jesse!'

Despite the fact that his father was from Swansea, he affected a Yorkshire accent as he felt it gave him more authority.

Before Peter's morale could continue its toboggan-like descent, something caught his eye.

A small white dot bobbed up and down in the distance. Even when Peter turned to face it, it was difficult to tell how distant it was. What was it? The mystery object moved at speed down the middle of the muddy aisle of tents. Peter squinted to confirm what he was seeing. It appeared to be a white paper bag moving, of its own volition, above the muddy ground, like an out-of-control hovercraft.

Then, Peter heard the rasping, purposeful breath of a dog running at speed. A second later, a black Patterdale terrier sped past him. In its jaws, half a loaf of industrial white bread clad in its plastic cover. The terrier seemed surprised to see him and slid to a halt a safe distance away. The dog dropped its prize on the ground just long enough to look Peter up and down and then cough, unproductively. Taking up the loaf, the terrier continued on its way.

'What that was all about?' thought Peter.

'Outside' had not really been an option when he was growing up. There'd been a garden, yes. But that comprised a small, manicured lawn surrounded by ornamental beds kept rigorously in check by Peter's father and his gardening chum, Mr. West. Together, they shared the same objectives as Agent Orange as they pulled, sprayed, chopped and burnt any plant that dared to set a leaf, root or tendril across the line of its appointed place. Many gardeners admire and love plants and gain enormous pleasure from their study. Messrs. Figgis and West were of the school which believed that nature is a fine and wonderful thing but it must know its place and it must never be given an inch. The garden, like a parterre, was for admiring, not for playing in. The only exception to this rule was when the Figgis & West partnership had one of its regular spats about who got to use the lawnmower.

The sit-upon Suffolk was the mechanical object of both of their desires and both parties would sulk for weeks if they thought that their rights of access had been in any way diminished by the other. The young Peter used these brief periods of unrestricted garden access to discover hornets, wasps, bees, his allergy to larch pollen, the giant hogweed by the compost patch and any other life-form that could sting, harm or poison.

There was little requirement for 'outside' in the laboratorial, metro-sexual world of The Civil Service. 'Outside' was something one passed through to get from one department to another. 'Outside' separated the office from home. He had managed to avoid the arduous team-building weekends in the Brecon Beacons during which small groups of bewildered civil servants would be abandoned in the middle of nowhere and instructed to use their 'skills, judgement and teamwork' to survive outside for 48 hours. It took a near fatal case of hypothermia, the discovery of teeth marks on the shin of an executive assistant and some pretty nasty accusations before this programme was shut down.

Peter knew from television weather forecasters that conditions 'outside' were called 'weather' but this rarely impacted on his work. Occasionally he would get caught in a downpour whilst running for the bus but occasionally too, he would get paid a day's holiday when the department's Health & Safety supremos shut the office because the temperature dropped below freezing and snow and ice became a distinct and, to their mind, deadly possibility.

He trudged back through the Warwickshire mud to the LDV van and clambered up into the driver's seat. His feet were wet and freezing. The rest of him was just wet.

This trip had already confirmed that the van was more slot machine than motor vehicle. As soon as he had coaxed the engine into life at four o'clock that morning, red lights began to appear on the dashboard. The symbols might as well have been ancient hieroglyphs for all the meaning they conveyed to him. One of the red lights disappeared when he released the handbrake. That left only three to decipher. A top-up of oil got rid of another one and tipping some water into the radiator seemed to get rid of the third although it still flickered malevolently when the van was going around sharp right-hand bends. The final warning light remained resolutely 'on'.

Then there were the noises. By the time he had reached Beaconsfield, the van had developed a number of noises. An annoying squeak, similar to that of a sparrow being slowly tortured to death by a cat, made its presence known a few more miles up the M40. A dripping noise came from somewhere inside the vehicle but more than that Peter could not discern without the benefit of daylight. The whole journey in this strange vehicle was quite unnerving and Peter was really beginning to feel the early start by the time he reached his destination. Before stopping the engine he reverted to traditional agricultural methods of vehicle maintenance and gave the offending red warning light a good thump with his fist. The light remained on. The water and oil lights came back on plus a yellow warning light which Peter hadn't seen before.

On the far side of the show ring, a Land Rover pick-up stood with its engine pushing out a trickle of exhaust fumes. Peter flashed his lights but, receiving no response from the other vehicle, he got out of the cab and started to walk anti-clockwise around the main ring. On turning the final corner, he looked back to his starting point. In the gloom, he saw a large figure waving his hands above his head. To Peter's annoyance, the Land Rover beeped twice in recognition and immediately drove off anti-clockwise around the main ring no doubt to offer assistance.

'To Hell with this,' thought Peter as he climbed carefully through the wire fence and marched purposefully across the main ring. As he approached, he heard, above the rising wind and drizzle, what appeared to be an animated discussion between the driver of the Land Rover and the mystery figure. It soon became clear that it was more than that. It was a fully-fledged argument complete with ill-temper and expletives. Before he could get there, he heard the mystery figure shout something at the Land Rover driver and walk off. Peter was only twenty feet away from the rear bumper but that was ten feet too many as the Land Rover moved off again.

'Oy!' he shouted. 'Stop! Stop!' but it was too late. The Land Rover returned to its original vantage point on the other side of the main ring.

But the mystery figure had heard Peter. It stopped in its tracks and wheeled around to face him.

'What?' shouted an angry man clad almost entirely in camouflaged waterproofs. 'But I warn you. It had better be good… because I am in a foul, fucking mood! I can tell you this for nothing. I am not moving my fucking pitch again.'

The trader before Peter was enormous. A goatee beard and two dark eyes glared out from the front of his Elmer Fudd style hunting hat. The camouflage clothing attempted to conceal thirty stone of angry goose-shooter.

'I just wanted to ask that bloke where my pitch is.'

'Who? Numb-nuts in the Land Rover? He couldn't find his own arsehole in a well-lit room with both hands. Follow me, there's a map over here.'

A map had been put up on a board but the plastic sheeting which covered it wasn't exactly rain proof. The camouflaged man produced a Maglite and studied the smeared layout.

'Who are you, then?'

'I'm Peter. Nice to meet you ...'

The camouflaged man turned to Peter.

'It's a game fair, not a fucking cocktail party. What's the name of your business?'

'Oh, it's Belt Up.'

'Well, Peter. It looks like you and me are opposite one another for the duration of this rainfest. I'm Kevin. Kevin Wilcox. Shoot 'em All.'

'Hi,' said Peter awkwardly. 'Who or what are we shooting exactly?'

'No. That's the name of my business. Shoot 'Em All. I sell wild-fowling equipment. What do you sell?'

'Belts ... leather belts,' said Peter trying to sound unrehearsed.

As dawn broke, Peter and Kevin found their pitches and started setting up in the heavy wind. Peter left the LDV lights on so he could see what he was doing. The glow from an open caravan door also shed some light on the proceedings. As he started to unload the iron bars from the back of the van, the smell of frying bacon from next door was particularly enticing. The conversation less so.

'Oh bollocks! You've forgotten t' bread again!' said a man's voice with a heavy Yorkshire accent. 'Every weekend it's the bloody same.'

'No, I haven't,' retorted a female voice in the same patois. 'It's in cool box.'

'No it isn't. I'm looking in there now,' said the man.

'I don't believe it. It's him again. He's been here. He's taken it,' said the woman, her voice breaking into a wail.

'Oh God! Here we go again,' responded the man. 'How many times do I have to hear this? Look, Glenda,' he said, his voice softening a touch. 'You just forgot. It hasn't been stolen. Not even the cheap buggers at these shows'd steal half a loaf. But you have to understand, if there was this dog, like you say, at these shows, he'd have better things to do than steal bread. There is no terrier. It's all in your mind, love.'

'But I've seen him, Reg. I've seen him ...' Her voice tailed off into a sob.

'Course you have, love. Of course, you have. Now, where are your pills.'

The caravan door swung closed. Peter was left to the task in hand.

Setting up the stand had been a lot easier in Slough with Abe's help. Peter now wished that he'd done a full test-run. After what seemed like hours, Peter succeeded in erecting the market-stall frame. As he stepped back to admire his work, the caravan door opened and out stepped the rotund figure of Reg with a rubbish bag in one hand and a roll-up in the other. His Sou'wester hat sat incongruously with the fleece 'Hello Kitty' dressing gown and gum boots which covered the rest of his five-foot four-inch frame.

'Have you got a roof for it, then?' said Peter's new neighbour.

'Yes,' replied Peter. 'Can you give me a hand pulling it over to the top?'

'Not in this weather, mate.' The wind was gathering strength and gusting powerfully.

'You should have put the roof sheet on before you put them legs in,' explained Reg. He drew heavily on the roll-up but seeing that it was soaked through dropped it. 'You see that fellah opposite?' pointing across the aisle.

'Yes,' said Peter, looking at Kevin struggling against the wind to pull the sheet across the top of his stand.

'That's exactly how you don't do it.'

Peter saw the roof canvas opposite fill with wind like a sail, rip itself from Kevin's grasp and lurch, like some alien apparition, into the mud at the centre of the main ring.

'Bollocks!' bellowed Kevin as he climbed into the ring to retrieve the canvas.

'See?' said Reg.

'I see,' said Peter.

'You take out those back legs, get the sheet clamped down nice and tight to the frame and then put the legs in and you won't have that problem,' said Reg.

It was the first time Peter had ever taken advice from a man wearing a 'Hello Kitty' dressing gown but he was pleased he did. Within minutes, his stand had a roof and a rear wall which provided shelter from the wind. He wondered whether now would be an appropriate time to mention to Reg his own dog/bread encounter earlier that morning. But then thought better of it.

'Fuuuuck!'

His thoughts were interrupted by another scream of rage from across the aisle as Kevin repeated his earlier mistake and headed off, for the second time that morning, to the centre of the show ring to retrieve the errant and now muddy canvas.

Making good the stand and dressing it with stock seemed to take forever. Peter was exhausted. Even though it was now daylight, he slumped into his folding chair and fell asleep. A few minutes later, he was nudged awake by Kevin's muddy boot.

'What a bloody performance, eh?' said Kevin handing over a polystyrene cup of tea from the catering van. 'I thought I'd never get that bastard canvas on. Anyhow, are you all set?'

'Yes, I am,' said Peter groggily. 'Thanks for the tea.'

'No problem,' said Kevin. 'Is this your first day trading then?'

'Yes,' said Peter.

'Me, too,' he said.

'That's odd,' said Peter. 'I had you down as a veteran.'

'No, not with all that bollocks with the canvas,' he said, laughing. 'Still, let's hope we make a bit of money today.'

The show opened at nine o' clock. The public proceeded to drift in like a bank of fog. Special Investigator Figgis had begun his mission.

6. GEWGAW

GEWGAW Events was founded by Sir Quentin Massey-Itch in 1950. Twenty years later the company had become Britain's leading organiser of game fairs and country shows. Sir Quentin would have liked to add 'pinko lynchings' to the company's list of activities but was dissuaded by his underlings. A banker by trade, Sir Quentin had made millions in the inter-war period by investing in human misery. He was adept at using his network of 'the great and the good' to ensure that he did so with impunity.

Running boxes of assault rifles to the Republican Government in Barcelona in the Spanish Civil War was a highly productive scam. Sir Quentin's friends and colleagues feared that he might be going 'all leftie' on them before it was reported that the firing pins on the rifles broke as soon as they were fired. Sir Quentin was paid well for duplicity by his Falangist chums and as a sweetener was allowed to keep the huge payment he had received from Republican coffers.

The run-up to World War Two were boom years. They combined two of his favourite pastimes; making easy profits and boring anyone who would listen (normally other bankers) about his powerful contacts. Discovered some years after his death, his draft autobiography entitled *So I Said to Winston* remained unpublished after The Home Office issued a D-Notice. Her Majesty's Government considered the publication of the work 'not conducive to the public good'. The editor who had been working on the text was declared insane shortly afterwards and removed to a Swiss clinic where, after thirteen suicide attempts, he mysteriously died of natural causes.

Greed was Sir Quentin's undoing. At the end of the War, he was persuaded by the conman, Moreton Lugg, to invest heavily in what turned out to be a classic Ponzi scheme. Lugg pretended to have discovered Third Reich gold bullion in sunken vessels. Sir Quentin could barely conceal his glee as what he took to be profits came rolling in. When Lugg finally did a runner, the smile disappeared from Sir Quentin's moustachioed features as quickly as the money from his account.

In Paraguay, two years later there was a news story about a botched murder attempt. The victim turned out to be none other than Lugg. The assassin had at first tried to shoot Lugg with an old assault rifle but, when the firing pin of the weapon broke, he enthusiastically and comprehensively bludgeoned the conman to death instead.

Sir Quentin now sank what remained of his fortune into sizeable country estates and took up an 'embarrassment' of City directorships. His twin children, Croesus and Penelope, were dispatched to boarding schools and emerged both literate and house-trained some years later. They never knew their mother.

'Just as well, really. Daddy's bad enough!' Penelope would say in her matter-of-fact manner. After a stint at MI6, supposedly as a secretary, she saw nothing wrong in settling down to the serious matter of breeding horses.

Her brother, Croesus, was more 'sensitive'. His childhood clumsiness persisted. 'Accident prone' was the kindest description that could be found in his school reports. His early career was patchy. Jobs never seemed to last for more than a matter of weeks. His two years working as an assistant in the pressed flower collection at the Victoria & Albert ended messily, after a small fire. Croesus returned to the country and resumed his natural position of playing second fiddle to his more assertive sister.

Before his death, Sir Quentin's fortune had dwindled to what he referred to as 'small change' thanks to some fashionable new inheritance taxes but it was still a respectable sum. He invited his children to his country seat, Raphe Episcopi Hall, to discuss the family finances. The house was an acquired taste described by Pevsner as:

'An affront to the senses on nearly every level. A ghastly waste of time, effort and materials'.

With his usual acumen, Sir Quentin had made all his estates self-financing. Realising that traditional country fairs were a welcome diversion from the drab life of post-war, austerity Britain, he had taken on ex-POW's on starvation wages to set-up and run a series of entertainments throughout the year at each and every country estate he owned. For this he charged a handsome gate fee. Food and drink sales alone paid the set-up costs. Gewgaw Events Limited was not that limited. Its dozen sites around the country with their associated country and game fairs, driving competitions, horse and dog shows and agricultural events continued to provide a good income for Penelope and Croesus. He revealed to the twins the source of their living as they took tea in the sweltering heat of the Guava Room at Raphe Episcopi.

'As I said to Profumo only the other day, if you want to get on in the world, you've got to know who you're 'getting into bed with'. As you two know everything about each other, there should be no nasty shocks in the future.'

He paused to cram an entire chocolate éclair into his mouth. Penelope looked away. Croesus wanted to but could not. He was transfixed by the sight of cream, chocolate and choux pastry oozing from his father's mouth onto the adjacent moustache. Sir Quentin stooped low and picked up by the scruff of its neck one of the squirming retinue of Jack Russell terriers that usually followed him about the house. The terrier was held in place as it licked the remains of the éclair from around Sir Quentin's moustache before being returned to its yapping mob of fellows.

'You'll have forty-nine percent of the shares in Gewgaw each, of course, so you, Penelope, will have to take time off from watching your nags copulate to make sure that the business prospers and you, Croesus, will have to take time off from whatever it is you do to help out as you can. Understood?'

'Understood, Daddy,' they both intoned dutifully.

'The remaining two per cent will be left to our solicitors, Spon, Charters & Haemorrhage, to ensure that the business is kept on an even keel. As you know, Old Mr. Spon died last year but the new senior partner, Young Mr. Spon, has agreed to take on the task.'

The arrangement with the solicitor made little impression on either of the twins who had both found it nearly impossible to tell the difference between Old and Young Mr. Spon despite the forty-year age gap.

Over the years, it was Penelope who had made the running at Gewgaw Events. Even during her short stint with the Security Services she had made sure that the staff at the family business were well-paid and were motivated by a career path. She oversaw the contracts for maintenance, marquees, utilities for the houses and their grounds. She even oversaw and okay'd the acts that took place in the ring to ensure that each and every event had that 'Gewgaw touch'. Her successful stud business gave her a substantial income in her own right. This she retained. Not quite the marrying kind, a string of schoolgirl crushes and rumours of a later lesbian affair suggested that she might prefer the distaff side of things. She had had the misfortune to inherit her father's looks and, before a stint of laser surgery, his facial hair. Her looks were as striking as her manner was forthright.

Croesus looked after the gardens.

As a stranger to promise from his earliest years, he descended the ladder of education swiftly from the great schools, where he was bullied mercilessly, to the last chance saloon of private tutoring.

'He's an arse and not even a horse's one at that!' his sister would say of him when news of some fresh disaster reached her ears. Croesus took on Raphe Episcopi after

Sir Quentin was taken off by an unexpected tax bill. It soon became clear to Penelope after a mysterious fire in the East Wing that he was incapable of looking after himself let alone the estate without an overseer or 'keeper' as she insisted on calling the role.

Croesus's only interest was in flowers and their preservation by the method of pressing which he had learnt thoroughly before his removal from the V&A. He resented his sister's domineering nature and always had a yearning to redress the balance but not in a way that would give him more power or obligations, just on a personal level.

At first he disliked his overseer, Walton, but this was a passing phase. Walton's bluff American humour combined with old-style Southern manners soon began to meet with Croesus's approval. He was delighted to find that Walton had studied Botany at Don University, allegedly the Harvard of America's southern Mid- West, and had a fund of interesting facts and anecdotes about the plant world which kept him enthralled. Even Penelope felt that Walton was a force for good and that her brother was finally settled in a role where he could do himself and others no harm. Walton came with excellent references and seemed to be living up to them.

But things were not as they seemed. Walton's interest extended beyond the care of his charge. Over time, conversations with Croesus were skewed towards the details and financing of Gewgaw and its events. Gradually, Walton's role as an amanuensis extended deeper and deeper into his charge's ownership of nearly half the country show business which, in recent years, had started to make a loss.

'Of course, it's all Penelope's fault. She's run the thing into the ground,' Croesus would say emphatically without any real understanding. Walton remained silent letting the worm of cynicism burrow deeper into the tiny, shiny lentil of Croesus's brain. Walton always presented the Gewgaw business in a negative or unflattering light to Croesus. He would drop in the occasional fact which would often have to be repeated several times before Croesus took it up and ran with it.

By the time that Penelope realised that her brother was nothing more than a mouthpiece for his 'keeper', the damage had been done and an unbridgeable rift opened up between her and her dim-witted brother. He, under the constant encouragement of Walton, blamed Penelope for the declining performance of Gewgaw. Penelope could see that Walton was making mischief but was not able to prevent her brother doing the American's bidding.

The crisis came to a head when Penelope's beloved stud inexplicably burst into flames one night. The insurance companies squirmed and dragged their feet and, eventually, Penelope received only a fraction of the rebuild and stock cost.

Money, for the first time in their lives, became an issue for the Massey-Itch twins. But it was not just the money. Penelope grieved for the loss of her beautiful horses for several months. When she started to take more of an interest again, she had a nasty shock. Under Walton's guidance, her brother had sought outside finance to shore up Gewgaw's flagging performance.

What she hadn't realised was just how completely Croesus had fallen under the influence of Walton and his real boss, Ieuan Henge. She wasn't prepared for the *fait accompli* which now confronted her; a new regime under which her brother's interest in Gewgaw would be controlled by Henge Enterprises. She was surprised, however, to discover that Young Mr. Spon with his two percent stake in the business had also apparently thrown in his lot with Henge Enterprises.

'I know that Croesus is about as much use as tits on a boar when it comes to running the business,' she said angrily to Young Mr. Spon, 'but surely you must see how important it is that the family retains the controlling interest in the company.'

'Well Penelope, I'm not sure that I do. After all, your absence from the board in recent months has resulted in a sad lack of direction for the business. I firmly believe that a strong connection with Henge Enterprises can only be to the all-round benefit of Gewgaw. Mr. Henge is very well connected and, if his other business interventions are anything to go by, he seems to have something of a Midas touch.'

What Young Mr. Spon had not revealed to Penelope was the deal he had been forced into by Ieuan Henge at a meeting not a week before.

Young Mr. Spon had stood on his honour and flatly rejected Henge's offer of money to secure the takeover of Gewgaw Events. However, this refusal brought about a demonic change. Henge's manner changed from emollient and polite to something altogether more threatening. His icy demeanour seemed to send the ambient temperature of the room into free-fall.

His softly-spoken description of Young Mr. Spon's immediate future included words like 'metal fire escape', 'spinal damage' and 'unimaginable pain'. In addition to the lawyer's natural survival instinct, Young Mr. Spon had been a card-carrying physical coward all his life. He was also blessed with a very vivid imagination that had no difficulty whatsoever conceiving the type of pain that was being discussed here. Henge's description of Young Mr. Spon's medium and long-term future included words like 'wheel chair', 'liquidised food', 'straw', 'letter board' and 'catheter'.

Spon was paid well by Gewgaw. He even quite liked Penelope and her idiot brother. But no sense of duty or loyalty could be worth a future like this. He shook on the deal. As he did so, he noted that Henge's hand was cold and clammy like that of a corpse.

7. TRADERS

THE first day at Funless Hall Game Fair started slowly giving Peter ample opportunity to size up the other traders as potential VAT fraudsters. Across the aisle he could see the owner of Airgun Shooting Stall yawning luxuriously and then scratching his backside in the morning sunshine.

Hardly international tax criminal material, thought Peter. But then what does a VAT-dodging member of society actually look like? Unless you catch them red-handed filling in their real cash-book or, nowadays with their real spreadsheet on a screen, it's difficult.

His thoughts were disturbed by Reg from next door. 'I thought you might like a cup of tea before the show gets going,' he said. 'That's very kind of you,' said Peter.

'When do they start buying?' said Peter.

Reg smiled and shook his head.

'I can see it's your first show. The gates aren't open for another hour and I don't think we're going to be rushed off our feet. But you might get some business just before lunch. We might get a few more in if this sunshine keeps up and dries out the ground for this afternoon.'

Peter returned to his consideration of the traders opposite.

Here's a likely candidate, he thought, looking at the smart American 'Fifth Wheel' trailer across the aisle to his right. The long, space age, aerodynamic shape was a little at odds with the Land Rover pick-up which pulled it. Although Peter noticed that even this was in near perfect condition with gleaming white paintwork on straight, flat panels. On the bed, was a substantial articulated hitch to receive the trailer coupling.

The owner was opening the white canvases to reveal 'Countrymun'; an immaculately presented shop selling dog and kennel equipment. He was accompanied by an odd-looking, shaggy light grey lurcher; odd-looking because he had two light blue eyes. Peter had noticed the dog hanging around an old oak tree just as the sun was coming up that morning. He whistled to attract its attention but received only an imperious look by way of response followed by a belch.

'Pagan! You stay there,' said his owner. 'You'd best leave him alone. He's eaten something from under that old tree and it hasn't agreed with him. He's been rumbling away like an old septic tank all morning.'

Pagan wagged his whip-thin tail weakly and then as if to illustrate his master's point wretched painfully in an effort to regurgitate the offending meal.

'That's a lovely set-up you've got there,' said Peter admiringly.

'It's for sale if you're interested,' said the trader. He finished securing the canvas and walked gingerly across the aisle as if trying not to muddy the soft grass surface.

'I'm Irving,' said the trader extending his hand. 'And this is Pagan.' Pagan again wagged lazily at the sound of his name.

'Yes, if you got a spare fifteen grand, the entire rig can be yours; rebuilt Land Rover and American Fifth Wheel trailer complete with living accommodation and shop all in one handy unit. It's only a year old and is really worth twice that.'

'Then why are you selling it so cheap?' said Peter.

'Well, I've had enough with waiting,' replied Irving shaking his head.

'Waiting for what?'

'The Department of Transport, the police, the DVLA. Where would you like to start? The police keep on stopping me and telling me that the vehicle isn't road legal as it's currently made up. The DVLA disagree and say that it is road legal so the whole matter has been sent to the Department of Transport who are meant to be making a decision about it. But that was twelve months ago, I shouldn't be using it but I have to because I can't earn a living any other way, so here I am. It's a bargain basement price if you don't mind taking on the wonderful world of bureaucracy.'

Irving's explanation was interrupted by the sound of Pagan successfully ridding himself of his problematic meal in two hunched, herculean spasms. It looked like someone had dumped a baby alien right in the entrance to Peter's stall.

'Oh, sorry about that,' said Irving. 'If you hand me over a plastic bag, I'll clear that up for you.'

Peter silently complied. He was grateful for Irving's good manners. The smell of regurgitated rat, or whatever it was, lingered on the stall so Peter stepped into the middle of the aisle to enjoy the weak, February sunlight.

The gates were now open and the public were beginning to wander in. In the distance, shotguns punctuated the birdsong as the clay shoot line received its first customers of the day. Peter turned to look down the aisle bordered by ancient oaks which drew the viewer's eye to the Palladian facade of Funless Hall in the distance. 'Capability Cohen,' the eighteenth century's first and only Jewish landscape architect, had done a wonderful job indeed ... and cheap already, according to the guidebooks. Peter suddenly felt a thrill as if he was in the presence of something special; something that couldn't be repeated. The Great British Outdoors had just claimed another convert.

There was a loud rustling of canvas as Kevin emerged from the front of the Shoot 'Em All stand.

'Finally got everything sorted,' he said confidently. 'I've just got to get rid of the water from this roof. Do you mind giving me a hand?'

'Not at all,' said Peter pleased at how well he was fitting in. He pushed the canvas aside and entered a menagerie of plastic water-fowl decoys. Down one side of the stand, every species was represented from enormous 'magnum' black and white Canada geese ('to help the short-sighted ones', Kevin quipped) right down to the diminutive teal with a few odd ones thrown in. A large pink flamingo decoy occupied one corner.

'You can't shoot flamingos, can you?' asked Peter tentatively, not wanting to give away his newly acquired and eggshell-thin knowledge of wild fowl.

'No, you can't. But I thought if interior decorators and car manufacturers can go for the pink pound then I should give it a go.'

'Hunting pink?' ventured Peter.

'Oh very good,' replied Kevin. 'You could get on to radio with that sort of material ... Russian radio.'

Peter felt a funny sensation run through him. He was chuckling. There hadn't been a great deal of call for that sort of thing in his working life at the Department. It felt good.

'And herons?' said Peter pointing at another life-size decoy. 'Surely you can't shoot them?'

Kevin put down the box he was moving and turned to face Peter.

'You obviously don't get out much, do you, mate? Of course you don't shoot herons. You stick the decoy in your fish pond and move it around every other day to prevent the fuckers from coming in and swallowing two grands worth of your koi carp!'

Peter shut up. Questions about the three large boxes of yellow bath-time ducks and the black plastic crows clearly visible at the back of the stand would just have to wait.

'Let me just shift this last box and I'll show you what we've got to do,' said Kevin.

Peter looked down the chrome grid wall on the other side of the stand. This was hung with foul-weather clothing including huge waders, a small plastic boat, waterproof jackets, a bin with a rotating camouflaged seat on top of it, flotation devices as well as a bright display of what looked like lines and weights, presumably, thought Peter, to hold floating decoys in place in the water. There was also a wall of shiny wooden goose and duck calls looking like the medieval antecedents of the modern kazoo.

'Just look at this,' said Kevin finally. The early morning rain had pooled on top of the tent roof creating a huge bubble of water inside the stand which sagged precariously. It looked a considerable amount of liquid. The roof material was shiny and stretched and looked like it might give way at any moment.

'I think the best way of doing this,' said Kevin, 'is for both of us to see if we can push this bulge up and empty the water over the back and side. What do you think?'

'We can give it a go,' said Peter grabbing a broom.

Kevin needed no such equipment being tall enough and between them they gingerly manoeuvred the bulge towards to edge of the roof and, at the right moment, gave one almighty heave.

Both expected to hear the satisfying sound of a large quantity of water hitting the ground. Instead they heard a high-pitched yell followed by a stream of abuse in a foreign language, 'Madre de Dios! Que el hijo de puta que lo hizo?' (Mother of God! Which son of a bitch did this?)

Kevin looked at Peter and Peter looked back at Kevin.

'That doesn't sound good,' said Kevin. 'I don't know where he's from but he's definitely not happy.'

Kevin opened the back of the tent and they both stepped outside.

'Sorry about that!' said Kevin to a very large, wet, bald-headed man with tattoos and a moustache who was being held back by two colleagues both of whom glowered at Kevin and Peter.

One said to his dripping colleague, 'Pablo! El jefe dijo. Non causan problemas! Dejarlo solo!' (The boss said: Don't cause any problems. Just leave it!)

The dripping man wriggled and squirmed to escape his colleagues but they had a good purchase and held on as if someone's life depended on it. Peter's, as it happened. As they dragged Pablo away, he turned and pointed to Peter and yelled in broken English:

'I see you! You dog! I cut you!'

'Well,' said Kevin. 'Weren't they nice!'

The commotion had attracted a couple of stallholders who were looking on. One of them, called Paul, holding a dead pigeon in his hand, said to Peter, 'You'd better watch yourself, pal, when it gets dark. They're a nasty bunch of buggers, those Mexicans, when you get on the wrong side of them.'

'Mexicans!' chorused Kevin and Peter. 'What are they doing on the game fair circuit?' said Peter.

'They're meant to be running that Taco and Chilli trailer over there,' said Paul inspecting his dead pigeon.

He was joined by his other half, Helen, who added, 'But it's never open. They're something to do with the show organiser as well. They're meant to help set-up apparently but they don't seem to do much, just ponce about telling other people what to do.'

'He's right.' Peter turned as another female voice behind him said, 'At the end of last season, they gave Sid, who used to work with me, a proper going-over. He's so scared of 'em, he won't come back. I'm doing the trailer by myself this year.'

She was medium height and slim build with dark hair and large green eyes. Her jeans and Dubarry boots accentuated a pair of long legs. She had a delicate mole on her right cheek. Peter was struck dumb. Her words of warning seemed to wash over him as another uncharacteristic sensation ran through his body. She's gorgeous, he thought.

'But you've definitely pissed them off so I'd tread carefully if I were you,' she said walking away.

'If you do have any trouble, I'm over there on the Pigeon Destroyer stand. My name's Paul,' said the owner of the dead pigeon.

Peter shook his hand. He then spent the next ten minutes picking off congealed blood and feathers which seemed to have spread everywhere.

He stuck his head under the canvas to get back into the Shoot 'Em All stand. As he did so, his senses were sent reeling by an explosive sound. He staggered forward.

'What do you think of that?'

With his ears still ringing, Peter moved his mouth but a strange sound came out. He cushioned his right ear which had taken most of the impact.

'It's my new jumbo goose caller,' said Kevin apparently unaware that he had deafened Peter. 'It's for you. If you have any trouble with that crowd overnight, give a blast on this. I can see you're a dangerous man to know.'

'But it was your idea!' protested Peter. 'Why didn't the Mexican get angry with you?'

'Now, now,' said Kevin. 'You can't go round blaming your mistakes on other people. Anyway, you'd better get back to your stand, they've unleashed the buying public.'

He was right. Outside Peter could see people moving slowly down the line of stands. It was time to take some money.

8. OLD WINE, NEW BOTTLES

IEUAN HENGE entered his personal secretary roughly from behind much like old-time, Western gunslingers entered a saloon. Believe it or not, this was not the worst job the personal secretary had ever had. Russlana was an attractive, leggy forty-something. Her almond eyes were framed by long black eyelashes. Her hair had seen more colours than Jacob's coat. Her ample breasts were all her own and strangers to the surgeon's knife. She was like what enthusiast vehicle restorers call a 'barn find'. All the basics were there but time had taken its toll of the body work. Like a barn find, she smoked when in action.

She breathed out a cloud of tobacco smoke from her Austrian high tar cigarette as she looked around the expensive and showy rented Mayfair office from her vantage point, bent naked, over the back of a large, black leather Philippe Staerck sofa. All the usual stuff, she thought. Designer this, designer that and a few expensive paintings by people who claim to be artists because they have shared a lift or public urinal with Charles Saatchi. She shifted position disguising the move as a sign of pleasure with a well-practised moan.

Meanwhile, Henge admired his own oiled torso and upper body musculature in the mirrored wall.

'God,' he thought to himself, 'I look bloody superb this morning.'

As his thrusts became more urgent, he waved a hand above his head like a rodeo rider. Catching sight of himself in the mirror behind the large Danish teak desk, he wondered whether he should have bought that Stetson hat he had tried on in Jermyn Street not an hour before.

As matters gathered pace, he raised a foot onto the sofa arm for more purchase but resisted the temptation to give away his American antecedence by shouting 'Yee haa!' as he did so.

Russlana shifted position again, more out of the need for comfort than consideration. She had learnt just to put up with Henge's peremptory sexual demands and get on with it with the minimum of fuss, as she had always done. At this point, her thoughts were almost entirely taken up with the prospect of lunch.

She hailed from a backwater garrison town in Central Asia where her drunkard mother and violent father had taken only the most unhealthy of interests in her. She learnt early to compartmentalise her life in order to survive. A couple of madams found her work in St Petersburg before a lucky break with a wealthy punter took her to Dubai. She liked it and stayed. Her facility with languages and numbers enabled her to move into the legitimate economy becoming a PA with only the occasional relapse. Only if she liked the look of the punter and the money was good. This was how she found Ieuan Henge and combined the two activities. But it wasn't the perfect situation.

Henge had only a smattering of half a dozen languages fluently. In not one of them did he know the word for 'foreplay'. The sex was brutal but the money was excellent and after two years 'on the game' in the Middle East nothing phased her.

Henge finished. He withdrew with all the charm of a retreating Napoleonic Army and headed to the shower.

In preparation for his meeting with Croesus Massey-Itch, Ieuan Henge had spent much of the night memorising the Latin names and details of nearly 200 dried flower exhibits in the V&A. For a normal businessman this would have been unusual behaviour. But Ieuan was anything but a normal businessman. Obsessive attention to detail was his hallmark which enabled him to build his group of off-shore wealth management and finance companies in just a few years.

Based in the Turks and Caicos and other tax havens far from prying eyes, these companies provided him with a front for his anything but normal business activities. Drugs, arms and people-trafficking was where he made his money. The challenge for Henge was how to hide the enormous profits. He paid his consultants generously to find corporate targets which could provide a suitable front, identify the companies' weaknesses and exploit them to enable Henge Enterprises to move in with either a merger or takeover proposal. The offer, once made was rarely refused.

Gewgaw Events Limited had just been given such a 'going over' and, with the help of the spy, Walton, Henge was confident that Croesus Massey-Itch, who was way out of his depth, would hand over his interest in the company. Even if he didn't, Henge considered the sum he had paid the reptilian lawyer Spon as a worthwhile back-up.

The only unknown quantity was the Massey-Itch sister. She must be kept out of matters at all costs. Burning down her stables was meant to keep her out of the game permanently. The thought of all that burning horse flesh gave Henge a warm cuddly feeling inside before he remembered Walton's words of warning.

'She's tough. She'll get over the loss quickly and be back firing on all cylinders. If we want to get hold of Gewgaw Events we'll have to act quickly and decisively.'

Henge stepped out of the shower. He spent five minutes examining his profile with its closely-cropped, dyed fair hair, the pulsating veins in his neck, the shaved, sculpted torso in the flattering light of the wall-sized dressing mirror. Yes, everything was perfect. Well, perfect to a mind that rarely considered anything else but itself, anyway.

His early years, after the mysterious death of both parents, working in the Californian porn industry had left Henge with an ideal. He aspired, even now in his early forties, to the body of a male porn star. No exercise regime was hernia-inducing enough, no non-prescription, steroid-based, body-building was extreme enough in its symptoms to make him waver from his goal. After all, if you're a card-carrying psychopath to start with, no amount of muscle damage or surprise appearances of superfluous nipples on an otherwise perfectly toned buttock is going to put you off. Just chalk it up to the paranoia!

But for Henge, the most important decision of the day was this. To Albert? Or not to Albert?

During the working week, he abstained from wearing the small but satisfyingly weighty gold bar through the tip of his member. But for special parties at weekends, national holidays and for exceptional business occasions, Henge felt that he was incorrectly dressed without his piece of 'man vagazzle'.

The takeover of Gewgaw Events was special enough. Using this long-established company as a front, he would be able to provide his narco-partners with just the sort of services they demanded whilst establishing a firewall for himself by keeping the idiot Croesus, guided by his keeper Walton, at the helm. 'Sweet!' muttered Henge to himself as he gingerly manoeuvred the one-ounce gold Albert into position.

Croesus, Walton and Young Mr. Spon arrived at the V&A fifteen minutes early and made their way directly to the Pressed Flower Gallery. Croesus led the way like an enthusiastic six-year-old pushing open the swing doors and letting out a small cry of wonder as he entered the chamber. To him, no amount of time was ever wasted here in what he regarded as a hallowed sanctum. He nearly ran down the line of glazed, hardwood cabinets like an excited child.

Young Mr. Spon regarded him with a mixture of pity and indifference. How could such an idiot be in charge of Gewgaw Events? How could that same idiot just throw away his heritage, his living and, he considered darkly, possibly his life? This creature Henge was not exactly the patient or understanding type. Young Mr. Spon remembered Henge's threat about eating the rest of the meals in his life 'through a straw' and shivered. Given Croesus's gift for annoying even the most placid of people, things could very easily spiral out of control.

Young Mr. Spon wasn't even on the same page when it came to understanding Croesus's motives. Things like 'heritage' and 'income' were things that poor people worried about. If, like Croesus, you had been well provided for in the cocooned upbringing of the English landed classes, you had always had money; you always had entertainment and if anything even vaguely serious and therefore dull needed doing, you always had staff. To Croesus the situation was based on entirely different factors. A lifetime of gossip, envy, jealousy and petty-minded bitching at family, friends and acquaintances had left him with one analysis of the current situation and one alone. As he had recently confessed to Walton:

'You see, Wally (as he had taken to addressing his keeper), the important thing is that only now am I going to be given responsibilities for which I was ready years ago. I've been held back by Old Bag Features (his nick-name for Penelope) and those nasty, horrid lawyers for far too long. I think that you and I and your Mr. Henge will make a much better job of running things.'

Walton smiled. He realised early that sibling rivalry was the key to gaining his objective and once that was understood, the deal was, as his countrymen said, 'like taking candy from a baby'. If Croesus ever veered from the required line or became troublesome, all Walton had to do was mention the possible return of Penelope and this was enough to bring his witless charge to heel. Walton realised that Croesus would have accepted an investment deal from The Devil himself if it meant keeping his older sister and her tart summations of her little brother's inadequacies at bay.

'Croesus? Is that you?'

Henge's mid-Atlantic tones emerged from a warm, dark and distant corner of the Pressed Flower Gallery.

‘It is!’ responded Croesus. ‘Is that you, Ieuan?’

‘It is, damn it. It is!’ said Henge with his mock-Texan bonhomie fully deployed. He stepped forward into the light of the main gallery.

‘It’s an honour to meet you,’ said Croesus.

‘I know it is,’ replied Henge through his fixed smile. He took and shook Croesus’s delicate extended hand. Croesus had not been expecting something as cold and clammy but soon recovered.

‘You must call me Croesus.’

‘I am already,’ said Henge. ‘Hell, it’s just like we’re old friends like me and old Spon here.’

Henge threw an arm around Young Mr. Spon’s rounded shoulders and squeezed. It was all a bit too much for Spon’s system. He emitted a high-pitched squeak followed by a short baritone fart of surprise. Walton and Croesus looked at Young Mr. Spon. His face was red. His mouth was open but words came there none.

‘You see the type of idiot I’ve had to work with over the years,’ said Croesus.

‘Barely house-trained! It’ll be wonderful to work with someone like yourself who has real business skills, Ieuan. But there is just one thing ...’

Henge’s smile diminished a notch as he cast a sideways stare at Walton who looked concerned. He knew that Henge was not keen on hitches especially of the last-minute variety.

‘I thought we’d been through everything already, Croesus,’ Walton muttered. ‘Surely there can’t be anything else you’re unclear about?’

‘Well, Wally,’ came the answer, ‘it’s just the small matter of the cheque. The investment, you know. When do I get it?’

‘Of course,’ said Henge. ‘That’s very naughty of me, isn’t it? I had it here in my pocket all the time. Here it is.’

Croesus snatched the proffered envelope and with one easy motion extracted the cheque within.

‘Well, that all seems fine,’ he said.

Walton could feel his pulse come back to normal as Henge, once again smiling, placed a fraternal arm around

Croesus's shoulder and diverted his victim's attention to the cabinets of pressed flowers surrounding them.

'Of course, pressing flowers was my passion as a boy ...' said Henge.

'Really?' said Croesus being drawn further into the trap. 'How extraordinary! It was mine too!'

'Look over here,' said Henge playing his role to the full. 'Have you ever seen a better example of *artemisia absinthium* or this fabulous *rheum raponticum*?'

'Wonderful, wonderful,' gushed Croesus.

Thank God for that, thought Walton. My work here is done.

He shoved Young Mr. Spon towards the exit.

'And for God's sake, Spon. Go to the john before you turn up to your next meeting with your new boss. He isn't always that forgiving and he generally hates any reference to bodily functions.'

'Any in particular?' asked Young Mr. Spon daringly.

'Yes' said Walton. 'Bodily functions which aren't his. Now let's get to work. It's showtime.'

'It all seems to be going remarkably well,' thought Walton congratulating himself as he drove back to Raphe Episcopi. 'The shows will act as handy distribution points across the country for our products. The cover is excellent as you could hide anything amidst the chaos of a country show without anyone suspecting. Now all we have to sort out is the investors and we are 'good to go'.

He was surprised at how easy it was to persuade Croesus to have a shooting party at Raphe Episcopi even if it was out-of-season. The Massey-Itches had never fretted over such details. Over the decades, the estate had become knee-deep with pheasant. This was partly due to the assistant gamekeeper, Stanley Forage, and his interest in antiquated and, for the most part highly illegal, traps which had cut a swathe through the local predator population. In his later years, Sir Quentin had lost his love of shooting things and, more recently, Croesus's aversion to any loud noises had resulted in shooting days being few and far between. But the cover and grounds had been kept in tip-top condition.

'We should have a shooting party, Croesus,' he suggested. 'That way, you can meet all of Ieuan's friends and investors in one go. It'll be like a big series of house parties with everyone dressed up for the occasion.'

Little did Walton suspect but he had inadvertently used one of Croesus's trigger phrases by mentioning the words 'dressed up'. Instantly, Croesus was reminded of his childhood love of fancy-dress parties. Frankly, he didn't much care what people dressed up as, providing they dressed up. If they wanted to relax between set-piece meals by murdering a few hundred pheasant, that was fine by him just as long as the 'dressing up' fun continued.

The shooting party was confirmed then and there.

9. FUNLESS

MUCH to his surprise, Peter's first day of trading at Funless Hall Game Fair had improved from a difficult start. It took him some time to sort out his sales patter. As a tax inspector, he was only used to dealing with people via email, telephone or, preferably, letter. The Department favoured the 'professional distance' approach as it prevented the public from having the opportunity to plead or beg which, as the findings of several expensive internal reports showed, upset the staff.

Peter, for the first time in his working life, came face-to-face with the great British consumer. Belt Up had been open for business nearly an hour before the first punters wandered into view.

'Belts' droned a middle-aged couple almost in unison as their eyes fell on Peter's wares. 'And probably the finest belts available on the show,' responded Peter cheerily.

Both looked at him with undisguised amazement. It looked as if they had merely thought 'belts' and never actually meant to say the word. They were now confronted with a salesman who was not only selling belts but who could read minds as well. After a moment's silence, the woman – rather incongruously – said 'No' and they both continued on their way.

A family advanced down the line of tents with noisy children running out in front like cavalry pickets.

'Cor! Look Dad! Belts!' said the youngest child more

noticeable for the dabs of iodine on his neck and face than for his stature.

'Bostin! Just the thing,' responded the father in a rich Black Country accent. He was a large man who seemed to be losing a battle with gravity for the possession of his jeans. ''Ow much are they, mate?'

Peter floundered. 'What, for a belt?'

'No mate, for a massage and happy ending,' said the man.

'Ron!' said his wife man-handling the pushchair through the mud, '... not in front of the kids. And pull those bloody jeans up.'

'What do you think? Yes, a belt. That belt there. Have you got one of those to go round me?'

'Fat chance,' muttered an attendant teenager whose intervention was cut short with a clip around the ear from his father.

'I'm pretty sure we have,' said Peter. 'Let me just have a look.'

He lifted up a coil of belts which Abe had made for him and looked at the sizing imprint behind each buckle.

'Before you do that,' said the man. 'How much are they? A black one, mate.'

'They're thirty quid,' said Peter.

'Thirty quid? Do you have anything a bit cheaper? It's a bit more than I wanted to spend.'

Peter replaced the coil and picked up another coil of belts he had made. They didn't look as good as Abe's but this was reflected in the price.

'You can have one of these for twenty ... if I've got the right size.'

Peter handed over the longest belt in the coil.

'That's more like it, mate. Let's 'ave a go with one of those then.'

Hoisting his trousers up to around where his waist had once been, the customer, helped by his family, threaded the belt through the jean loops and secured the buckle. It was a perfect fit.

'I'll take that, then,' said the customer. 'June ... Pay the man.'

June's hand dived into the bag suspended from the handlebar of the pushchair and brought out a purse from which she extracted two ten-pound notes which she handed to Peter. The man hoisted his jeans up for a final time before the group moved on with the kids running ahead as before.

Peter looked at the two curled and creased tenners in his hand and felt a new sensation wash over him. Short of Christmases and birthdays, he had never been given cash in his hand. Even though it was a sale, it felt more like a present. It was a strange feeling of satisfaction unlike any sensation he had encountered before. It was as if he was looking at money for the first time. He was used to dealing with vast amounts of money in his job but these were just rows and rows of figures on a computer screen. There was no personal connection with it. But taking two tenners from a customer, who was happy to pay for the goods, which had been offered without the use of threatening letters, fines or an early morning raid by The Knock, was something new and pleasurable to him.

Peter's larger sizes of belt were popular and he was struck by how embarrassed customers were by their weight, asking, almost apologetically, if he had their size. Some were a bit more brazen.

'Do you do a belt like that in Fat Bastard size?' asked one large potential buyer. Delighted to find a belt that fitted, he immediately bought three.

'That's me sorted for the rest of my natural,' he commented to his companion as they walked away.

Most women customers were more covert about their purchasing.

'I've just parked himself and the kids at the beer tent and wanted to come back to get him a belt because I can never find a decent one in his size and he's holding his drawers up with baler twine ... even when he goes to his lodge meetings.'

Peter savoured the masonic image of trowel, set square, apron and baler twine as he bagged the purchase.

Some shoppers nearly bought but failed to commit at the last moment, using an array of awkward excuses to escape parting with their cash.

'That's just what I'm looking for,' said one tweed-suited man. 'Is it available on your website?'

'Yes, it is. But you could buy it here, now, and avoid the postage cost.'

'Oh, so it would be more expensive then?'

'No. It wouldn't,' Peter replied. 'But you'd have to pay postage.'

'Oh well. I'm not quite sure about that.'

Suit yourself, thought Peter. By early afternoon, he already appreciated the decisive buyers and found happily that they were the majority at this particular show. He only had one 'finesser'.

'That's just what I'm looking for. But do you have it in a slightly lighter shade of brown,' said the well-spoken woman in the waxed hat with a pheasant feather.

'Well, yes. Actually, I do,' responded Peter reaching into a coil to produce the required belt.

'Oh,' said the customer apparently put out that her challenge was so easily met.

'Well that's a little lighter than I wanted do you have something between the two?'

'I do,' responded Peter remembering that Abe had carefully explained that one batch of leather had been made in nearly every shade between dark havana and chestnut. He spread out a choice of six different shades across the counter from which the customer could choose.

A look of panic came over her face as she about-heeled and walked off.

'You get a lot of them time-wasters,' said Reg arriving from next door with another welcome cup of tea. 'Twenty minutes of blather and no sale to show for it at the end. They drive me nuts.'

Just as Peter was finishing his tea a couple in matching 'his and hers' tweed shooting jackets arrived on the stand with the largest bull mastiff that Peter had ever seen. In fact, it was the first bull mastiff he had ever seen.

‘These belts then?’ sneered the man. The mastiff stuck its muzzle over the counter and gently oozed snot and saliva over the coils on the table.

‘Could I ask you to pull your dog back? It’s dribbling on my stock,’ asked Peter.

‘Oooh!’ said the women sarcastically, ‘Aren’t we all lardy-da! They’re only belts and not much cop at that.’

Peter broke through his natural reserve and actively started disliking these people. As he tried to think of a suitable response, he saw to his horror the mastiff move into position, raise its leg and pee all over the front of the counter. The arc of urine shot up and over the first couple of rows of belt coils.

‘For God’s sake!’ said Peter, ‘Pull him away!’

‘Why?’ said the man making little or no effort to move his dog.

‘It’s only a bit of pee and he hasn’t finished yet. You shouldn’t come to game fairs if a bit of pee bothers you.’

Peter was trembling as the couple walked away, outraged by their lack of consideration. He had never had to deal with people like this and their leaky pets. At this early stage in his selling career, he certainly had no clear idea of how to deal with the situation. It was just before the show shut for the day that he received the instruction he needed.

Standing in front of his stall, he placed his hands behind his head for a long, luxurious stretch. He noticed Paul, the dead pigeon man, had a bad infestation of what Reg called ‘space invaders’. Two friends who had met on the Pigeon Destroyer stand and had decided to spend half an hour catching up on old times whilst they, together with their dogs, prevented any buying customers from getting onto the stand.

‘You watch this, son,’ said Reg from next door. ‘You’ll learn something useful now.’

Peter watched as Paul stood in front of his counter, arms folded, looking not at the men now deep in discussion but their dogs. The spaniel and the terrier had long ago expended the entertainment value of sniffing each other's privates and were now listlessly waiting for their owners to shut up and move on. Minutes passed. Paul yawned and scratched his nose but maintained his close surveillance of the dogs, the spaniel in particular. This had now moved to the counter and was sniffing at the green cloth covering it. Paul stood stock still like a snake coiled and ready to strike. Up went the spaniel's rear leg to pee down the green cloth but before it could deliver its load, Paul's foot hooked the dog's raised leg and carried on the upward arc. The shocked spaniel fell over with a shriek more of surprise than pain. The owner was none the wiser when he turned to face Paul who now looked puzzled. Shrugging his shoulders, he said:

'What are they like? Eh? Aren't they funny?'

The dog got up, shook itself and skulked off with the owner audibly giving it a dressing down.

'Spaniel-tipping,' said Reg. 'He nearly invented the sport. He hasn't had a dog pee on his stand for nearly four years. He's a bugger at it.'

Half an hour later, Peter had cleaned his stand and stock and noticed that the other stalls were beginning to shut for the day. He glanced across the aisle at Kevin who was counting his takings. Along wandered the couple who had visited Peter's stand at the beginning of the day.

'Decoys,' they intoned as they looked inside the Shoot 'Em All stand. The woman pointed at the grid-wall adding 'Goose calls'.

Kevin turned to them and in a perfect mimic of Darth Vader responded: 'Your powers of observation serve you well, young Jedi!'

There was a pause while the couple stared expressionless at Kevin before the man – this time – said 'No' and they ambled off.

'What do people do in the evening here?' Peter asked Reg.

'Well, I'm cooking this evening for 'er indoors but there's a food tent which does food and a bar with decent beer and cider. There's also a space heater.'

The very word 'cider' filled Peter with dread. He remembered the effects of his last foray into the sordid world of cider drinking with Abe. The sun was sinking and the wind was beginning to pick up. There was nothing for it.

Peter and Kevin entered the bar. It was a traditional show-tent made of faded canvas with what looked like two ships' masts providing support for the roof. A wooden bar had been set up with barrels and a row of optics behind it. White plastic tables and chairs in various stages of decay were dotted around on the flattened grass floor. Most were occupied. The bar had obviously had a successful day.

In one corner, a large corn dryer had been set up to provide a steady, desiccating stream of hot air for the huddled patrons. At the other corner lay an unconscious bearded man of some girth whose head seemed glued to the ground by a pool of congealed vomit – hopefully his own. No one seemed bothered that he had fought the fight with Rat's Scrotum Draft Scrumpy and lost. No one seemed that bothered if he spent the night there.

'What do you want?' asked Kevin.

'I'll have a lager shandy,' said Peter, mindful of his recent experimentation with cider.

'No you won't,' said Kevin curtly. 'You'll have proper drink if I'm buying.'

'What can I get you?' said the heavily tattooed barman Peter had never met someone who had facial tattoos until this moment. An oriental dragon design swirled up the left side of the barman's neck culminating in the Chinese character for 'soup' on his left cheek. This was the only Chinese character Peter recognised. He always ordered soup in Chinese restaurants and had taken the precaution of learning the character so he could point it out on a menu.

The barman, sensing Peter's interest, said, 'It means *courage* in Chinese.'

'Oh,' said Peter deciding that silence was the best course of action.

'I'll have a pint of whatever that cider is in the barrel and Little Lord Fauntleroy here will have ...'

'Lager, please,' said Peter, 'a half of lager.'

'Sorry. The lager's finished; so is the bitter and so is ...' he nodded at the body on the floor,'... the scrumpy.'

'Two pints of cider, then,' said Kevin completing the order. Peter braced himself for his second 'man versus cider' experience as he and Kevin found seats within spitting distance of the corn dryer.

As they sipped their drinks, more and more people arrived but the temperature remained hovering around zero. Peter recognised some punters and other stall holders. In the dark space behind the corn dryer, he also recognised the Mexicans huddled around a table drinking corona beer and shots of mescal. Peter noted gratefully that they were keeping themselves to themselves. He quite liked the cider and, as the alcohol began to enter his bloodstream, he started to relax. The first pint slipped down easily and soon he had bought a second pint for him and Kevin.

'Where are the loos?' he asked Kevin as he placed the plastic glasses on the wobbly plastic table.

'Over that way,' said Kevin. 'Towards the car park. I'll look after your drink.'

It was getting dark when Peter made it over the muddy ground to the row of evil-smelling, blue plastic portaloos. As the horizon began to darken, Peter saw three familiar shapes gathered around a Subaru estate in the car park. It was the unpleasant tweed-clad couple and their bull mastiff. To secure the mastiff in the dog cage, they'd left the tailgate and rear doors of the car open.

'I'm just going to the loo before we set off,' said the man making towards the line of portaloos.

'Alright. I'm just here chatting to Sandra,' said his partner.

'That's right,' thought Peter, 'you chat away. It's payback time'.

Despite its size, appearance and lack of bladder control, the bull mastiff was a friendly soul and even wagged gently at Peter as he approached the open door of the vehicle. The dog was more puzzled than bothered by this strange visitor. A nervous whine escaped its drooping jowls as it saw the visitor unzip his trousers and pee all over the rear seat of the car. The dog only emitted a tentative bark when Peter had finished and zipped up his trousers. What Peter hadn't expected was the early return of the driver from the portaloos.

'Oy! You! What the bloody hell do you think you're ...' shouted the driver still some way off.

'It's just a bit of pee!' shouted Peter triumphantly. 'You shouldn't come to game fairs if it bothers you.'

With that, Peter ran as fast as his legs would carry him into the shadows between the rows of vehicles leaving the tweed-clad couple to rant by their soiled Subaru. Peter took a circuitous route back to the bar to make sure that he wasn't seen by his victims and returned to his seat flushed with success to enjoy his waiting pint. He found his pint and its twin sitting waiting for him on the table top.

'I got bored of waiting so I got another one in,' said Kevin.

As they finished their third pint, a gap opened up on the table nearest the corn dryer.

'Come on,' said Kevin, 'I'm bloody freezing.'

They occupied the free seats with a cursory greeting to the drinkers on either side.

'Fucking tastes like varnish, this stuff,' said Kevin chucking his empty plastic glass towards the dustbin. 'I'm going to get a scotch. Do you want one?'

'No, I'm fine,' said Peter. His act of revenge had put him in a sociable mood so he struck up a conversation with a taciturn, stubbly man to his left.

'Are you trading here?' shouted Peter above the roar of the corn dryer.

'No. I'm working on the fun fair ... on the dodgems.'

'Oh,' yelled Peter. 'How long have you been doing that?'

'About six months. My name's Frank,' responded the man extending his hand.

'What did you do before that?' asked Peter.

'I was inside,' said Frank.

'What working inside?' said Peter. The cider and the roar of the corn dryer had conspired to addle his brain.

'No, mate,' said Frank, 'I was in prison.'

'In prism?' yelled Peter. 'What's that? I've never heard...'

'No,' said Frank turning to face Peter as if to remove any barrier to understanding. 'In prison.'

'Oh,' said Peter glumly. 'Sorry about that. It's a bit noisy here so ...'

'Don't worry,' said Frank, 'that's alright.'

'Well, if I stop asking questions now,' thought Peter, 'it'll just seem plain rude or stand-offish. But if I carry on this conversation, on the other hand, he might get angry about me sticking my nose into his business. Oh what the hell!'

'How long were you in for?'

'Fourteen years,' said Frank. Even now a small panicky voice inside Peter's head began to plead 'Be quiet! For God's sake.' But it was too late. The alcohol level reached that part of the scale which read 'Talk yourself into trouble' and Peter found his mouth saying: 'Christ! What did you do? Kill someone!'

'Er... yeah, actually,' said Frank beginning to shift uncomfortably in his seat.

'For the love of God!' screamed the panicky voice inside Peter's head, 'Just zip it! Shut the fuck up!'

But Peter's mouth would not be silenced: 'Was it anyone you knew?'

Frank shot a stare at Peter. He couldn't decide if he was mentally challenged or pissed. Before he could decide, a tweed-clad arm appeared from nowhere, fixed itself around Peter's neck dragging him backwards out his seat in a swirl of cider.

'There you are, you little fucker!'

The owner of the mastiff and a soiled Subaru had finally tracked down his quarry. He was about to bring his fist down onto Peter's sprawling form when Frank stood up revealing a frame honed by years of dedicated gym work-out in an assortment of Her Majesty's prisons. Frank seized Peter's assailant delicately by the throat and hoisted him off the ground.

'Do you know how rude it is to interrupt a conversation?' said Frank.

All the tweed clad man could do by way of reply was a purple-faced gasp.

'I don't particularly mind if you want to kick the crap out of him as he's a nosy little sod. But you have to wait until we've finished our conversation. Savvy?'

The tweed clad man with the purple face nodded and broke wind by way of reply.

'Now sod off before I do something you'll regret.'

Tweed-clad man beat a hasty retreat to the exit and disappeared into the night beyond.

'Now,' said Frank turning back to Peter. 'Where were we?'

Kevin arrived just in time to prevent Peter from making matters worse.

'I'm sorry,' he said jerking Peter to his feet. 'He's pissed again. He just can't hold his cider, this one. He'll be bloody useless all day tomorrow as well. I hope he wasn't bothering you.'

Kevin frog-marched Peter out of the exit.

'Let go of me!' Peter remonstrated. 'I was the victim there not the trouble-maker,' he added, aggrieved.

'That's as may be but all that kerfuffle with the bloke in the tweed jacket had started to attract attention from the Mexicans ... and we don't want that, do we?'

'Oh, no. We most certainly do not.'

'Anyway, why did the guy in the tweed jacket have a go at you?'

Peter told him about the bull mastiff and his moment of sweet revenge. Kevin chuckled.

'You're a dangerous man to hang about with, aren't you, Belt Man.'

Peter agreed weakly. It had been a long and eventful day and even though it was now pitch black, it was only half past eight and Peter was ready for bed.

Inside the tent, the Mexicans had been attracted by the attack on Peter and its speedy resolution.

'Isn't that the hombre who soaked Pablo this morning?' asked Juan.

'I think joo are right. But it's important that we don't cause problems here for the boss. Keep a low profile. For God's sake, try and keep Pablo away from this gringo or things will get difficult around here,' said Jesus.

As Juan sat his substantial rear end back into the plastic chair to resume drinking mescal and bitching about the weather, he and his colleagues failed to notice a small clear plastic sachet work itself free of his rear pocket and onto the grass below. In fact, no human eye in the bar saw this unfortunate event. But not all eyes in the bar that evening were human. Behind the folded canvases of the entrance lay a small dark form, ever alert for opportunities.

Stealthily, Mackerel the Patterdale Terrier crawled slowly around the edge of the bar tent being careful to stick to the shadows. As he approached the Mexicans' table he edged forward and delicately picked up the sachet of white powder between his front teeth before withdrawing with his prize to the safety of the shadows. There was no other entertainment available; no larger dogs to bark at; no smaller dogs to menace or sexually abuse; no children to beg or steal food from. So Mackerel settled himself down behind the pile of canvases to chew through the sachet and find out if the contents were edible.

10. WILDLIFE

'WE estimate that the creature – whatever it was – left the tent about here,' said PC Wilson sticking his muddy boot through the dinner-plate-sized hole in the canvas wall at ground level of the beer tent which had appeared overnight. 'Even allowing for the fact that the canvas was old and weak, it seems obvious to me that it was moving at quite some speed.'

'So you don't think it was thieves then?' said the tattooed barman. 'What about all those packets of nuts and crisps which have just been ripped open and left?'

'No,' said the constable decisively. 'It was definitely a wild animal of some sort about the size of a ...'

He hesitated as if trying to remember something and then finished the sentence, '... a wolverine.'

'Wolverine?' said the barman with the soup tattoo on his neck. 'I don't think we have any of them in Warwickshire, do we?'

'No, not a wolverine,' said the policeman apologetically. He placed his fingers on his brow as if making a major mental effort.

'It's similar to a wolverine but smaller ... You know, related to a weasel ... hang on a minute.' He spoke into the radio on his lapel.

'This is 1 – 4. 1 – 4, over.'

A voice muttered a crackled response.

'Do you or any of the lads know the names of the weasel family, over?'

'Is it a cat?' asked a passing cleaner.

'No ... not a cat. You know the one I mean ...' The harder PC Wilson tried to remember the name, the more elusive it became.

'It can't be a pine marten, can it?' said the barman. 'They're too small. The same goes for stoats.'

'Come on,' said the policeman. 'You know the one. It's got a black and white face.'

'A panda?' said the cleaner. 'But the hole'd be a damn sight bigger if a panda had made it. Anyway, aren't they all banged up in zoos?'

The radio on the policeman's lapel burst into life, 'Hallo 1 – 4. Are you there, over?'

'I am, over,' replied the constable.

'We've asked around the station. The father's called Norris and the son who was nicked last week is Cedric. Their dog, the big ugly bugger that bit DC Williams when he went to make the arrest is called Alan. Does that help?'

'What?' said the policeman. 'What are you going on about, over?' There was a pause before the voice on the radio answered in aggrieved tone. 'You asked for the names of the Weasel family; they're the shoplifters who live on the Churchill Estate, right, over.'

'Not them, over,' the policeman's exasperation increasing. 'I was asking the names of animals which are closely related to weasels! You know, that one with the black and white face.'

'Oh. Standby, over,' crackled the radio.

'Oh for God's sake! What is wrong with my memory? You must know what I mean. They spread TB to cattle and they're shooting them in the West Country to keep the numbers down.'

'The Welsh?' said the barman, hesitantly. 'I'd heard that medieval thing about it being illegal for a Welshman to be in Hereford with a bow but I've never heard about any cull.'

The radio sputtered again, 'Black and white, you say. The Sarge thinks it's a dwarf panda. DC Williams says it sounds like one of the Pokemon but he couldn't remember the name either. Any good? Over.'

The group stood in silence for a moment.

'Welsh people generally aren't black and white, either,' said the barman.

'Just forget the Welsh!' snapped the policeman. 'I'm talking about the animal that made that hole in the canvas!'

He stopped and took several deep breaths before continuing.

'So what have we got so far? I am a medium-sized animal capable of moving with speed and force; I've got a black and white face and I'm currently being culled in the West Country because I'm suspected of spreading TB to cattle? What am I?'

The barman scratched his 'soup' tattoo nervously whilst gazing into the middle distance. The cleaner leant on her mop and sucked her teeth.

'It wouldn't be an otter, would it?'

'No,' chorused the other two in unison.

'I heard a very funny story about otters the other day,' continued the cleaner, unperturbed. The other two looked at her. She continued:

'What's the difference between an opera soprano and an otter?'

Her audience seemed stunned.

'One has a moustache and smells of fish. The other lives in a river!'

The cleaner's spasm of laughter had barely abated when a poker-faced PC Williams said:

'Look. This isn't some sort of rural edition of Britain's Got Talent. We're trying to solve a crime here.'

He pointed to the hole to illustrate his point.

'As things stand, progress in this case seems to depend on us remembering this one member of the weasel family. We seem to have remembered every single one except the one which is relevant to this case.'

'Well I was only passing and I thought I might be able to help,' said the cleaner aggrieved. 'If I knew that you were just going to end up badgering me about some stupid animal I wouldn't have bothered.'

'That's it!' shouted the policeman in triumph. 'Badger!'

'I hate to piss on your chips,' said the barman. 'But a badger would have burrowed its way out rather than run through the canvas, wouldn't it?'

'He does have a point there,' said the cleaner. 'Have you finished with that white powder and all those bits of plastic bag in the corner. If you have, I'll clean up it.'

'That's fine,' said the policeman. 'Carry on. I don't think that's relevant.'

About five miles away, Mackerel, the Patterdale Terrier, came to with a jolt. The fact that his surroundings were unfamiliar was not necessarily a problem. Being a Patterdale Terrier, he viewed this as part and parcel of life's rich tapestry. He saw the new day's challenges merely as another opportunity to showcase his super-hero-like abilities. That being said, he did feel a bit strange.

His memories of the previous evening were blurred at best. After chewing that sachet of white powder, events seemed to move into fast-forward mode. As the bar closed and the traders made their way back to their caravans, vans or tents, he saw his opportunity to deliver a devastating blow to the box of snacks kept behind the bar.

Even after liberating snacks all over the counter and tables, he wasn't in the slightest bit interested in eating any them.

A slight movement had caught his eye as a rat crawled beneath the tent canvas. Generations of customers had, over the years, 'hosed down' that particular section of tarpaulin to the extent that it was now fragile. The rat was lucky. It hadn't even seen Mackerel starting his run. Had the wired Patterdale hit and bounced off the canvas, it would have been curtains for the rat. Mackerel's supercharged condition meant that he hit the tarpaulin at such a speed that it gave way and the terrier suddenly found himself in the chill outdoors. The rat vanished into the shadows.

Mackerel's memory failed him as to what happened next. He remembered passing that caravan which always had the nice white bread. As he approached, the woman standing in the doorway was smoking a roll-up. Their eyes locked across the dark, trampled grass before she let out a terrified cry, 'Reg, Reg! It's him. He's here again!'

He passed by, attracted by the lights in the distance and the promise of adventure.

As the sun rose, he lay on his back in a comfortable pet bed. He noticed that his mouth, no stranger to foulness, tasted, on this particular morning, like it had been used as a cat latrine. He opened one sticky eyelid and saw, from the view, that this might be a distinct possibility.

On top of the fridge perched an elderly long-coated Siamese cat glaring daggers at the interloper some feet below who had taken over its bed. The cat had difficulty in sitting properly and was clearly in some distress. The events of the previous night came back to Mackerel.

On approaching the house, he had spotted a cat's rear-end protruding from the cat-flap. Monty, the elderly Siamese tomcat in question, had led a pampered existence and was over-fed to the point of diabetes. Despite his girth and age, he could still use the cat flap but only carefully and slowly. So slowly indeed that Mackerel found an opportunity to exercise his baser nature – something he did without bothering about age, gender, species or pack hierarchy.

Monty found himself trapped in the cat-flap, whilst his rear end was subjected a most disagreeable sensation. So disagreeable in fact that, for the first time in eight years, he had managed to negotiate the cat flap in record time and seek sanctuary on top of the fridge. Here, Monty remained *fridged* for several hours whilst his assailant paced the floor below. No matter how thoroughly the cat cleaned his backside, it still felt like it had been hit with a .22 airgun pellet.

Meanwhile, at floor level, the effects of the sachet contents were beginning to wear off. The first signs were not good. Mackerel emitted a long, languorous fart that seemed to leave his body a deflated husk. If only it were so. The diarrhoea that followed came without warning. Its range and quantity were prodigious. Within seconds it became clear to Monty, from his vantage point, that his owners' expensively decorated kitchen would need further attention in the coming days.

Dehydrated and disorientated, Mackerel slumped backwards into the cat bed where he slept the sleep of roadkill.

Seeing that his assailant was out for the count, Monty carefully descended the north face of the fridge to wreak a terrible revenge on his erstwhile assailant. Having relieved himself into the snoring maw of the comatose terrier, he started the long ascent back to the safety of the fridge to continue his long night's vigil.

But this morning, Monty's moment of triumph was denied him. He managed a long, slow menacing hiss at the terrier before the sounds of the household coming to life intervened. Mackerel heard approaching footsteps and just made it to the cat-flap in time. His head swam as he hit the chill morning air and tried to orientate himself. Inside, he could hear human noise.

'Oh, for the love of Jehovah! Poppy! Poppy! Get down here right away and clear this up. Your fleabag cat has shat all over the new kitchen!'

There was a gasp of exasperation as Monty's owner saw the extent of the desecration followed by a none-too-friendly rhetorical question, 'What the hell are you doing up there?'

From the soiled kitchen came the high-pitched squeal of an elderly cat being grabbed roughly by the scruff of its neck. This was followed by the scream of an adult male human when it has just had its forearm razored by flailing claws and been punctured by the three remaining teeth of an elderly cat. The clatter of the cat-flap went almost unnoticed in the hubbub.

Mackerel moved through the undergrowth, nose working overtime trying to retrace his trail to Funless Hall Country Show and Game Fair.

***

'Hello? Terry? Is that you?'

Terry had just got to sleep after a long evening and early

morning entertaining a group of foreign businessman – Scots for the most part. He gazed across the tumulus form of Mrs. Dudley-Vaughan at the alarm clock.

'Yes. Yes, it is. It's also two-thirty in the morning so this had better be important.'

Fired with the success of his first day, Peter had been unable to get to sleep. After a couple of hours, he gave up the struggle, extricated himself from the five-season sleeping bag and sat shivering on the camp bed in the back of the van. Despite the lateness of the hour, he had decided to report in. After all, his new, well-connected friend 'Terry' had told him to ring 'at any time'.

'It's me, Terry. Peter. I thought I'd better let you know that I've just completed my first day on the shows. I can't say it's been very productive regarding the investigation. I spoke to lots of traders but few seemed to be VAT registered and those that were seemed to be on the straight and narrow.'

'So, let me make sure that I understand this clearly,' said Terry. 'You've telephoned me at two-thirty in the morning to tell me that you have discovered absolutely nothing. Is that right?'

'Yes, Terry,' said Peter. 'You did say that I should call you at any time and I thought it best to leave it until now to prevent the possibility of being overheard.'

'I suppose you have a point,' said Terry testily. 'But in future, let's keep the nocturnal communications to a minimum shall we?'

'Message received and understood, Terry. I'll ring you after the Milbourne Saint Nonce point to point on Saturday,' answered Peter.

'No need,' cautioned Terry. 'No need. I'm sure that the antics of our VAT fraudsters will stay fresh for discussion during the working week.'

The line was already dead.

11. SHOOTING PARTY

IT had been a busy week for Walton. Of all the master criminals he had ever worked for, not one had ever realised the amount of work and organisation that went into being bad. Without the hard work and commitment of people like himself, most criminal bosses would find it difficult to carry on. When he started working for the Californian porn baron, Willard Dong, he was amazed to discover that the so-called boss had about as much idea about how money from wholesale drug deals was laundered through the books of his porn empire as that scrawny rat of a lapdog from which he was inseparable. This was part of a discernible trend throughout history.

Al Capone moved his lips as he counted on his fingers well into adulthood and, as an organised crime boss, was useless without the help of his accountants. The irony of his being thrown in prison for tax evasion was not lost on Walton who always maintained that you need to squirrel away some information about your boss which one day might be useful as 'leverage' if things got messy.

As he steered the Aston Martin into the driveway of Raphe Episcopi Hall, he reflected that in the past seven days, he had hit a veritable gold mine of just such information. After the meeting at the Pressed Flower Gallery of the V&A, he had confirmed to Ieuan that he had the ideal front for an investors' meeting in the form of a shooting party. Ieuan seemed genuinely impressed with Walton's ability to 'move things on' as he would say in his mid-Atlantic drawl.

Walton was an extremely astute judge of character. Within minutes of meeting Croesus he had pigeon-holed him variously as an 'idiot', 'loser' and more worryingly 'potential pyromaniac'. Ieuan was more of a challenge but it was only this week that Walton had pigeon-holed his boss as 'narcissist' and 'sociopath' with 'psychopathic tendencies'. As he watched Ieuan Henge seated on his sofa, he noticed that his boss seemed incapable of tearing his gaze away from himself in the various mirrors dotted around the walls and tables and how he was always fiddling with his appearance, pinching the creases in his trousers, smoothing his shortly-cropped blond hair or even testing his breath on the palm of his hand. The guy was like an overstretched ship's hawser which, if it snapped, would cut in half anyone who was standing too close.

'Yes,' he thought to himself as he walked up the back stairs to his staff quarters, 'it's just as well that organising this shooting party has given me access to all Ieuan's contacts. These could be very useful if I'm ever backed into a corner.'

The past seven days had shown him just how far the tentacles of Henge Enterprises extended and penetrated the international establishment. Russlana, Ieuan's own personal 'blow-up doll' or 'bud' as the other staff had rather cruelly nicknamed her, had handed him a file of people that Ieuan would want to see at the proposed bash. It was mind-boggling.

Minor Arab princes with their Syrian advisers, jostled for position with the eldest offspring of Middle Eastern, Central Asian and Eastern European dictators.

'Don't these people have enough money without being criminal?' thought Walton. His own background was humble and his family life virtually non-existent thanks to drink and drugs. It was only due to the commitment of a single teacher at his high school that Walton had ended up sitting that scholarship exam. It was a matter of amazement to everyone except Walton himself and the Chinese student he'd paid to take the paper for him on-line, that he found himself with a full scholarship to Don University in America's Mid-West.

On the guest list, he noted some 'usual suspects'. Mexican Mescal exporters. 'How do you make that much money from spiky plants?' he wondered.

But as he scanned the list of activities and corporations belonging to Felipe Ramirez or as he was more generally known, 'El Cameleon', the answer became apparent.

This was no one-trick pony. He had interests in pharmaceuticals, shipping, logistics, restaurant chains and even a useful chain of funeral directors. The fact that 'El Cameleon' personally comprised a substantial proportion of the Mexican economy meant that he wasn't much bothered about who knew that his wealth came from drugs. He had bought local and national governments throughout central America so assiduously, it was difficult to find anyone in public office with a bad word to say about him. The uninitiated thought Felipe's nickname came from his uncanny skill in disguising his drug interests with arcane and complex corporate fronts. Actually, he was called 'El Cameleon' because he was born with a divergent squint of such savagery that even as an adult he appeared to be able to move each eye independently.

'It's true,' Ieuan once revealed to Walton. 'He had to put up with a lot of ribbing on the way up. One hombre ...'

Walton recoiled at the gratuitous use of this Wild West Americanism.

'... in Guadalajara thought it might be fun to spread a false explanation of Felipe's nickname. He said that Pablo was called 'El Cameleon' because his tongue was so quick at darting out to lick the arse of any passing official. Everyone had a good time laughing at that one ... before they found the hombre in question and his family seated around a large wooden table in their own garden. Their tongues had been pulled out and nailed to the table top before each had their throat slit. No one much laughed at Felipe's nickname after that.'

Next was a list of sub-Saharan African potentates so comprehensive that it looked like a document from the International Criminal Court in The Hague. 'All blood diamonds and bling,' thought Walton. 'The problem is that crime at this level just isn't funny.' But before he could get any more serious, he spotted the comic turn. After all, no gathering of the corrupt and evil would be complete without a representative from the 'Mother of all Parliaments'.

Grenville Cheese was christened with the less impressive name of Richard. The reasons behind his decision to change his name by deed poll at the age of eighteen will be clear to anyone who has undergone a minor public-school education and suffered the type of name-calling that goes on there. His decision to pursue a career in politics just made matters worse.

'Lordy!' thought Walton. 'How old nicknames stick.'

'Smeg' was his nickname in the third form. 'Smeg' was his nickname when he joined the Conservative backbenches having, against the odds, took the safe Labour seat of Chamfertown & Puce in County Durham with a majority of 12 for the Tories.

Still what he lacked in name, he certainly made up for in personal avarice. Any whacky cause would find a ready advocate in Grenville Cheese MP providing the brown envelope was thick enough. Tory Whips soon noted him down as having too many skeletons in the cupboard for even the most minor ministerial post. Not even they could deal with interests like seal pup clubbing for the disabled, whaling cruises for the over seventies and the introduction of a free market for drugs and prostitution. Grenville took any and every opportunity to mingle with the criminally wealthy. True to form, his was the first acceptance received by Walton, a bare twenty hours after the invitations to the shooting party had been issued.

In fact, nearly all the invitations were accepted apart from Marat Komoushinsky, the Russian oligarch. He sent a rather emotional response in hand-written Russian. Russlana had translated.

‘Owing to some difficulties with our Government, I shall be unable to attend your shooting party. I would have loved to come along but I have been informed by the authorities here that, as a result of my activities with the Novosibirsk Electricity Board during the late 1990’s, that I may have a nasty accident with a metal fire escape sometime in the near future. It has been an honour, Ieuan, knowing and working with you over the years. I would like to leave you something to remember me by so have arranged to have my two gundogs Mishka and Kochka flown over to you from their kennels in Yekaterinburg. Remember me!’

Walton was pretty sure that this was a diplomatic paraphrase as when he looked at the original he had noticed, even with his rudimentary skills in the Russian language, that it contained phrases like ‘gold-plated Makarov 9mm’, ‘accidental exposure to radioactive isotopes’ and ‘gold bars in cupboard under the stairs’.

When Walton mentioned this to Ieuan and showed him Russlana’s translation, his response was typical: ‘Who?’

‘Komoushinsky,’ repeated Walton.

‘Never heard of him,’ said Ieuan.

‘You’re godfather to his daughter,’ said Walton.

‘Oh yeah! That Komou ... whatever his name is. Right. How old’s she now?’ said Ieuan. ‘When the dogs arrive send them across to Croesus’s gamekeeper. If they’re any good, sell ’em. If not, have him shoot them, will you?’

‘Jeez!’ thought Walton. ‘The arseholes I have to deal with.’

12. POINT TO POINT

MILBOURNE SAINT NONCE is one of those notable ancient place names that tourists come across when visiting the West Country. As Peter discovered, just before sunrise on a freezing morning, the name is just about the only thing which is notable about the place at all. He had found the village without any difficulty using a road map but there were few notices along the route guiding the would-be trader to the site of the point to point. It was only as the light level increased that he managed to spot the marquee which was to provide the stewards with some shelter for the day and easy access to the adjoining bar.

The LDV lurched reluctantly along the icy track and around the hedge to reveal what Peter felt was a bit of a poor show. There was the one marquee. Behind it was a row of portaloos which, overnight, had been comprehensively vandalised by a group of bullocks. Only two of the portaloos were left in operable condition. This was an academic point as all had frozen solid overnight and, only an hour after the padlocks had been removed by the stewards, now represented a clear and present danger to local ground water quality.

This was Peter's initiation into the weird trading culture of point to point horse racing.

The courses comprise land that is good for little else and is usually isolated on exposed uplands or in the muddiest of valleys. These race meetings have developed quite a following amongst hardcore punters who see point to points as the poor relation to National Hunt racing. Some meets attract these committed gamblers who plough their lonely furrow between the bookies gathered around a paddock and the beer tent. Some attract the aspiring middle classes. Never missing a chance for a party, they turn up with booze, picnics and inappropriate footwear. Their four-by-fours are suspiciously clean. Even when the January wind is gusting at over forty miles an hour and the wind-chill factor has driven the temperature down to Siberian levels, you can usually hear the braying and air-kissing of these latter-day hoorays determined to let everyone within hearing distance know that they are having a good time.

Trading at these events, Peter discovered, was a bit touch-and-go. On the right day, sales could be good even if the rain and wind were making standing around uncomfortable. On the wrong day, the crowd could be huge, the sun could be blazing down and sales would be non-existent. Those traders who bothered to turn up were either those who knew and were known in the local area or those who, after a winter of subsistence trading on high street markets, were desperate enough to try anything to get a few sales.

By ten o'clock, Peter was shocked to see that there were only six tents set up. He'd expected fewer than the Funless Hall show the previous week but more than half a dozen. A couple wearing 'dog's ear' woolly hats started to set up next to him. During a pause in the proceedings, they introduced themselves as Pat and Aly.

'... and that's Bobby in the cab,' said Aly.

Peter peered through the glass and saw a medium-sized shaggy mongrel, eyes hidden by a long grey and brown fringe but lower teeth clearly visible from a prominent under-slung jaw. Pat and Aly were selling woolly hats and, rather optimistically, sun glasses. These retreated to the back of the van as the drizzle set in to be replaced by a tub of umbrellas.

One the other side, a tent was being erected by a well-dressed fifty-something in a fedora. He was selling hats as well. He was obviously the token perfectionist at this point to point as his white marquee housed a professional display of headgear ranging from furry headbands for the girls right the way through to bowler hats for hunt servants. The sign above the entrance proudly announced the presence of Lidd & Co., 'Hats for Town & Country'.

Further down the line, Peter could see another stand selling paintings and prints. This stand too had a selection of hats on spinners prominently displayed at each end of the stand. And beyond that a stand with a wonderful display of knitted woolen goods. On a central table, Peter noted, was an offering of ... hats.

Peter began to discern a pattern. Pausing from his set-up for a moment he stepped out in front of the row of tents to glance at the stands at the end of the line. Sure enough, the cup-cake seller at one end of the line had just put out a spinner of wax hats. At the other end, the stand selling riding tack was now festooned with a wall of women's hats and fascinators.

Before he could comment on this to his neighbour, the proprietor of Lidd & Co., sprang across the inner span of his stand to where a passing spaniel was just about to raise its leg against one of the immaculately ironed counter cloths.

'Oh no you bloody don't,' he said emphatically yanking the dog away by its lead. The spaniel and its owners gawped confrontationally at the hat vendor as if he had transgressed some ancient law.

'I take it,' said the hat seller, 'that you don't let your dog slash all over your soft furnishings at home so I'd be obliged if you extended the same courtesy to me.' The gawping continued but response came there none as the spaniel and its staff wandered off.

'Sorry about that,' said the hat man extending his hand. 'John Halifax's the name.'

'Oh! What a coincidence,' said Peter. 'Like the inventor of the tricorn.'

'Yes,' replied John calmly. 'But it's only coincidence. It's not like running into a railway engineer called Isambard Kingdom Brunel or a mass murderer called Heinrich

Himmler now, is it? Anyway, I must crack on and get this sorted out if you'll excuse me.'

Peter retreated to his stand and was just putting out the last few coils of belts when he was interrupted, 'Pete!'

Peter whipped around to see the portly, bearded frame of Pat behind him examining the leather goods. He obviously had a message and moved closer with a conspiratorial air.

'Do you know what Aly and I have got in the back of the van?'

Peter's mind raced. Before he could unleash his over-active imagination on this question, Pat continued, 'We've got two spinners full of hats.'

'Oh,' said Peter.

'How would you like to have those outside your stand for the duration, eh?'

'Well, that's very kind of you, Pat, but hats, you see, aren't really my thing and I'd feel ...'

'No, no,' said Pat placing a fraternal arm around Peter's shoulder and guiding him outside to stand in front of the row of stands. 'That's fine. I just thought I'd ask because if you had said 'yes' ... then every fucking stand at this event would be selling hats!'

He spread out his arms to encompass the row. It was true. Every single stand was selling hats in one form or another. Pat let out a laugh which was slightly too high-pitched for comfort and squelched off back to his stand.

Peter returned to his stand and checked the canvases. As the sun got higher in the sky, the wind picked up. He passed the rest of the morning selling belts to the few punters who found their way to the line of trade stands and asking his neighbours if they were registered for VAT. The hat man was. The rest weren't.

Even the absence of scary Mexicans failed to lift Peter's spirits. Who the hell would live like this? The hours are Hell, the trade is as unstable as a teenager's hormones and even after that, you have to pay tax on any pitiful level of profit you do manage to make. For the first time, Peter could feel his enthusiasm for his special mission waning slightly.

13. DRIVING MISTER CROESUS

AT the Henge Enterprises Mayfair headquarters, Russlana was having a difficult day. It was impossible to find a couple of days when so many rich, powerful people were available. After she discussed this with Ieuan, Walton's original idea for one large shooting party had become Ieuan's idea for a number of smaller shooting parties. This way, Ieuan explained at the planning meeting, they would be able to meet up with all the important investors who could be, as he liked to put it, 'briefed and fleeced' at leisure.

As the words fell from his lips, a high-pitched whine like an excited cocker spaniel about to wet itself came from the corner occupied by Croesus. 'This is just wonderful,' he gushed. 'We haven't done this sort of entertaining at Raphe Episcopi since insider trading was legal.' Ieuan smiled at Croesus whilst taking Walton to one side. 'You don't have to bring him everywhere with you, Old Sport, do you?' he whispered.

Walton replied, 'It's best I do. We wouldn't like Croesus to initiate anything himself, would we? This way, I can always refer to your orders and remind him that he was present. God knows, he's difficult enough to control as it is.'

'What do you mean?' replied Henge.

'After we came up with the idea of the shooting party, he disappeared off to London and spent nearly six grand having fancy dress costumes made up! He's got a Lawrence of Arabia get-up for when the Arabs are here and an Ivan the Terrible suit for when the Russians visit. I dread to think what he's got in mind for the weekend when El Cameleon and his Mexicans are around.'

Ieuan guided Walton out to the hallway:

'But this is a fucking nightmare! I can't have him rolling around like a loose cannon while we're trying the secure funding. It's down to you, Walton. You really need to get a handle on this jerk or he'll ruin everything. We can't have Croesus treating the investors like they're a bunch of his weirdo school chums, for God's sake. They'd never agree to put into the scheme after that. What are you going to do?'

Walton felt his palms moisten. He knew of old that when Ieuan started to panic people got hurt. And nothing was going to get Ieuan panicking more than the prospect of being shown up by Croesus at what were likely to be the most important meetings in his criminal career. Before he could stop himself, Walton heard his mouth say the worst words it could come up with at this moment:

'Don't panic, Ieuan, I'll keep him out of ...'

Too late. Henge's fist thumped into Walton's solar plexus winding him. He slumped against the wall, fighting for breath.

'You should know by now, sport. I don't panic. I leave that to others. Make sure that idiot Croesus is under control. No excuses.'

I really must remember just how thin-skinned he is, thought Walton as his vision cleared and he made his way back to the meeting room. Perhaps it was about time that Croesus met some gamekeepers. They could keep him out of the way.

***

'So we'll have to keep an eye on Croesus all the time?'

Andy Gudger sounded concerned. He knew that something was up. Getting an invite from Croesus's new partners to 'meet for a pint' in the Snug Bar of The Poor Struggler Arms was always grounds for concern.

'But we'll have our hands full running the shoot, won't we. Surely that's got to take priority, hasn't it?'

'Quite right,' said Walton in his most conciliatory manner. 'All I'm asking is that you find someone to add to your team so that they can make sure that Croesus doesn't ... get in the way.'

'Anyway, shouldn't he be with his guests.' The high-pitched Welsh voice of the groundsman, Barry Parry, cut in. 'After all, they're his guests aren't they? Why isn't he with them, then?'

Walton was prepared for this. He had done his research.

'Were any of you employed here when Croesus last picked up a shotgun? Can anyone here remember what happened?'

Gudger was the only one old enough. He raised his hand as he swallowed the remains of his beer and addressed his half-dozen colleagues.

'Walton's right. Nothing on the face of God's earth would persuade me to place a shotgun into the hands of Croesus after what happened, ooh, it must have been twenty-odd years ago now.'

'Tell them,' said Walton surveying the blank faces of the estate staff. 'Go on.'

'It was the last time that the old boy, Sir Quentin, had his chums down from London for a big day. It was early in the season and quite warm, I remember. The birds were behaving themselves. Everyone was having a good time; especially Sir Quentin's close friend, The Secretary of State for Fish and Ag., I can't remember his name. Anyway, Croesus wasn't up when the shoot began and only joined the party half-way through.'

'What did he do, then?' said Barry Parry, 'shoot the Secretary of State? He'd have to get in the queue nowadays, wouldn't he?'

After the giggling died away, Gudger continued. 'That's exactly what happened. I never knew Croesus take a shooting lesson. I never knew Croesus to be capable of remembering anything from one day to the next. As birds came up and over, he swung through and everyone hit the dirt. Mercifully, he had the safety on or it would have been curtains for someone. Two minutes after that, there was a shot followed by a scream and the Secretary of State went down like a sack of shit.'

Gudger's audience was spell-bound.

'Buggeration!' said Barry Parry.

'Was he dead?' said another.

'Who's round is it?' said a third.

'Tell 'em the gory details,' said Walton.

'Luckily, the gun was pointing to the ground when Croesus succeeded in his struggle with the safety catch. Unluckily, the barrels were pointing at a large stone and several bits of it ricocheted in the direction of the Secretary of State's family jewels.'

Gudger looked at Walton who nodded his approval. Gudger leaned forward, conspiratorially, and shared an interesting historical fact with his workmates:

'To this day, that politician, whose name still escapes me, is the only British politician since Henry Fitz-Allwin de Londonestone in 1189 to lose a testicle whilst in office.'

Having lodged a couple of fifty-pound notes behind the bar to cover the rest of the evening, Walton returned to his rooms at Raphe Episcopi Hall.

14. THE NORTH

SOMETHING was not right. Peter had never felt like this before in his working life. During his dismal day at Milbourne St.Nonce point to point, he had retreated to the privacy of the LDV cab and tried to ring Terry on several occasions to report in but the Assistant Secretary's line was permanently unavailable. As the day drew to a close, he was sitting in the LDV cab, mobile phone in hand.

'Oh well,' he thought. 'What else can I do?'

He dialled the office number. Janice Twinge answered. Nigel Grind wasn't available so Peter had to leave a message. Peter was never quite sure whether Janice was all there. His call was hampered by a really appalling telephone line which had a lot of interference on it. The interference sounded like someone moving their hand across the receiver to disguise sniggering or laughter in the background.

'You're sure you're alone and that this call is secure?' Peter had asked Janice. 'Yes, yes. It's fine. By the way, I've got a list here of events that you might want to attend for whatever it is you're investigating, Peter. There's one in Wick.'

'But that's nearly in Norway it's so far north,' remonstrated Peter. 'I'm not sure if the van'll make it.'

'Not to worry, you can do the Dross Game Show on the way back and there's another one in Dumfries and Galloway. After that, there's a country show in Northern Ireland. No need to do anything your end. I've booked you in to them all on the Assistant Secretary's instructions. All you have to do is turn up.'

The interference kicked off again. Now it sounded like a crossed line with lots of people sniggering and laughing.

'You are alone at your end, aren't you? There's nobody else there, right?' said Peter. 'You'll pass my note to the Assistant Secretary; to him and nobody else?'

'Yes, yes,' soothed Janet but now it sounded as if she was sniggering.

Peter heard a hand clamp over the mouthpiece and what sounded like a very familiar voice; Dave Rosser's voice, say something ending in 'wanker' before the line went dead.

'That's odd,' thought Peter. 'I thought Dave Rosser had left for a job in the private sector. He can't still be in the office.'

Sitting alone in the cab of the LDV, Peter let out a long sigh. This was not how things were meant to be. The 'special mission' was turning out to be anything but 'special'. The shows were hard work. The living conditions were dreadful. He'd still found no evidence of traders trying to fiddle their VAT. He'd hardly found any traders making enough money to make it worthwhile registering for VAT. What was going on?

He turned the key in the van ignition. After a couple of seconds the yellow light went out and he started the engine. As usual, the dashboard lit up like the Christmas decorations at Hamley's toy shop but he was used to it by now. He waited for the warning lights to go out. After fifteen minutes of waiting, it became clear that this was not going to happen. His eye caught a movement on the dashboard. It was the needle on the engine temperature gauge jerking into the red. Even in twilight, Peter saw a jet of steam snake its way out from beneath the bonnet.

He phoned the AA.

***

'Kev,' said Peter from the passenger seat of the brand-new Mercedes Sprinter van. 'I really am very grateful for this. It's got me out of a real fix. I've already paid for the shows so I would have taken a real smacking if I'd missed them because of the van breaking down.'

'Well, if you don't mind me saying, that van of yours really is a heap of shit. You want to ditch it,' replied Kevin. 'You were just lucky that I had to come and collect some stock just down the road from you and that I had enough room for your stuff as well.'

The extra-long wheelbase Sprinter complete with thirty-foot caravan in tow moved swiftly through the rain and spray of the M6 into the fast lane and bore down at speed on the Yugoslavian Fiat which was struggling to overtake the governed lorry to its left.

'Absolutely,' said Peter, his knuckles whitening as his grip tightened on the door handle. 'How fast are you allowed to go legally when you've got a caravan hitched up as well?'

Kev's off-hand 'Dunno, mate' indicated that he had his sights set on the Yugoslavian Fiat. Over the years he had established a happy medium between decisive driving and road rage and was always keen to deploy it.

'Look at this muppet in front. He doesn't have a clue that I'm here.'

As the speedometer passed eighty miles an hour, Peter noticed a trail of smoke from the rear of the Yugoslavian Fiat similar to that seen in old footage of World War One dogfights when one of the bi-planes gets hit. He couldn't possibly imagine that, even with the view obscured by spray, the driver was unaware of the several tons of brightly illuminated van and caravan that were inching aggressively towards his rear bumper. Suddenly the car swerved dangerously all over the fast lane.

'Hallo!' said Kev. 'He's just woken up and looked in his rear-view mirror. I bet he's crapped himself.'

The Yugoslavian Fiat pulled sharply in front of a lorry which let out a horn-blast of displeasure as the Sprinter/caravan combo sailed serenely past unfettered by other vehicles, speed limits or other road traffic regulations.

One hour later, they pulled off the motorway at Carlisle and decided to do some shopping for the expedition to The North and have lunch at the US-style cash-and-carry, Spend-Mo.

'I'm going to try out a new idea for disposable floats on decoys and anchor-lines,' said Kev heading off to the toiletries section. Peter was surprised to see two large boxes each holding a gross of condoms hit the bottom of the shopping trolley.

'I've got to get some lubricant to help the line go through the eyelets as well,' said Kev. Seconds later a couple of two-gallon tubs of Vaseline joined the earlier purchases.

As they walked down the aisles, Peter could not help feeling a bit awkward. Their fellow shoppers had begun to notice the two, large, middle-aged men, one with boyish features, the other with a full set of what was often referred to as 'buggers' grips' wandering along sharing a shopping trolley which contained an odd array of purchases. Carlisle is a traditional place with a conservative outlook. Peter sensed that conclusions were being not even roughly sketched but definitely drawn by local shoppers as they caught sight of the contents of the trolley. The staring started. Covertly, at first, but then full-on.

'We need chocolates,' announced Kev decisively. Peter pointed to the wholesale boxes of Yorkie Bars in the vain hope of butching-up Kev's increasingly ambiguous purchases. Kev was searching for a present for their hostess for the evening.

'No, not those,' said Kev. 'We need something prettier. Something with a bow on the box.'

There was a snort of disgust from an elderly woman passing by with her husband whose stern features made clear his thoughts.

'You people are disgusting. Not content with breaking every tenet of nature when it comes to intimacy, you now flaunt your abomination. We all know exactly what he means about the chocolate. When you've run out of condoms and lubricant making the unnatural beast with two backs you intend to wallow around in your own feculence feeding each other sweets!'

Peter had already noticed that the spirit of the European Directive on Gender Equality in the Workplace had yet to reach Carlisle and that the good burghers of that town were now swerving to avoid any contact with Kev and himself or even their shopping trolley.

Matters were not improved when Kevin went in search of the perfectly formed potato in the Veg department. There were rumours that someone would be bringing a potato gun to one of the shows and Kevin didn't want to miss the chance of having a go. He held up a large King Edward to show Peter announcing, as he did so in a loud clear voice, 'That's the sort of size I'm looking for. Remember the trick is that it's got to be a nice, snug, tight fit but at the same time it has to slide in and out easily without lubrication. If it's too big and you force it, you might end up splitting the sides.'

His explanation was interrupted by the sound of a man retching. A woman with a pram had also got the wrong end of the stick. Wiping her mouth on a disposable nappy she lurched past Peter and Kev muttering something along the lines of 'flogging being too good for perverts like ...'

'What's up with her?' said Kevin oblivious of the gathering of shoppers who were beginning to get their 'mob' on.

'I think we should leave,' said Peter.

'Why?' said Kev.

'I'll tell you in the van.'

'All I said was that I thought this would be a perfect fit ...'

'No more talk. Just go,' muttered Peter propelling the shopping trolley towards the checkout.

In the car park, Peter caught a waft of smoke at the back of his throat but thought nothing of it. As they approached the Sprinter, they both noticed a diminutive figure standing by the van.

'Now what?' said Kev as they approached.

'Ees thees joo van, meester?' said Juan. His Mexican accent was instantly recognisable. Peter pulled his hat low over his eyes.

'Yeah,' said Kev. 'What's it to you, mate?'

'My compadre ees not very happy,' continued the Mexican pointing to his colleague leaning against a nearby car shakily smoking a cigarette. 'He say joo run him off the road some mile back.'

'Don't think so, mate,' bluffed Kev. 'Must have been someone else.'

Peter could now definitely smell burning.

The other larger Mexican finished his cigarette and approached with a gait that suggested that he had recently suffered a severe shock resulting in a pants problem. As he got closer, he squinted at Kevin and then at Peter. Peter looked at the ground but it was too late.

'Madre de Dios!' exclaimed Pablo. 'It ees heem! The one with the water.'

Juan was slow on the uptake.

'Who Pablo? Who? Every day we have to go through thees. You have a photographic memory and a national library of grudges. Who is it thees time?'

'The one who tip water all over ...' He let the mime finish the sentence for him.

'Oh! Him! Well, my friend, it ees, as you say in joo country, not "joo lucky day".'

Peter meanwhile had found the source of the burning smell. It lay eight parking bays away on the right.

'Nor yours, amigo,' he said. 'Isn't that your car?'

Peter helpfully pointed to the Yugoslavian Fiat. The thin trail of smoke that Peter had observed when the car was in front of them, had now grown to a billowing plume beneath which bright yellow and red flames were clearly visible.

'Ees an old trick. I know thees trick,' drawled Juan. Slowly his hand dropped menacingly into his jacket pocket.

'Ees right! The car!' shouted Pablo.

They both turned around just in time to see the fire really take hold. Both ran towards the burning car but there was little they could do.

'What was he going to take out of his pocket?' asked Peter as he and Kev heaved the shopping and themselves into the cab.

'Dunno, mate. But I'm not hanging around to find out.'

As the Sprinter and caravan sped towards the car park exit, the flames reached the petrol tank of the Yugoslavian

Fiat which exploded. Peter saw two forlorn figures standing close by before they too sprinted to leave the car park via the perimeter fence.

'And,' said Peter, 'with a single bound, they were free.'

'Not quite,' cautioned Kev. 'What were they doing there in the first place. Let's be honest, you don't travel to Carlisle for the weather.'

'Good point,' replied Peter. Then the penny dropped. Reaching into his pocket for the Dross Game Fair paperwork, he pointed to the letterhead which read 'Gewgaw Country Events' and then underneath in barely perceptible fine print 'A Henge Enterprises Corporation'.

'Oh shit!' said Kevin. 'I think we'll be meeting up with our Mexican friends again before we get back to England!'

15. WOOKY HARAM

IEUAN HENGE had decided to wear his vintage Huntsman tweeds for the shooting party. He had bought these at auction for an immense sum believing them to have been originally made for Edward VIII. Even if the Amir was a little down the social scale from Princes of the blood royal, he still did things properly when abroad. Ieuan expected the Amir would turn up in a perfectly-tailored shooting suit and he had no intention of letting the side down ... whatever side that was.

Ieuan's psychotic side rather admired the fact that, at home, his Arab guests would think nothing of having someone stoned to death for some actual or imaginary transgression of religious law but, when in London, they would do far worse.

Abdul Abulbul Amir's parties were notorious. Entire floors of one of the best central London hotels would be taken as the venue for a forty-eight-hour orgy of impropriety involving drink, gambling, drugs and hookers. Even thinking about this stuff at home in the Arabian Peninsula could get you beheaded. Ieuan made a mental note to keep Russlana out of sight.

The Prince had rather taken to her when they had last met skiing in Gstaad and Ieuan had no intention, knowing Russlana's predilection for loads of money, of losing a useful and flexible member of his team to one of his investors.

The previous day's negotiations at the Prince's country house just north of London had gone well. The Prince's investment in Ieuan's new drugs distribution scheme had been agreed without the tedium of negotiation. Although the Prince was present, it was his secretary Anwar Aban, a talented Syrian negotiator, who took the lead. When Ieuan had attempted to provide more details about the scheme, the Prince had cut him short:

'Ieuan. I do not need to know the fine detail. Tell this to Anwar. He enjoys this sort of thing. It is sufficient that you tell me that for a certain investment I will get a certain return. I trust you so that is all I need to know.'

Ieuan accepted the gracious invitation to stay on for a sumptuous traditional dinner. The ground floor of the Edwardian country house had been substantially altered and now comprised a large, luxuriously carpeted and furnished space into which, later that evening, huge platters of coloured and spiced rice were brought directly from the nearby kitchens accompanied by steaming cauldrons of meat. There was far more food than the thirty or so guests could ever account for and easily enough for the attendant household staff who would eat afterwards.

Ieuan noticed that a large amount of food ended up on the carpet as it was carried from the kitchens. Obsessed with cleanliness, he wondered how the stains and marks were removed. He was impressed by Anwar Aban's answer, 'We just recarpet the ground floor after each banquet. It's just easier that way.'

Anwar Aban entertained himself for the rest of the meal by watching Ieuan resisting the gag reflex as he ate with his fingers from the communal platter.

Back at Raphe Episcopi, on the same evening, Walton had taken the precaution of placing Croesus in the care of the gamekeepers, beaters and picker-uppers on the shoot. Over several hours in the pub, they had taken time to explain to their nominal employer how the shooting party would proceed.

Croesus, still obsessed with the fancy dress element, seemed to have missed the point of the whole proceedings. He recoiled at the suggestion that hundreds of pheasants were about to embark on the first step towards oven-readiness in a hail of shot and cordite. He seemed more interested in what would happen to all the feathers afterwards. It wasn't until picker-upper Ron gave forth on his memories of helping out at a shoot for another Arab dignitary some years ago that the vexed question as to whether downed game birds are truly *halal* or *haram* (forbidden) according to Muslim requirement that Croesus's goldfish-like powers of concentration became fully engaged.

At seven o'clock the following morning, the shoot staff gathered in the rear yard at Raphe Episcopi. There was a genuine buzz of excitement about the day to come. This was the first shooting party that had been held on the estate since Sir Quentin's time and everyone was determined to make a good show of it.

Everyone had turned up in 'full fig' for Walton's pre-shoot pep-talk. Andy Gudger looked every inch the shoot captain turned out smartly in his dad's tweeds which had been given to him back in the fifties by General Franco. Ron and the other beaters and pickers-up had made a special effort donning Barbours where the original colour of the fabric was still just visible.

There was the occasional blip. Ron's twenty-two-year-old son, Little Ron, had turned up dressed as Chewbakka the Wooky from Star Wars. His six-foot-five frame was actually a little too big for the hairy XXXL fancy dress suit. However, by cutting off the feet and wearing a pair of rigger boots, the effect was still quite convincing. This promising young rugby player had never been 'quite right' after that fateful Young Farmers' meeting some years ago during which someone had spiked his drink with several horse tranquilisers. He was more than tolerated on the estate as he was easy to get along with and as strong as an ox.

Barry Parry, the under-keeper, had no such excuse and had let the side down somewhat by wearing a migraine-inducing orange camouflage jacket and breeks which he had won in a game of cards on a trip to the US.

'I'm a bit nervous about these foreign buggers,' Barry had confided to Walton the previous afternoon in his high-pitched Welsh accent, 'I want them to know I'm 'ere.'

At half past seven, the advanced party of the Prince's retinue arrived to check out security. No expense was spared on this after an unfortunate incident a couple of years earlier when the Prince had been mistaken for the owner of a well-known Knightsbridge store by a disgruntled ex-employee who egged him savagely and then tried to finish him off with a hand-held blender. The Prince only suffered minor bruising but his doctor said it could have been much worse if the hand-held blender had been plugged in.

Exactly ten minutes later, the Rolls Royce limousine glided onto the gravel of Raphe Episcopi Hall's driveway. The Prince emerged from the car, immaculately clad. Ieuan stepped forward to shake the proffered hand.

'Ieuan,' said the Amir, 'you are a most generous and gracious host. It is so kind of you to organise some shooting for me at such short notice. It is as if you know how much I love your English country sports.'

Ieuan smiled taking the Prince's hand but inwardly bristled not just at his guest's gracious manners which made his own mid-Atlantic pretension seem shabby but also at the fact that the Prince's tailoring bordered on the perfect.

As the small-talk continued, Walton stepped forward to help the Prince's staff unload his guns and take them to the gun room. Ieuan felt better as he saw the estate staff take control of the proceedings.

By the time he, the Prince and Anwar Aban were at the first drive, he even felt a little flicker of pride at the arrangements which Walton had overseen. Just a flicker. The better Walton performed, the more Ieuan's deep-rooted paranoia kicked in, forever worried about his talented employee's motives and whether he was really 'on board' or just pretending.

The birds on the first drive were fast and low providing a real test for the host and his guests alike. The morning seemed to be going well and Ieuan started to relax when Anwar Aban, handing his gun to his loader, stepped towards Ieuan pointing.

'Mr. Henge. What is going on over there? I have never seen anything like this before. Please can you explain?'

Ieuan turned and saw the hunched form of Croesus's elderly Labrador, Suddaby, readying himself, with all the speed and deliberation of a dockyard crane, to produce an extravagantly large turd in the middle of the vista.

'Oh yes,' said Ieuan. 'I'm sorry about that. It probably wasn't walked sufficiently this morning.'

'No, Mr. Henge. Not the dog. There by those bushes.'

Amidst the retrievers retrieving and the pickers-up picker-uppering, a figure in Arabian robes was clearly visible moving from pheasant carcass to pheasant carcass apparently slitting the throat of each dead or wounded bird in turn.

Through his rising rage, Ieuan barely heard Andy Gudger mutter 'Fuckin' hell fire!' as he too saw the figure. 'What the hell is going on here?' hissed Ieuan.

'It's Croesus,' replied the shoot captain.

'No shit!' said Ieuan. 'I didn't think it was Peter O'fucking Toole! I don't care if it's freekin' Rudolph Valentino, I just want him gone.'

'I'm onto it,' said Gudger as he muttered into his walkie-talkie. 'Come in, Little Ron. Come in, Little Ron. Over.'

Anwar Aban was waiting for his answer.

'It's just a little tradition we have here at Raphe Episcopi,' said Ieuan confidently. 'It's a sort of post-first drive pantomime in which one of our number impersonates the guests.'

'Oh really?' said Anwar. 'I have been shooting in your country for thirty years and I thought I knew of all your strange customs from the giving of the full contents of one's wallet to the loaders at the end of the day through to the bafflingly paltry donation of a new car to the shoot captain but this I have never seen.'

'Oh yes,' said Ieuan glaring at the advancing robe-clad figure who was now waving at him. 'It's a Midlands tradition really. Like your people, we like to keep the old customs alive.'

'Ah yes,' said Anwar politely feigning satisfaction with the explanation. 'Tell me, Mr. Henge. These customs, are they like your Britain's Got Talent or The Voice. I like it very much when the fat ladies, they sing.'

As words fell from his lips, Ieuan saw a large hairy

creature emerge from a thicket just behind Croesus's robed form. Over a distance of 20 yards, the yeti or bigfoot or whatever it was, built up a considerable speed.

'What the ..?' chorused Ieuan and Anwar Aban. Their perfectly justifiable question was lost in the howl of pain let out by Croesus as he was felled by a flying tackle perfectly executed by what appeared to be a character from the popular motion picture, Star Wars.

Barry Parry stepped forward and said quietly to Ieuan, 'Well, Bach. There's something you don't see every day.'

' Not every day, no', said Ieuan, nonplussed.

He recovered his senses quickly. 'What's your name?'

'Oh sorry,' said Barry. 'I'm Barry Parry, the under-keeper. There's lovely to meet you.' He extended his hand.

'Well, Barry,' said Ieuan ignoring the handshake. 'You're fired!'

As Ieuan rejoined the rest of the party, Barry shouted after him.

'Why's that, then? What have I done?'

'It's not what you've done. It's what you're wearing' shouted over his shoulder.

A little way off, Ron was applying smelling salts to the prone form of Croesus.

'Christ, Boy. I told you to stop him not kill him.'

'Sorry, Dad,' said Little Ron. 'The muscle memory just kicked in. I couldn't stop myself.'

'Dad,' continued Little Ron. A high-pitched wail of pain indicated that Croesus had rejoined the world of the living.

'Yes, son.'

'Should his arm be facing that way?'

Little Ron, with his years of experience in club rugby, was no stranger to breakages and dislocations. Even through the voluminous robes, it was clear that Croesus's shoulder and probably a good deal more of him would be needing hospital attention.

16. SYRUP

PETER and Kevin stood in their shared stand space at Dross Game Fair looking at the locals. Some kilted, others in trews, they meandered around the main ring through the drizzle and into the beer tent. There they stayed for much of the morning periodically appearing to urinate down the canvas sides of the bar tent before diving inside once again for a refill.

'How many hours did it take us to get here?' asked Kev.

'Twelve,' replied Peter.

'It would have been eight if I hadn't listened to you,' muttered Kevin bitterly. 'I slept like a log last night and I'm still knackered.' Peter hung his head in shame. Kevin was not in a forgiving mood. He was a remarkably good mimic.

'Don't follow the sat nav, Kev,' said Kevin in a high-pitched imitation of Peter's southern accent. 'I know where we're going. I used to come here on holiday when I was a kid. I know where Port of Moncrieff is!'

He switched back into his laconic Leicestershire patois.

'It's just a fucking shame we were looking for the Port of 'Montieth', wasn't it. You knob-head! The other one's only two hundred and eighty miles away and probably doesn't have a narrow ford where you can get a Mercedes Sprinter and caravan stuck!'

Peter could understand that a certain level of bitterness might be in order given the nasty scrape down the side of Kev's new van and the dent to the front of the caravan but he hoped that Kev would lighten up a little as the show progressed.

The drizzle stopped. In the ring, equipment was being moved about with some urgency as they wanted to get the demonstrations started. Across the far side of the ring a small black dog ran across the open space looking like he was late for a Young Dogs' Christian Association meeting. Peter watched the familiar black shape head directly into the bar at a brisk trot. The terrier's arrival was greeted with hilarity by the drinkers therein.

'They obviously don't get out much around here,' he said to Kevin trying to lighten the mood. He needn't have bothered.

Peter took the opportunity to take a walk to clear the atmosphere. Unlike Kevin, who had slept in the caravan, Peter got the cab in which he slept fitfully. At around two o'clock, he was woken by an alien presence in his sleeping bag. It was his own hand and arm which, deprived of a blood supply, had gone to sleep. By four in the morning the handbrake of the van felt like it had entered his soul. So it was good to get some fresh air before the day got going.

Walking down the line of stalls he was just about to greet Paul and Helen, in front of the Pigeon Destroyer stand, when the Tannoy burst into life.

'... pervert, right?' said a man with a local accent. In the background, the clinking of glasses was clearly audible.

'And he's doon all the heavy breathing doon the phoon to this wee lassie. He says to her 'I bet you've got a tight arse with no hair.' And she says, 'You're reet. I have. He's lying on the sofa watching the footie. Who shall I say is calling?"

Uproarious laughter filled the air for a few seconds before another voice cut in, 'Is that light meant to be on?'

The Tannoy resumed its earlier silence as a figure of authority strode across the ring and jumped into the commentary box. Thanks to the soundproofing, passers-by were treated to a Marcel Marceau-style mime of one angry man shouting at two very contrite men. Eventually, the figure of authority settled himself behind the microphone and, in mellifluous tones, addressed the crowd:

'Ladies and Gentlemen, Gewgaw Events welcomes you to the twelfth Dross Castle Game Fair here in beautiful Scotland.'

From the beer tent, there was loud cheer. A man wearing a kilt with a fox-head sporran strode into the aisle and yelled: 'speak up, you posh twat. We canna hear ya!'

The figure of authority persevered, 'Despite the occasional shower, we're going to get matters underway at ten o'clock with our first event which is Obadiah Chubb's Wonderful World of Long-Netting. Obi has worked all over the world with long-nets. He's just back from Greenland, he tells me. They don't have any rabbits in Greenland, of course, nor long-netting, for that matter. He was meant to go to Iceland. Obi tells me it was a mistake at check-in at Copenhagen airport. He'll be demonstrating his patented, one-man, long-netting system for catching rabbits with the assistance of his two dogs, Widdle and Puke.'

The Tannoy fell silent. The commentary box mime now showed a man being passed a piece of paper.

'I'm sorry,' said the commentator. 'The dogs' names are Fiddle and Duke. When Obi vacates the ring at around a quarter to eleven, there'll be a falconry display by ...'

More bits of paper were being passed around in the commentary box.

'... by ... Ray Bomber-Harris from Trussocks Falconry. You'll recognise from Ray's accent that he's originally from Essex but he's been running a falconry and rescue centre in the Trussocks now for two decades and has become part of the local landscape there. He is assisted today by his charming partner, Wendy.'

'It seems OK now,' said Helen toying with the dead pigeon, 'but you wait 'til the end of the season when you know every act, every word, off by heart. It eats into your soul.'

''Ere,' chipped in Paul. 'You know your Mexican mates? They're 'ere 'n all. I saw them arrive yesterday by taxi. They were in a right state. Couldn't pay the fare. Things got quite ugly.'

'I thought they might put in an appearance,' said Peter. 'We bumped into them on the way up here.'

When he reached the far side of the ring, Peter decided that a peace offering might be in order for Kevin. So he bought two coffees. The liquid in the cups bore no resemblance to coffee he had ever tried before but he took it on trust. He even managed to get a till receipt for his purchase.

By the time he got back to the stand, the drizzle had returned and the long-netting display was coming to a sodden conclusion. Watched by a man in a wheelchair parked by the ring outside the bar and the traders on their stands, Obidiah Chubb was carefully folding the long net and placing it back in the bag around his shoulder. As he removed the sticks from which the net was hung, he placed them carefully in his quiver. The masterly impression was sadly undermined by his two terriers. Ignoring all instructions from Obi to 'fetch', 'kill' and more obscurely to 'leave it a-fuckin' lone', Fiddle and Duke had spent most of the demonstration defecating around the ring and rolling in fox-shit.

'Kev. I got you coffee.'

'Oh thanks. My hands are bloody freezing.'

Pleased to see that a thaw had set in between them, Peter continued: 'Any customers?'

'Nah. They're all getting beered up in the bar.'

As he spoke, the sun suddenly broke through the clouds. Brilliant sunshine and departing drizzle combined to create a scene of which any advertising agency would have been proud. Scotland's wild and beautiful landscape was brought briefly into sharp and compelling focus. As if this wasn't enough, a huge double rainbow appeared across the distant hills. Even the hardened drinkers in the bar waddled outside to 'ooh' and 'aah' at the unexpected meteorological bonus.

'Ray seems to have worked his magic again, Ladies and Gentlemen.' soothed the announcer over the Tannoy. 'He's brought some perfect flying weather with him. So, without more ado, please welcome Ray Bomber-Harris, Wendy and the Trussocks Falconry Display Team.'

Forgetting to switch over the microphone to Ray, the announcer carried on in less velvety tones, '... I don't care. You've been warned about drinking during set-up before. You're not the only set-up guy in this part of Scotland, you know.'

Ray and Wendy entered the ring wearing green medieval costumes. They looked like they had escaped from a Hollywood production of Robin Hood.

Back on the Tannoy, the set-up guy answered back, 'Actually, I am. I've keeled all tha others.'

The conversation might have carried on had they not noticed Ray advancing on the commentary box, waving his arms.

'... ucking time too!' said Ray as his mike became live. Ray was not a 'merry man' but he was professional. In the business of falconry, no mews is bad mews.

'Good Morning everybod-ay! We are Trussoch Falconry and we'll be demonstrating for you, this morning, vee ancient art of falconry. In fact, it is very old indeed going back four fousand years at least to Ancient China. Vey probably had less of a problem with microphone hand-overs in vose days but were just as skillful at persuading vese perfectly evolved aerial predators to do veir biddin'.'

Wendy, an attractive thirty-something, approached in her tight green body stocking. On her left wrist she carried a hooded raptor.

'Now!' said Ray *hamming up* his rich estuarial tones.

'Vis is Wen-day, my charmin' and talented assistant.'

There are hoots and wolf-whistles from the crowd now loitering by the bar entrance.

'And this is,' continues Ray removing the falcon's hood, '... is Fursday. And Fursday is a cross between a Gyr Falcon and a Saker Falcon. Gyrs are big and Sakers are strong. So Fursday here is a big, strong girl who can quite easily chase her prey to exhaustion if necessary. While the weather's nice, I'm going to give Fursday some exercise using a loo-ah.'

Ray launched the falcon which immediately began to gain height. The air was still cold from the earlier rain but the sunshine was beginning to create eddies and thermals which the falcon could exploit.

Back on the ground, Ray held up the lure which looked like the front quarter of a rabbit attached to a long line.

'Vis,' he continued, 'to the uninitiated, is a loo-ah. It's actually a piece of weighted rabbit skin. But Fursday don't know that. To her, the loo-ah is something tasty, flying around in the air which she can catch and eat. As a rule, most raptors love to eat fresh and I fink it's fair to say that if Peter Rabbit popped up in the middle of the ring, Fursday 'ere would probably go for that rather than my manky, old loo-ah.'

Ray jerked the line to pull the lure out of the path of the stooping falcon which streaked past before flapping away to recover height. Peter noticed the satin sheen of the falcon's light golden plumage as it shone in the sunlight. As one stoop followed another, Peter could see its head turn and keep focus on the lure with its powerful eyesight. With each succeeding stoop, more of the drinkers were lured away from the safety of the bar to the ringside outside to watch this masterful display of man and bird working in perfect harmony. Peter even noticed the sun glinting on the red hair of one of the drinkers as he lolled against his large, spandex-clad female friend.

Ray continued to whirl the lure but now the falcon seemed hesitant.

'Now Fursday can be a bit of a diva when she wants to be,' said Ray. 'She used to 'ave a boyfriend. But she killed and ate him.'

Peter could see that Ray's arm was beginning to tire.

'I don't know what's going on here,' said Ray, 'but her eye seems to have wandered a bit.'

'I love this bit,' said Kevin at the front of the stand.

'What bit's that, then?' asked Peter.

'When the falcon sees something more interesting in the distance and fucks off.'

'Really?' said Peter. 'Does that happen often, then?'

'More times than you'd think,' said Kevin.

Back in the ring, the whirling of the lure was beginning

to tell on Ray whose arm was beginning to cramp up. Sweat gleamed on his forehead.

'Vis usually brings her in ... Hey!' he shouted down the mike. 'Hey!' he repeated but to little effect.

The expensive, hybrid falcon had now climbed to a great height and was barely visible; just a speck against the clear blue sky. Thursday seemed to be looking for something. Something other than the – by Ray's own admission – 'manky, old' lure.

Peter could not have known but the same glint of copper from the drinker's hair had also caught Thursday's attention and triggered a vigorous, primeval hunting response in this airborne killer. Perhaps the hair was the same colour as lemmings in Summer. Or perhaps, the ginger glint triggered a memory of a good feed at the expense of a pet guinea pig. Perhaps we shall never know. One thing we do know is that the gingery, hairy thing on top of the drinker's head looked a damned sight more interesting than that old piece of rabbit skin and seemed tantalizingly oblivious of the 'clear and present' danger which the falcon represented.

Even at that height Ray could see that Thursday had begun her stoop. Half with relief and half with exhaustion, he said, 'At last! Here she comes. Although she seems to be coming in at a funny angle. Hey!'

He moved smartly backwards towards the bar end of the ring.

'Hey!' he shouted for a final time.

Peter thought it odd that the falconer should be going to the falcon rather than the other way round. As he looked up, he could see the approaching falcon's wings were held back against its body to maximise speed. He thought he saw vapour trails from the wing tips. But whilst the falcon's speed was like that of an artillery projectile, the angle of approach was off.

The sound of the Gyr/Saker hybrid hitting the top of the drinker's head was similar to the popping of a crisp packet and clearly audible to all around the ring as was the tearing sound as the falcon appeared to scalp the ginger man.

With a cry of 'Ma heed!' the drinker sank to the floor.

'Yer hair, Barney! That bird's gone an' scalped yer!' screamed the spandex-clad woman. 'It's taken yer lovely reed hair!'

'No, it hasn't,' said a bearded drinker. 'It's a wig, yar dozy bint.' At this, the spandex-clad woman set up a wail of which a banshee would have been proud. Meanwhile, two heavily overweight St. John's Ambulance men arrived, puffing and wheezing, to minister to Barney and drip sweat on to him.

Ray was left speechless in the ring as he watched Thursday drag her prize to the roof of the food tent where, holding it down with her feet, she energetically pulled out tufts of ginger hair in search of something edible.

'Told you,' said Kevin. 'More times than you'd think.'

Later that afternoon, Peter met up with Jayne at her stand.

'So what did you do before you traded at game fairs?' he asked.

'Aren't you the nosey one. It's all questions with you, isn't it?' she said passing a sandwich and cup of tea to a waiting customer. 'I think I'm allowed some secrets, after all. Where are you next?'

'Do you know,' said Peter relaxing a little. 'I couldn't tell you off the top of my head. I am so knackered my mind has gone blank.'

'Aah. Poor lamb,' she teased, 'You'll get used to it. You'll have to learn to save your strength for the more enjoyable aspects of life.'

She winked at Peter whose pulse-rate immediately quickened.

17. IF I HAD A SIXPENCE

ON his way back to the stand, Peter tried to concentrate on his mission but found it impossible to keep his mind from wandering back to Jayne. He'd always prided himself on his powers of concentration and his ability to set a plan and stick to it. Still, this was probably the first time he had noticed a girl flirting with him and it threw his thoughts into a jumble.

As he trudged back through the mud to the stand with two soggy kebabs, he felt that something big was about to happen in his life, something which would radically change his future.

Everything appeared to be unravelling. Even his loyalty to the department. He hadn't uncovered any evidence of VAT irregularities at any of the shows he had attended. Operation Wild Goose, despite its big build-up, seemed to be a red herring. He suspected that Terry wasn't being entirely honest with him. He felt that he was the butt of some complicated civil service joke.

The possibility that these shows might be a front for some other sort of criminal activity, a massive drugs distribution system, for instance, had taken him completely by surprise. He was also surprised and elated that Jayne, unlike most women he had bumped into, seemed to be not just helpfully disposed towards him but, dare he think it, attracted to him.

'I've bought you dinner to make up for my crap navigation yesterday,' he said to Kevin, as he entered the stand. At the back, Kevin presented an exotic vision; a large man clad in camouflage clothing who had obviously been rained on in the recent past sitting in a deck chair surrounded by hundreds of plastic geese and ducks. Between the widgeon and teal decoys at his feet, like some bizarre ancient tribute, a pile of crushed empty beer cans was beginning to form.

Kevin belched richly as he reached out for the soggy kebab. They ate in silence until Kevin rose from his chair to chuck the kebab wrappings in the bin.

'You know what, if that hadn't been soaked in rainwater for a good half hour, that would have been a really good kebab. Even as it was, it's cheered me up. Thanks for that. Where have you been anyway?'

'What?' said Peter, still deep in thought. 'Oh I just went for a wander. Bumped into Jayne and had a chat with her.'

'What? That nice-looking brunette on the food wagons?'

'Yes, that's the one,' said Peter nonchalantly.

'You dirty dog. You're sniffing round that, are you? Well good luck to you, mate. From what Paul at Pigeon Destroyer was saying the other week many are called but few have been chosen since she started on the shows a couple of years back.'

'A couple of years?' said Peter. 'She talks like she's been doing this for a decade or more.'

'Don't think so, mate,' said Kevin opening another can of beer and taking a swig. 'Paul was saying that she suddenly appeared at Belvoir Game Fair with that old boy, Sid, just eighteen months ago.'

'Oh,' said Peter now more confused than ever. 'Kev, I've just got to give my Ma a ring as it's her birthday today. I don't want to leave it any later.'

He ducked beneath the stand canvas out into the dark and walked a good distance away from the tents. Crouching down, he listened for a good few minutes to check that he was alone before taking out his mobile phone and ringing Terry's private line. Again, it came up as disconnected. He rang the office number.

'Is that you, Janice?'

'Hello Peter.'

Peter began to wonder whether Janice had any private life at all or whether, like him, she existed merely to work. At least the line was clear this time, without all of those unsettling crossed lines which seemed to plague him when he rang during the day.

'Janice, I need to speak to the Assistant Secretary as a matter of grave urgency but his mobile line appears to be disconnected. Can you get a message to him? He didn't reply to the last one I left with you.'

There was a long guilty silence at the other end of the line. To her surprise, Janice felt remorse at the officially-sanctioned cruel joke which was being perpetrated against Peter. There were obviously trace elements of pity left in her character despite her years with the department. She decided to act.

'You really don't get it, do you, Peter?'

Peter, puzzled by the pregnant pause, now became flustered at this digression.

'Get what?' If the game fairs had taught him anything, it was directness.

'They're running you ragged out there.'

'Who are? What are you talking about?' replied Peter.

'Terry ... and Maurice.'

'I don't know what you're on about,' said Peter shirtily, misconstruing Janice's attempt at honesty. 'Is it too much to ask that you get an urgent message to Terry without delay or we are going to have a serious situation on our hands here.'

He rang off.

'Wrist-artist,' muttered Janice as she reached for the departmental telephone directory.

***

Terry entered the party. Having parked Mrs. Dudley-Vaughan at her mother's in Sussex together with a medicinal case of her favourite Foxdenton gin, he had come up to town that afternoon under the pretence of an early start and a working Sunday in the office.

'Time and government stop for no man,' he muttered by way of explanation, kissing 'Mrs. D&V', as he called her, on the cheek as he departed.

On arriving at Victoria, he had taken a taxi to a discrete Mayfair mews house where the evening's party was to be held. No normal party this. Attractive young women and men from around the world in various stages of undress and inebriation populated every stairwell, corridor, sofa and closet. Unlike these godlike 'hosts' and 'hostesses', the 'guests' were less alluring. Bizarre combinations of costume, fetish wear and lingerie polluted the view. A high court judge in a Sylvester the Cat onesie here, a male front-bench member of Her Majesty's Loyal Opposition dressed as Margaret Thatcher there. Terry's bespoke latex trousers from Spank of New York (purchased at huge expense on a recent Trade Mission) and his chain mail singlet with nipple apertures looked positively tame by comparison.

He downed a Viagra with a swig from a champagne flute before being addressed by a familiar frame. Time and gravity had not been kind to Maurice. Not even the gaily coloured baby doll, suspenders and stocking combo could disguise the sagging burgundy belly, pendulous breasts and knees which would have won numerous prizes if there had been departmental seaside day trips.

'Good evening, M. Janet Reger?' inquired Terry.

'We live in times of austerity, Terry, in case you hadn't noticed. It's Victoria's Secret, actually.' Maurice's response was tetchy to say the least.

'Look, Terry,' he continued, adjusting a false eyelash. 'I don't want be a whiner but the beginning of the evening was frankly ruined for me. My secretary rang asking me about your whereabouts. I don't have to tell you how disconcerting that sort of thing can be. Apparently that tiresome drone, Figgis, has a matter of great import that he wishes to discuss with you.'

'Oh Lord,' said Terry. 'Is there no escape? What on earth does he want now? I had to ditch my mobile because of his constant, vacuous updates. I really will have to think about bringing this whole tiresome little project to an end.' As the Viagra kicked in, he shifted to the right redirecting the latex tent which had manifested itself away from his superior.

'Thank you,' said Maurice observing the civility. 'It's good to see that some of us still consider it rude to point. I hope you can sort out this Figgis matter sooner rather than later. Anyway, I hope you have a good evening. I shall try my best to recover my party spirit. I'm off upstairs to see Madame Xandra after a few more drinks.'

Terry shivered. Not at the mention of the famous Berlin dominatrice's name but from the cold draft blowing through the open window at the rear of the room.

'I'll be with you in a minute, Maurice', said Terry moving towards the open casement. But Maurice stopped him.

'Just a word of warning,' he said quietly. 'That Liberal peer is here again. He's already been warned about his behaviour which is frankly bizarre. He's lurking over there behind the curtain.'

Terry looked over M's shoulder and could see a figure in the shadows.

'As soon as anyone leans over to close the window,' warned Maurice, 'Well. You know. It's just like that version of the Eton Boating Song.'

18. POTATO GUN

BY ten o'clock that evening, Kevin had finished the canned beer. This left only Peter's emergency stock of dry cider. Peter took seriously Abe's advice during the course of his training, 'Never travel with less than twenty litres of good quality cider. You never know who you're going to bump into.'

Taking Abe at his word, the back of the LDV was always equipped with a large bag-in-a-box of cider from a reputable maker such as Roger Wilkins, known as the Saint of Mudgley or Raglan Cider Mill's Breakwell's Seedling. Both had been moved with the rest of Peter's stock into Kevin's van. Both were bone dry.

'This tastes like fucking varnish, too,' said Kevin forcing another pint down his throat. 'Here, top me up and put a bit of that other one in it to take the edge off it.'

Peter topped the dry cider with some of Weston's Old Rosie and passed the glass back.

The canvases rustled and a set of heads appeared through the gap. It was Helen and Paul. Paul had been at the gin and Helen had a box of white wine. The alcohol level increased as a party atmosphere began to develop. Bit by bit, Peter's mind was diverted from his unsettling discovery.

Paul entertained them with some indiscreet stories about shows where overnight thievery had been carried out by the estate owner's son and the summary punishment meted out. Everyone tut-tutted their disapproval at the decline of the landed gentry.

Kevin contributed his story about a character at his local rugby club nicknamed 'Parrot'. Helen asked where the nickname came from. Kevin explained with relish that if you looked closely at nearly every team photo taken between 1988 and 1994, Parrot's penis was always clearly visible resting on someone's shoulder.

Helen's disapproving blush soon gave way to a rather attractive giggle. She then regaled them with the tale of their recent exotic holiday in Sri Lanka. She had been plagued by an English couple who would talk about nothing but their bowel movements.

'Anyway, after nearly two weeks he still hadn't gone,' said Helen bringing the tale to a dramatic conclusion. 'It were only on the final day that he appeared by the pool and told me that he had finally been but that 'it were so hard', he said, 'you could whittle it like a stick!"

Amidst the laughter that greeted this punch line, Kevin's involuntary retching reflex nearly ruined the tone of the evening.

Peter was wondering if he should chip in when another head appeared through the gap in the canvases.

A vision clad in a three-piece, camouflaged shooting suit appeared before them. Carl Cox, show organiser, estate manager and deer-worrier had spent some years in a regiment of the British Army's lightest infantry, an experience which had brought out in him some eccentric interests.

These included gate-crashing wedding parties which coincided with game fairs. He and his friends Scottish Donald and professional Cornishman, Chris Green, would claim to be either a group of itinerant mummers hired to entertain the party or distant Canadian cousins from Magnetawan in the Province of Ontario. The resulting mayhem was usually the same with their forced ejection from the proceedings being mandatory.

In his hands, he held what looked like a child's toy resembling a very small plastic trench mortar.

After a glass of cider, Carl said: 'I'm just waiting for Chris to get here and then we'll begin.'

Chris Green arrived. Apart from his reputation for shooting and eating virtually anything that God invested with breath, Chris's out-of-hours interests included 'being Cornish' and 'blowing stuff up'. Carl's toy was a bit of a step down from the cordite and black powder big-bangs that Chris was used to but he decided to make the best of it.

'What on earth is that?' slurred Paul pointing at the plastic contraption.

'That, my friend, is the mother of all potato guns. Capable of firing a one-pound King Edward nearly three hundred yards, this is the last word in tuber projectile technology.'

Alcohol, drunks and a potato gun. What could possibly go wrong?

Eyes grew wide with amazement. 'Oohs' were 'oohed'. 'Aahs' were 'aahed'. The reception of the potato gun seemed unanimously positive until a voice from the wall of duck and goose decoys chipped in.

'That's bollocks, that is,' said Kevin. 'That poxy thing couldn't fire a potato three hundred yards. Look it's all ...' Alcohol suddenly rushed in and filled that part of Kevin's brain where words had previously been. '... plastic.'

Carl looked hurt. But he loved a challenge.

'Right,' he said. 'Follow me!'

Out they went, into the cold and dark, and straight to the casting pond which had been established on the perimeter of the showground. Under torchlight, Carl crouched down and producing a fine example of a one-pound King Edward potato from his game bag tested the fit down the capacious barrel of the gun.

'Not too tight, not too loose,' he said, leering at Helen.

She looked away snorting in disgust.

Carl suggestively eased the projectile into position down the gun muzzle.

Next he carefully unscrewed the combustion chamber and, producing a can of L'Oreal hairspray, squirted a small amount into the chamber before quickly securing the breech. Primed and ready, he presented the potato gun to the inebriated, tittering audience.

The casting lake was about a hundred yards long. At the far end was a caravan. Inside the caravan, shone a dim light. The type of light that says, 'We've gone out for the evening but we've left the smallest light on in the hope that it might deter any passing, opportunistically-inclined burglars.'

Framed by the dimly lit window was the silhouette of a territorial Yorkshire Terrier whose high-pitched yapping could be heard even at this distance.

'Ladies and Gentlemen. I give you the bouncing spud. Mr Green! Over to you.'

Chris stepped forward, inspected the Calibri cigarette-lighter trigger mechanism, before shouldering the weapon, aiming it at the surface of the casting pond some twenty yards off.

The report was of a deep, visceral kind which seemed to make everyone's ears pop. The potato was clearly visible as it shot out of the muzzle on its trajectory, a bit like a hand-launched ground-to-air missile.

The 'oohs' of delight and admiration soon turned to disappointed 'aahs' as the potato achieved only two bounces before disappearing beneath the water's surface.

Everyone became ten years old.

'I want a go! I want a go!'

Kevin remained aloof from the general enthusiasm, disdainful of Carl's great claims.

The potato gun was reloaded and handed to Paul.

'Now, my lover,' said Chris in full Cornish assistance mode, 'you want to take a shallower aim about twenty-five yards to get this bugger to bounce.'

The report of the gun seemed even louder this time as the potato left the barrel.

'Oooh!' went the crowd as the potato bounced like a gun dealer's cheque; once, twice, three times. It even tumbled through the air just like a miniature version of Barnes-Wallace's famous bouncing bomb.

The 'oohs' continued as the potato skimmed the surface of the casting pond.

'Five, six ... seven,' counted Carl.

'Eight, nine, ten,' counted Helen.

'It doesn't seem to be slowing down,' said Chris.

As the potato sped towards the dimly-lit caravan, the terrier's barking became frenzied as if it knew of its impending nemesis. The King Edward slammed into the side of the caravan like an Exocet punching a dinner plate-sized hole. Everyone held their breath in the post-impact silence.

But as soon as the terrier's yapping recommenced, they broke into applause.

'Nice shot, my bootiful,' said Chris Green patting Paul on the back.

'It's still not three hundred yards though.' Kevin was determined to remain unimpressed.

'Oh! Ye of little faith!' cried Carl as he rummaged round in his game bag for another projectile.

'Is this what you're looking for?' Kevin held in his hand the perfectly-shaped potato he had bought in Carlisle.

***

On the far side of the game fair site, Pablo was having a good evening; not a great evening but a good one, nonetheless.

Back in Mexico it was the Night of the Dead and everyone would be celebrating. The drug deal concluded, Pablo, Juan and Jesus saw no reason why they shouldn't celebrate this most traditional of Mexican festivals even though they were in deepest, darkest Scotland. They got together with some Mancunian dealers, cooked up a fiery chipotle stew, cracked open some of the better mescal and Mexican beer and things were flying.

The production of a cage-full of rats from the back of a van and their swift and messy dispatch at the jaws of Puppy, a Pit Bull cross had cheered Pablo up no end.

His knife-trick routine went off faultlessly impressing the Mancunians. One gringo had tried to copy the routine but had ended up stabbing the back of his hand with the wide-headed blade. Whilst not entirely necessary for a good time, Pablo couldn't remember any enjoyable events in his life in which blood, usually someone or something else's, had not played an integral part.

Both he and the gringos had laughed themselves to tears at the sight of the guy removing the knife from the back of his hand and then try, single-handed to stem the flow of blood from the wound with a roll of kitchen towel.

He was eventually half-dragged, half-carried across the showground to the St. John's ambulance where, Jesus noted, the obese ambulance crew also appeared to be celebrating the Night of the Dead with a huge box of cream cakes.

As Pablo staggered behind the food wagons to take a pee in the field beyond, he mulled over his United Kingdom experience so far. Ever since he and his colleagues had arrived in the UK from the shanty towns of Tijuana, he had been miserable. He didn't like the weather. He didn't like the food. He certainly didn't like the gringos but most of all he hated this weird new way of distributing drugs.

At home in Tijuana, the dealers queued up in an orderly fashion and were genuinely grateful for whatever you let them have. If they weren't, you drove them, together with their friends and relations, out into the desert, machine-gunned them and buried them. There was always another peon to take their place.

Back in Tijuana, being a gangster wasn't just a living. No, it was more than that. It was a profession. You only survived as a gangster after years of developing your machismo and observing and learning from the mistakes of others; often as you were cutting bits off them. Not over here though.

These gringos didn't play by the same rules. I mean, who brings a dog to a deal? He chuckled as he remembered Juan suggesting that the dog was the brains of the other team's operation. And then all of that unseemly squabbling about price. This was not how a man behaves. This is what women do ... when they are shopping ... at the market ... for underwear. He held that thought for a moment.

As his flow ebbed, he remembered the disaster with the car at Carlisle and all the excitement of concluding the deal. It had been a long day. He knew he would sleep well that night untroubled by the usual nightmares populated by his victims over the years.

Pablo was not wrong there. The one-pound King Edward smashed onto the top of his head with all the speed that the physical force gravity and L'Oreal hair spray could muster. He didn't even remember hitting the grass as he twisted and fell, face up, to the ground.

Some minutes later, Juan, too, decided to take a leak and edged away from the fluorescent lighting of the food wagon into the darkness beyond. Juan was the drinker of the crew. He had drunk a lot this evening but not that much that he didn't notice things. But standing still was difficult without swaying about. As he urinated, he was puzzled by how his flow hitting the ground when he swayed to the left sounded different to that when he swayed to the right. Peering onto the dark ground before him, the explanation soon became apparent. To the right, he was peeing onto grass. To the left, he was peeing on the prostrate form of Pablo.

'Gringo Bastards!' he thought. 'They laugh and drink with us but all the time they are planning to kill us and take the drugs and the money. Even now, they have murdered Pablo and are probably planning the same fate for me and Jesus.' He shook the last drops onto Pablo and did up his flies.

'We cannot use guns without blowing our cover,' he thought. 'We must do this the old-fashioned way. I wonder where the nearest desert is in this Scotland.'

After a few moments trying to plan things, he decided that he had had too much mescal and would just have to wing it.

'Hey, joo,' he said to Clint as he entered the food wagon. 'Does joo dog like snack? Can I feed joo dog?'

'Sure, pal. He'll eat anything,' said a relaxed and unsuspecting Clint. Juan tossed the dog a ketamine capsule nonchalantly. Nobody noticed. He then motioned to Jesus to join him outside for a smoke. Once outside, he looked carefully about to check that the Mancunian who had taken out Pablo wasn't hidden in the shadows and then showed Jesus the prone body of their compadre.

'What's this?' whispered Jesus.

'Is Pablo,' said Juan nonchalantly. 'Joo see. It ees like this. The gringos. They double-cross us. They want the drugs and the money!' whispered back Juan.

'Why does he smell of piss?' asked Jesus.

'It is their way,' said Juan. 'They dishonour their enemies even when they are dead.'

'Madre de Dios!' hissed Jesus. 'For this, they will pay.'

'Yes. Yes. But we must do it silently. It is fitting. It is The Night of the Dead, after all.'

It wasn't a difficult task. By the time they re-entered the food wagon, Pete, the head honcho of the Mancunian gang, was face-down on the table in a pool of chipotle stew and mescal which had only achieved the briefest of introductions to his stomach before being regurgitated. Mickey, the driver, was not in a much better state. Puppy was upside down beneath the table legs and jaws twitching away as he slumbered off the effects of the ketamine. In fact, Clint was the only member of the crew who was conscious.

After checking the others, Juan placed a brotherly arm around Clint's shoulders. 'Eh hombre. We have fun evening, yes?'

'Top crack, pal. Top crack,' said Clint.

'Joo come outside now,' said Juan all smiles. 'I wish to talk to joo about something private.'

19. NIGHT OF THE NEARLY DEAD

WHEN Pablo came to, he found himself beneath the Mexican food wagon. Juan and Jesus had dragged him there some hours earlier before driving off with the trussed and confused Mancunian drug dealers and Puppy.

Pablo tentatively examined the substantial lump on his head with his fingers. He also noticed something else which, after sniffing his fingers, he decided was ... raw potato. As his senses returned, he noticed another smell ... well, not as good as potato. 'Not as good'... with a hint of mescal. He tried to sit up but only succeeded in hitting his head on the wagon chassis.

Juan and Jesus, freshly returned from their quest to find a suitable sandy burial site for their victims, heard Pablo's howl of pain and came running.

'Pablo!' said Juan. 'Joo alive! We thought joo were dead, man! Izza miracle!'

'You're right,' chipped in Jesus in mysterious tones. 'It is a miracle. It is the Night of the Dead! They have sent Pablo back to us. Why is that? Don't they like heem?'

'Shut joo mouth, Jesus,' said Juan. 'Just be happy that they send Pablo back to us, eh?'

'The gringos? Have they left?' stammered Pablo, each word an effort.

'Er, yes,' said Juan. 'In a manner of speaking ...'

'What manner of speaking, Juan. Tell me straight, man, or I beat joo.'

'Well,' said Juan, his mind racing, 'when we saw that

they had killed you, we thought they wanted to take the drugs and the money ...'

Even through the thumping headache, the likely series of events became clear to Pablo.

'Joo killed them, didn't joo?' he said calmly cutting short Juan's explanation. 'Joo killed them and joo got rid of the bodies like we do back home.'

'Well, er ...' stammered Juan. 'Er ... yes. But not exactly like we do back home. We couldn't find a desert so we buried them in a small patch of sand in front of some buildings a long way from here.'

As the first light of dawn appeared on the horizon, Pablo wished that his mystery assailant had finished him off. It would certainly have been quicker and cleaner than what was heading his way when this king-size cock-up was reported back to El Cameleon.

***

Back in Mayfair, offices were just beginning to open up. For Walton, it had been an early start.

Some days, he just hated his job. Some days, Walton thought that his old Dean of Studies at Don University had been right.

'You'll end up a glorified messenger boy for someone who has power and influence but you'll never amount to much yourself.'

Some days, the messages were better than on others. Today the message was bad. Very bad. He had just ended a phone call with an angry man from Manchester. A man so angry that the limited vocabulary left to him by years of sustained steroid abuse seemed insufficient to express his anger.

For this reason, surmised Walton, the flow of verbal abuse from the man in Manchester was punctuated with shrieks, shouts and howls which would not have been out of place in the Primate House at Bristol Zoo. They certainly did nothing to clarify the view from Manchester about this morning's news story: the discovery of four local drug-dealers and a Pit Bull cross buried in the sandpit at St Athan's Church of Scotland Primary School in a small town just outside Glasgow. The name tag on the Pit Bull cross's collar read 'Puppy'.

'Must I do everything myself?' Ieuan's worst tantrums, Walton had noted, always started with a series of bellowed rhetorical questions. Heaven help anyone who actually suggested answers.

'I can't remember. Remind me someone. Did I actually ask El Cameleon to sort through his many thousands of employees and to select only those who were quite obviously incapable of carrying out the simplest commercial deal without totally fucking it up?'

'No. No. You asked for his best men,' chipped in Russlana, filing her nails. Sarcasm and rhetorical questions were two provinces in the same unvisited foreign country for her. 'I was there. I remember.'

Ieuan cast her a withering look. She alone might not fall victim to his rising anger.

'Now I have to take time out from important strategic matters to sort out these pissy little details. Why do I employ people? Can anyone tell me the answer? Don't I employ anyone who can sort this pissy little matter for me?'

Walton kept his mouth shut, his eyes down and leant forward to weather the imminent storm.

'Is it fair? I ask you. Is it fair that a business I've spent years building should now be in peril because no one thought to oversee the activities of a bunch of burro-fucking peons at one of our shows? Frankly, I am at a loss to understand just how even these insects thought it might in any way enhance my business interests by cutting the throats of some of the biggest drug retailers in the North West and then burying them and their domestic pets in a primary-school sandpit just outside Glasgow. Can anyone enlighten me?'

Walton ducked just at the right time to avoid a brass and rosewood humidor as it smashed against the panelled wall behind him spreading its Cuban contents like confetti. Russlana stopped filing her nails, looked at Walton and shrugged.

'I mean why stop at the dog?' continued Ieuan. 'Why not the cat, the gerbil and the fucking goldfish as well? But no. There must be a perfectly rational explanation. Perhaps they couldn't find a children's sandpit big enough to fit them all into!'

Ieuan was now red in the face, eyes blind with tears, out of control.

'If anyone has a better way of alerting every police force in the world to the presence of drugs being traded in the locale, perhaps they wouldn't mind sharing their insights with me now!'

Walton looked up just in time to see a Georgian occasional table heading towards him. He side-stepped deftly.

'Perhaps someone would like to hire a fucking laser show and put it up there in the clouds above each and every show we run. It could read 'Country Fair Organisers and Class A Drugs Wholesalers to the Gentry'. Do you think that would do the trick?'

***

'It's what we in the medical profession call a 'fog injury'.

The judgement was delivered by Sir John Stiffener, a rotund consultant surgeon dressed in an immaculate but quite elderly three-piece, pinstripe suit. He removed the watch from his waistcoat pocket to check the time.

'Mr Massey-Itch's shoulder at some stage was a completely different shape and that bit there should be seated nice and snugly into that socket there. The injuries you see before you are the type usually attributed to an articulated lorry when hitting flesh and bone at speed. Hence the expression 'fog injury'.

Young Mr. Spon and Penelope Massey-Itch gaped at him.

'But now,' said Sir John, 'I'm afraid I'm late for my next appointment so I must be ...'

'Not so fast, Sir John.' Penelope stepped between the surgeon and the door. 'Not, at least, until you have explained the deterioration in my brother's condition.'

'Well Madam,' said Sir John.

'That's 'Miss' to you, Sir John.'

'Er, well. Your brother is at an awkward age. One is never quite sure how elderly patients are going to react to a general anaesthetic.'

'Stuff and nonsense,' replied Penelope. 'On the day in question he was seen leaping around like a spring lamb before being felled by that flying tackle. I can't imagine that a little tackle like that would render him comatose. No. It's something that took place here in this hospital that caused the complications. And let me assure you, Sir John, I have the means and the motivation to find out.'

Suddenly, saving fifty quid on the bill by using that anaesthetist from Transdniestria seemed like less of a sound plan to Sir John. By the time it was obvious that the man with the gas had not the first clue what he was doing, Croesus was further under than Mozart and gaining fast on Ghengis Khan. It was only a matter of luck that his regular anaesthetist had been contactable and had managed to get in in time to save the day. Otherwise, this awkward discussion might be taking place in a morgue rather than a room in a private hospital.

Sir John never imagined that he would miss the NHS but he did. If there was a total balls-up, there was always a 'manager', civil servant or politician to take the blame. By the time the whole process was finished, most people had forgotten what the problem was in the first place.

Here in the private sector, the money was better but patients and their families expected results ... good ones. Now this Massey-Itch woman was kicking off about her brother and she looked like the living embodiment of trouble. But before he could reply, there was movement and sound from the bed behind them. Croesus coughed and then opened his eyes. He parted his parched lips and in a rather croaky voice said: 'Alan Titchmarsh.'

***

Later that day, at the head office of Henge Enterprises in Mayfair, matters had not improved.

'Don't I have enough to deal with already without this?'

The humidor salesman beat a hasty retreat from the panelled office as Walton battened down the hatches for another onslaught. He had handed Ieuan the print-out of an email from Spon.

'Dear Christ! As if it's not enough that I seem to be in business with the massed ranks of the retarded, now I have to deal with the lame too?'

'Is not lame that is problem,' Russlana pointed out, reading the document. She sat down. Her nylon-clad legs crossed momentarily creating enough electricity to run a small town.

'Business can continue with limpy man but not when he cannot speak so Spon is correct.'

Ieuan again gazed malevolently at her. However, Russlana's summing up of the situation was correct. Had Croesus's unfortunate experience resulted in his being afflicted by a gammy leg, then he might still have been able to play even the most nominal role in the running of Gewgaw Events. Sadly, the anaesthetist's suspected incompetence had resulted in a series of mini-strokes which had damaged the speech centres of Croesus's brain rendering him incapable of saying anything other than the name of celebrity gardener, broadcaster and writer, Alan Titchmarsh.

Young Mr. Spon's email pointed out that under the terms of the trust, Croesus's interest in Gewgaw would be taken over by his sister, Penelope.

20. DUPLICATION

TERRY leant back in his Charles & Ray Eames armchair and placed his immaculately-clad feet on the matching footstool.

'Hah!' he thought. 'You don't have to be born with a sense of entitlement. Nowadays, if you're careful enough climbing the greasy pole, you can acquire one. You've done okay for yourself, Terry, my son.'

He had checked earlier that morning. The diary was nearly empty. Just a ten o'clock and then nothing. 'Looks like a long lunch at that charming little Korean place on Leadenhall Street.'

Through the glass wall, he could see his ten o'clock appointment already waiting. He drew back his cuff to reveal the vintage Patek Philippe on his wrist.

'Keen,' he thought to himself. 'Half an hour early. Let him wait. I had to.' His secretary smiled at him; a picture of unhurried efficiency. Or was it the calm before the storm?

His phone rang. He picked up the receiver.

'I've got that call you wanted, sir,' said the switchboard.

'Oh good. What's the name of the restaurant again?'

'Not the restaurant, sir. That mobile number.'

'Oh,' said Terry disappointedly. He'd forgotten that he'd asked the switchboard to track down that annoyance, Figgis. 'Oh ... alright then.'

Through the glass wall, he now saw two badly-suited men with utilitarian, close-cropped hair in animated discussion with his secretary. One of them was pointing, red-faced, through the glass, directly at him.

'Bloody cheek,' muttered Terry.

'Sorry, Terry. Have I caught you at an inconvenient time?' said Peter down the phone.

'No, no ...' said Terry distantly, wondering just why he had given this underling permission to be on first name terms. 'No that's fine. How's it all going, Peter?'

'Well, thanks and I have exciting news to report, Terry. You know that all along we've suspected that these events have been a hotbed of VAT fraud.'

'We have? Oh yes, we have ... of course we have,' recovered Terry.

'Well, they're nothing of the sort.' said Peter triumphantly. 'It's much more serious than that. The shows are being used as a front for a massive nationwide drug-dealing operation.'

'What?' Terry could hardly believe his ears. 'What drugs? You're meant to be keeping your eyes open for VAT irregularities not conducting a drugs investigation. For God's sake, Peter. I've been backing you up to the hilt back here at HQ despite your lack of results but if you are going to start getting distracted by a couple of funfair attendants toking on the occasional spliff, then I feel the department's resources are being badly misused.'

Through the glass wall, Terry could see that his secretary was now involved in a fully-fledged shouting match with the visiting duo. The fat visitor was presenting what looked like a warrant card to the secretary and motioning towards the office door.

'It's not marijuana. And it's not just private use,' said Peter emphatically. 'We're talking about large quantities here. Yesterday evening, I saw with my own eyes a group of dealers from Manchester buy several kilos of cocaine ...'

The penny dropped. Terry leant over his desk and grabbed that morning's Daily Maul. Ignoring the hysterical headline which shrieked 'Death's Too Good For Them!' he scanned the story before asking Peter ...

'Did they have a dog?'

'What?' said Peter. 'Oh yes, Terry, they did as a matter of fact.'

'Did you catch its name?'

'I'm not following you here, Terry ...'

'Did you hear any of them call the dog's name?' said Sir Terry.

The office door handle rattled ominously. Terry could now see that his secretary had placed herself between the insistent visitors and his office door and an unseemly scuffle had broken out. His solitude was about to be invaded.

'Yes ...' said Peter. 'Funny that but one of them did call the dog. Its name was Puppy.'

Terry turned off his phone strode across the floor and opened his office door.

'... ing bitch has bitten me, sir' were the first words he heard.

'Don't be such a girl, Sergeant,' said the other policeman.

The thinner of the two plain clothes policemen had the secretary in an arm-lock with her face pressed against a Turkmen rug.

'What on earth is going on here?' Terry put on his sternest patrician manner.

'These men were trying to muscle in on your ten o'clock slot,' said his secretary from floor level.

Before he could remonstrate, a warrant card filled his field of vision.

'Bellend, Sir. Chief Inspector Frank Bellend of Serious Narcotics Investigation Force.'

The executive officer who had had ringside seats throughout the morning's events whilst waiting for his ten o'clock appointment sniggered. He was rendered into silence by a glare from the Chief Inspector's humourless features.

'SNIF, eh?' said Terry. 'That's very good.'

'I'm sorry, sir. What?

'SNIF. It's the acronym of your organisation.'

'Acro-what? Oh yeah. Funny that. No one's ever pointed that out before.'

Not to be further delayed or diverted, Chief Inspector Bellend stepped through the open door into Terry's office.

'And this,' he said, 'is Detective Sergeant Rimmer.'

Terry looked on as the policeman leant down to lift the now handcuffed and weeping form of his secretary from the floor. Behind them, Terry saw the executive officer's shoulders heaving in silent laughter as he pretended to read the paper.

'Was this really necessary, Chief Inspector?' he asked.

'Well, sir. She was being obstructive and Rimmer likes to keep his hand in.'

'Well come in, then, Chief Inspector,' said Terry guiding them into his office.

'But your ten o'clock ...' blubbered his secretary now handcuffed to her typing chair.

'Can you please ask him to reschedule.'

Terry began, 'So, how can I help, Chief Inspector?'

'Well, sir. It's slightly awkward. I'm going to have to ask you to exercise your discretion regarding the information I'm about to divulge.'

Terry nodded acquiescently and the police officer continued:

'You see, we've been tracking a group of Manchester drug dealers for about eighteen months now trying to find out about their supply and distribution network.'

Terry held up his hand.

'Before we get any further, would you like some coffee? We've just got a new machine.'

'Oh that's very kind of you, sir. White with three sugars, thank you.'

Terry leant forward and pressed the intercom. There was no answer. He pressed again before looking up and through the glass wall where he saw his secretary still handcuffed to her typing chair attempting to operate the intercom with her nose.

'Oh, of course. How silly of me. Would your Sergeant oblige me?' Terry motioned towards the secretary.

'Oh yes. Of course, sir.'

Bellend turned to his colleague.

'Would you mind, Sergeant? To continue then. The operation has been a goldmine for us. We'd had evidence pouring in from all directions. We thought at first that it was just a regional network which had been set up in Manchester but we now know that Manchester is just one of five regional hubs distributing drugs which are shipped in from all over Central and South America. These hubs are supplied by one kingpin and we are now very close to discovering his identity.'

'Has this got anything to do with those drug dealers who were buried in Scotland?' asked Terry.

'Well actually, it does, sir.'

Terry's attention was momentarily diverted by the sight of his now liberated secretary using her new Jimmy Choo's to kick Sergeant Rimmer squarely between the legs. The policeman hit the Turkomen rug like a sack of dog food and remained their clutching his groin.

'Oh dear, Chief Inspector. It looks like coffee will be delayed. But do go on.'

'These dealers from Manchester were our most productive source of information. Now they're gone, it's going to set us back a good two months in uncovering the kingpin of the operation. We've also been informed of a 'wild card'.

'A wild card?' repeated Terry, with one eye on the life and death struggle taking place beyond the glass wall. He saw - not without satisfaction - that Sergeant Rimmer was now handcuffed to the typing chair sporting a wire mesh, wastepaper basket over his head at rather a jaunty angle.

'I'm afraid I'm not as up-to-date on my poker terminology as I should be. Please be more specific, Chief Inspector ... or may I call you Bellend.'

The policeman winced.

'Chief Inspector is fine, sir. This intelligence comes directly from one of our undercover sources. The 'wild card' or unknown factor to which I am referring ... er ... to appears to be one of your own officers operating under the codename Figgis.'

Terry felt faint.

'I don't know if we've got a parallel investigation going on here.' said Bellend, 'and I haven't had time to check with Parallel Liaison, Operations and Duplications to see whether they have anything on their books.'

'Oh yes. Another corker' said Terry. If there's one thing I love, it's a good acronym.'

'Sorry sir?' said Bellend, oblivious.

'Well,' continued Terry, 'I suppose I could check with our Duplications Unit to see if anything comes up but it doesn't ring any bells.'

'Whoever it is nearly got himself killed with some pretty piss-poor 'obo' work. I'm told he soaked a group of foreign suspects with a roof-full of cold water and that our operative had to save his skin and risk ruining five years of work.'

'No, no,' said Terry playing for time. 'I'm still a bell-free zone. Let me just give our Duplication people a call and I'll get back to you. Is that all okay with you, Chief Inspector?'

21. THE GODFATHER

'THINK carefully, Walton. What exactly are you saying here?'

A sleepless night necessitated that the blinds were still drawn mid-morning in Ieuan Henge's Mayfair office. The last couple of days had taken the gloss off Ieuan's Teflon-coated narcissism and left him in a tetchy, highly-strung state which could easily turn to violence. The only member of his permanent staff who seemed immune from his wrath was Russlana, probably for no better reason than her compliance with his bizarre sexual appetites.

'Penelope has called in an independent auditor,' muttered Walton, his eyes downcast. 'Penelope has called in an independent auditor and he has requested full access to the Gewgaw books and lots of other information that we really don't want any outsider seeing.'

Thanks to Penelope's intervention on behalf of Croesus, the last few days had seen Walton's stock fall by several points on the Henge Index. He noticed that Ieuan no longer left matters to him but now demanded daily, sometimes hourly, reports. He had gone from trusted lieutenant to office whipping boy in a matter of hours and, remembering that none of his predecessors in this position had needed a retirement plan, he was becoming desperate to avoid being the bearer of any more bad tidings.

'So what are we going to do about it?' growled Ieuan, pacing around the victim of his bullying, just daring Walton to meet his gaze.

Walton looked at the floor and muttered, 'I'm afraid it would be best if she went.'

'I'm afraid it would be best if she went,' Ieuan mimicked Walton's voice. 'What the hell does that mean, pray tell?'

'She needs to disappear,' said Walton trying a new euphemism.

'Disappear?' said Ieuan his voice growing in volume.

'... to be tapped?' suggested Walton. 'Retired?'

'For God's sake, Walton!' bellowed Ieuan. 'No one really minds that this total fuck-up is your *meisterwerk* but at least be good enough to grow a pair when we are talking about how to put things right.'

Ieuan had always hated euphemisms and Walton's circumlocution was like tipping petrol on glowing embers.

'Not retire! Not tap! Not disappear! We are talking about killing the bitch! And that traitor, Spon. I'm tired of your crapola, Walton. God! If you want something done properly nowadays, you might as well do it yourself!'

***

El Castello was a generic Mediterranean restaurant in a cul-de-sac off Charlotte Street in London's West End. The original owner was Spanish; the current owner Italian; the staff were Albanian and Croatian and the kitchen manned by North Africans. Pizza and tagines rubbed shoulders with chicken provençal and bouillabaisse on the menu yet everything tasted very faintly of curry. Raffia-clad wine bottles from Italy hung on mock-wooden beams. North African blue and white crockery gathered incongruously around a whole Pata Negra ham from Northern Spain on its wooden carving stand. The media folk of W1 had quickly tired of this car-crash of culinary cultures and even on Friday lunchtime, it was quiet. As business declined, the owner had borrowed heavily to keep the business afloat. Unfortunately for him, he had borrowed from Ieuan Henge.

Ieuan, who had always loved films or 'movies' as he preferred to call them, planned to murder Penelope and Spon by re-enacting Michael Corleone's first murder from the Godfather Part One.

'It's your fuck-up, Walton, so it's about time you got your hands dirty.'

Ieuan loved piling on the pressure. He knew that Walton was a good back-room boy and that he was a reasonably efficient organiser, but killer?

'Well,' thought Ieuan, 'Let's see how he gets on with a bit of Mafia live action replay.'

During the planning meeting, Ieuan hadn't even mentioned the Godfather re-enactment idea when Walton interrupted. Interrupting Ieuan was never a good idea.

'Oh I get it,' said Walton. 'I come into the restaurant looking like I'm not 'carrying' but then excuse myself to go to the John and the gun's taped to the cistern. Just like in the Godfather!'

'Yes, it's sort of homage, if you will, to Francis Ford Coppola,' said Ieuan.

'Lobster?' chipped in Russlana. 'Homard means Lobster? What is Francis Ford Coppola doing with lobster? I thought he was into wine?'

'Not homard, homage,' Walton corrected.

Ieuan let out a sigh of exasperation. He was impressed that Walton had rumbled his Godfather theme but keen not to show it.

'Let's see how young Walton deals with point-blank, up-front, 'blood and brains all over your best shirt' murder,' he thought. He suspected that this would be way outside Walton's comfort zone and half-hoped that Walton would make a complete hash of it. Ieuan could then enjoy the prospect of his employee's confidence ebbing away, day by day, under a barrage of minor slights and insults until his inevitable disappearance and replacement by a new factotum.

On the appointed day, Ieuan, Russlana and the driver, Igor, were waiting at the table. Usually El Castello was deserted on a Wednesday lunchtime. Annoyingly, this Wednesday was an exception. A group of badly hungover oafs were regaling each other with stories of their exploits from what appeared to be a stag party the previous evening.

'What is 'stag party'?' asked Russlana. Even with her previous experience in gentleman's entertainment in the Emirates, she had never heard this term.

'It's nothing,' replied Ieuan. 'It's just a party where venison is served for a main course.' He wanted these oafs to disappear and quickly.

Spon had telephoned to say that they were running late but it looked like the oafs were settling in for the afternoon.

''Ere, these grapes taste off!' said one.

'You plonker!' replied his fellow. 'They're olives.'

'Hope she don't mind,' said the third gurgling with laughter.

After their hilarity had died down the first said, ''Ere mate! I don't feel well. I wish I hadn't had that kebab now. It must 'ave been off.'

He got up from the red-chequered table top and hurried towards the sign which announced, rather unhelpfully, in Albanian, '*Tualet*'. As everyone in the dining room heard the cubicle door slam shut, Ieuan dispatched Igor to their table with a monosyllabic message the gist of which was that they would be ill-advised to remain in the restaurant a moment longer. The oafs fled leaving their gastrically-challenged colleague to his fate.

Spon and Penelope arrived. Both were slightly disorientated by the gloom of the basement dining room compared to the bright sunshine which managed to permeate the traffic fumes of Charlotte Street.

Spon introduced Penelope to Ieuan.

'A delight to meet you,' he said turning on the charm.

'I wish I could say the same,' said Penelope with her usual directness, 'but I find this whole affair about as sordid and shoddy as the decor of this alleged restaurant.'

Ieuan ignored the slight until the introductions were completed and his two victims were seated.

'Walton sends his apologies. He's running a bit late as well.'

'Oh dear. I hope he won't be too long,' said Spon.

Ieuan glared at Spon.

'Let me assure you there's nothing to worry about ... even for turncoats and traitors.'

Spon emitted a tiny, high-pitched fart of terror.

'Well, I hope it's not going to be like that peace negotiation in the Godfather when Michael Corleone blows away the opposition,' said Penelope.

Ieuan flashed his whiter-than-white teeth and laughed disarmingly for just a little too long. Russlana shook her ample bosom and joined in. Even Igor's granite-like features cracked momentarily.

'No. No, nothing like that,' soothed Ieuan annoyed that his homage to Francis Ford Coppola's masterpiece was transparently obvious even to the victim. 'After all, if we can't sit down and sort out our differences like civilised human beings what is the alternative?'

Russlana had always found the rhetorical question a bit of a challenge so decided to supply an answer.

'Then we, how you say, 'shoot their arses full of lead'. That is how we do it back in Russia.'

Igor nodded enthusiastically before catching Ieuan's glare.

A waiter arrived with what appeared to be an old-fashioned milk bottle filled with water and a tray of glasses which he arranged in the centre of the table. The waiter then saw Ieuan's glare, collected the glasses and the water bottle and beat a hasty retreat through the swing doors to the safety of the kitchen.

There was a baleful groan from the door marked 'Tualet'.

'Oh God, Mate! I'm dying ...'

The end of the sentence was obscured by the sound of something warm and liquid escaping a small and unhappy valve before hitting a variety of surfaces ranging from water through to vitreous enamel, painted brickwork and, finally, tiled flooring.

'Oh good. Here's Walton now,' said Ieuan nervously. He felt matters slipping from his grasp. Perhaps the arrival of Walton would get things back on track.

'Sorry I'm late,' said Walton. 'The traffic is grid-locked out there.'

He took off his coat and slung it around the back of a nearby chair revealing a slim-fit shirt, chinos and boat shoes. There could be no doubt that here was an unarmed man.

'Would anyone mind if I went to the john before we get started?' asked Walton.

'Only if you're not going in there to get the gun taped to the back of the cistern,' said Penelope.

There was the tiniest of pauses. Again, everyone laughed just a little too enthusiastically and too long. Walton regained his composure, pointed at Penelope as if in appreciation and moved towards the door marked Tualet.

Neither of his intended victims nor his colleagues heard him gag as he opened the loo door. The smell that assaulted his senses seemed to emanate directly from the bowels of Satan himself. Trying to control himself and wiping the tears from his eyes he made his way towards the cubicle which, to his consternation, he found locked. His polite but insistent knock on the door was met by the sounds of a mid-sized human being involved in the difficult task of regurgitating something with a similar volume to that of a small car. The gagging finally stopped. The sound of more warm liquid hitting the floor was accompanied by the acrid smell of vomit. Walton stepped back.

'Hey Buddy. Are you okay in there?'

As he knocked on the door again, he noticed that the vomit was beginning to flow across the floor through the space at the foot of the cubicle wall. He stepped further back.

'Hey Buddy. I really need to get in there, man. I'm desperate here too, you know.'

'Just go away. Can't you hear. I'm dyin' in 'ere.'

The occupant's words were followed by another cacophony of sound. From the noise of escaping gases, Walton worked out that this time the occupant's insides had chosen the southern exit to leave the premises.

'Uuuuuurgh,' groaned the occupant. Walton heard something heavy behind the door slump forward and slide floorwards where it joined the small lake of stomach acids, cheap lager, red wine, a tube of semi-digested Tic-Tacs and masticated meat and salad from what had obviously once been a kebab.

'Bollocks!' thought Walton. He just wasn't cut out for this sort of activity.

'I'll kick the door in,' he thought. Backing up a little he took a run up and delivered a flying kick to the cubicle door. It offered no resistance and burst open easily. However, the recumbent oaf within prevented the door from opening more than an inch.

Carefully avoiding the growing puddle of ordure, Walton now decided that he might be able to get to the cistern by going over the cubicle wall.

If he was lucky, he would be able to close the loo seat and use this as a platform from which to retrieve the gun. Using the corner of the wall-mounted porcelain urinal as a step he managed to kneel on top of the cubicle wall for less than a second before the sound of cheap plywood panels and metal brackets giving way alerted him to the fact that his descent into the cubicle space would be less controlled than he had hoped.

The recumbent oaf broke his fall but Walton's foot had wedged itself into the bend of the water closet and was now lying twisted at a painful and unnatural angle to his ankle. Nothing could be done for his clothes which were now as mired as an enamel kidney dish in a tropical diseases ward. On regaining his senses, he noticed that the cistern was a low-profile model which had no gap between it and the wall. He carefully shifted position and saw that Igor had taped the gun to the bottom of the cistern. But the pain in his foot and ankle confirmed that this total failure to execute the plan would probably be added to Icuan's growing list of his failures.

Out in the restaurant, host and guests alike had sat askance as they listened to this series of events unfolding in the chamber within.

'I think we've seen and heard enough, Spon. Don't you?' barked Penelope. 'It's quite obvious that there's no talking to these people and that our first instincts were correct. We're leaving.'

Young Mr. Spon made directly for the steps back to street level but found his path blocked by Igor. Penelope pushed Spon aside and delivered a crippling blow to the intimidating chauffeur using a leather bag full of pound coins which she kept specially for such occasions and charitable donations. Igor fell to his knees. Penelope, followed by the ageing solicitor, took the steps two at a time and burst into the sunlight and traffic pollution of a London afternoon.

Meanwhile, Russlana had teetered into the *tualet,* surveyed the scene of destruction therein and re-emerged holding her nose.

Ieuan sat, incandescent with rage.

'Well?' he said looking at Russlana.

'Is total fuck-up,' she replied.

22. WHEN THE CARAVAN'S ROCKIN', DON'T COME KNOCKIN'

'THIS is all very civilised,' thought Peter to himself. He and Jayne were sitting behind the recently recommissioned LDV parked on Row N sipping excellent coffee made with Abe's old-fashioned, cooker-top espresso machine and looking at the game fair life about them on a balmy late morning at Bixley Show in Surrey.

Two pitches down, trader Ken could be heard gently coaxing his reluctant generator into life:

'Fucking heap of crap. Why in God's name won't you work? WORK! DAMN YOU!'

The flow of obloquy was broken by the sound of something blunt, cheap and heavy coming into contact with something expensive, metallic and generator-like. From inside the stand, Glenda, Ken's female companion, could be heard:

'Have you switched the fuel valve to 'On'?'

After a couple more unsuccessful attempts, the generator burst into life.

There was an outbreak of applause from adjacent stands and vehicles. Glenda appeared by the entrance to her tent and curtsied.

Jayne smiled at Peter. Peter smiled back. They had grown close since witnessing the drug dealers at work behind the food wagons and Peter was slowly but surely becoming besotted with Jayne. He had never shared so much of his life with another person let alone a woman and the thrill of his secret identity only made the whole scenario only sweeter.

'Peter,' said Jayne putting her coffee mug down on the upturned feed bucket which was standing in for a table. 'I've been meaning to talk to you about the other evening.'

'Yes,' said Peter.

'I feel that the experience has drawn us together, somehow.' She continued looking around to check that they weren't being overheard.

'I'm pleased you feel that way because ...' said Peter. 'I feel the same way... that we have something in common.'

'Well,' continued Jayne drawing her chair closer, leaning forward to whisper something. 'There's something I feel that I need to tell you.'

Peter too drew his chair forward a little and leant forward expectantly.

'Peter,' she said with her voice dropping to a husky whisper. 'I know who you are.'

This was not what Peter had been expecting to hear.

'Oh,' he replied innocently. 'And who might that be?'

'I'm very fond of you, Peter. You're cute. But I know that Her Majesty the Queen probably has better credentials as a game fair trader than you do. Your van, your product, the way you dress, it's all too contrived. My best guess is that you are doing some sort of undercover work for a government department. If the other evening is anything to go by, you need a bit more training or you might end up as a statistic.'

Peter came back to reality with a bump.

'Well,' he said, summoning as much composure as he could, 'I think you're very beautiful and intelligent but if it's a matter of perfect cover-stories, you need to up your game as well. You might 'talk the talk' about selling food at the shows 'for years' but I know from several sources you've only been doing it for two years maximum not the seven or so that you claim.'

'Oh,' said Jayne. It was her turn to adopt a mask of innocence.

'In fact,' continued Peter quietly. 'If I had to guess, I'd say that you were an undercover operative. Probably police but I'm not sure. After all, you seem to know more about drug deals than is likely or healthy for a fast food vendor.'

Both remained leaning forward, staring into each other's eyes, faces expressionless, poised a few inches apart. Jayne was first to break the silence:

'My caravan ... Now!'

***

Mackerel, the Patterdale Terrier, had been enjoying a late morning snooze beneath the caravan behind the food stands. His slumber was now interrupted by the sound of two people making a rapid entry into the caravan followed, a few minutes later, by the sound of one person making a rapid entry into the other. This was not new territory for the Patterdale. He knew these sounds of old. Any minute now the caravan would start squeaking and groaning making sleep impossible. Sure enough, the elderly Cheltenham Safari caravan started, gently at first and then with a greater sense of urgency to rock from side to side. The two human occupants, Mackerel noticed, also started to squeak and groan.

With an air of resignation, the small, black dog rose to his feet, shook himself, sniffed at and urinated over the caravan steps and moved off to find an alternative vantage point. After a few minutes wandering, he settled himself down beneath another caravan behind row P to watch the antics of another human.

***

It was with a sense of achievement that Kev had found the missing Gaucho Brand Steak Pie in the cab of the Mercedes Sprinter. Ever since he had transferred the kit from the old van to this new one, he knew the pie had been in there somewhere, safe and sound in its tin, he had just not been able to lay his hands upon it. Having arrived at Bixley a day early he was already set up and so had decided to occupy his time this morning cooking a proper lunch for himself. He may have found the pie but the can-opener had eluded him. Now as morning became afternoon Kev was running out of alternative can-opening strategies and he was not happy.

He had checked nearly every item of goose-shooting equipment on his stand against the properties required in a can-opener and had, frankly, drawn a blank. He did remember seeing a programme once in which a man opened a tin by rubbing the end of it against a stone. An hour and a half of rubbing the edge of the tin with a stone had achieved nothing. He had also considered the screwdriver option but had discounted it. Gaucho Brand were known for their cavalier attitude towards the contents of their steak pies but even a mixture of road-kill from the Southern hemisphere, meat which had a strange bluish tinge to it and what appeared, on one occasion, to be a human toe nail was unlikely to be improved by the addition of tin alloy swarf.

There was always the option of borrowing a can-opener but the loss of face entailed in admitting to another trader that you needed a fully equipped modern kitchen to de-tin and prepare a Gaucho Brand Steak Pie would be too much. The final option was the oar which had been left in the back of his van at a previous show. If he could only dent the tin sufficiently he could then bend it in half and slowly work the can in such a way that it would break in half and he could extract the pie that way.

Mackerel's slumber was disturbed for the second time that day when the Gaucho Brand Steak Pie, having received a glancing blow from the oar wielded by Kev, had taken to the air like a meat and pastry-filled UFO. It had hit the neighbouring caravan under which the terrier was sleeping at some speed leaving a small indentation in the duck-egg blue panel work. Luckily, the neighbours weren't in. Kevin retrieved the errant comestible for another attempt. He was shocked to discover that the tin seemed entirely unscathed despite all his effort.

'Right!' he said with determination as once again he bore down on the unfortunate Argie food import with the oar. He missed the trajectory and direction of the steak pie this time as his attention was almost completely taken up with the disintegration of the oar on impact. It was only when he saw the long gash in the paintwork along the side of his new van that he was able to find the seemingly indestructible pie-in-a-tin.

'Aaaaagh!' Kev emitted a cry of impotent rage as he grabbed the still unblemished tin and strode to the front of the Mercedes where he picked up a four-pound club hammer recently used by the neighbouring pitch. Having cleared the oar remnants from his hair and beard, he placed the Gaucho Brand Steak Pie on a convenient stone much as an Aztec priest would place a sacrificial victim.

This wasn't tin-opening. This was an execution. Kev raised the club hammer high above his head and brought it crashing down with all the force he could muster on the unfortunate tinned main course. Chaos ensued. Although the tin was mortally wounded, the blow had again been off-centre sending the metal clad steak pie missile spewing a trail of brown sauce exhaust directly for the new Mercedes van's windscreen.

Kev reached out instinctively as if to prevent the inevitable but to no avail. The Gaucho Brand Steak Pie hit the windscreen square on. At the very same microsecond that separated the impact from the explosion of the glass, Kev's lips moved into the correct shape for letting out a long howl of anguish.

***

Back in the caravan behind the food stall, Peter and Jayne lay back on Jayne's bed deep in post-coital thought. Never in his sheltered life had Peter experienced 'spur of the moment' sex. Jayne's frame might be diminutive but she certainly kept in shape. Peter's with his years of sedentary lifestyle had frankly had difficulty keeping up.

Jayne leant across lazily and pecked him on the cheek.

'You're a bit of dark horse, aren't you? Whoever you are,' she teased. Then, kneeling on the bed with her hair tousled and her face and breasts glowing, she adopted a mocking formal manner.

'I think it's best we get this rather awkward moment over and done with. Don't you?'

She extended her hand:

'I'm Detective Sergeant Jayne Harvey, Serious Narcotics Investigation Force.'

'SNIF!' Peter giggled still enjoying the post-coital moment.

'Why?' said Jane turning to look in a mirror. 'Is there something on my nose?'

'No,' said Peter. 'It's the acronym of your organisation. S.N.I.F. Good eh?'

'Oh yeah,' she said. 'Funny. No one's ever pointed that out before.'

'Are you serious?' said Peter. 'Surely, someone ...'

Jayne was not to be distracted so easily. Reaching for her tee-shirt, she said, 'And whom might I have the pleasure of just shagging?'

Her frankness took him aback but he decided that honesty was probably the best course of action in the current situation.

'I'm Special Investigator Peter Figgis, Her Majesty's Department of Tax & Revenue Affairs.'

Jayne gave him an old-fashioned look and drew him closer as if she was going to hug him.

'Are you sure?' she said. 'I've had you checked out and there's no mention on the database of your department having any 'special investigators'. You're not telling me porkies, are you?'

'No, I am not,' replied Peter earnestly.

'Now come on and tell Auntie Jayne exactly what you are up to at these piss awful events and I'll tell you what I can so at least we'll be singing from the same hymn sheet,' she teased.

'I'm meant to be investigating VAT fraud on the game fair circuit but couldn't find any. I stumbled upon the drug dealing instead,' blurted out Peter.

'What?' said Jayne pushing him away. 'I don't believe it. We spend seven years setting up this operation and you just blunder into it by accident? Unbelievable!'

‘Well, I’m sorry,’ said Peter, shuffling to the side of the bed and pulling on his pants and trousers. ‘The criminal community were fresh out of fraud so the multi-million-pound international drug distribution system possibly involving a British hub seemed the next best thing. God, I wish I hadn’t bothered. No one at head office seems interested and now I’m getting the third degree from you!’

Jayne reached for her electronic cigarette. After a couple of puffs, she adopted a more conciliatory tone, ‘It is what it is. We’ll just have to get on with it but it would be good if we could pool resources. Do you agree?’

Peter nodded childishly. After they had washed and dressed, Peter and Jayne exited the caravan. As he stood on the caravan steps, he saw that the sun had lit up the showground in a golden glow. The English countryside had never looked better to Peter. His perfect moment was only slightly disturbed by three loud noises in quick succession from the direction of Row P.

Smack! The sound of something hammer-shaped mishitting something pie-like in a tin.

Smash! The sound of something pie-like in a tin breaking something big and expensive made of glass and ...

‘Noooooooooooooo!’ The scream of a soul in torment.

As darkness fell, Peter wandered back to the LDV to check that everything was in order. He bumped into Paul and Helen who were still setting up. This was unusual as Peter noticed that they always allowed an extra day for shows and were amongst the first to be ready. Paul, as was his wont, was holding a dead pigeon.

‘I hope that isn’t the same one you had at Funless,’ said Peter,

Paul looked at the feathered corpse, sniffed it and replied, ‘No. It’s a fresh one. We do have standards you know. We change the pigeons on the decoys for every show. There are no flies on us.’ He grinned.

‘Why are you so late setting up?’

‘We had to wait for a delivery to arrive back at house,’ said Paul in his broad Yorkshire accent.

Helen added: ‘And a right cock-up, that’s been. We’re expecting camouflage jackets and the idiots have sent us a forty-foot container half-filled with ghillie suits.’

‘Never,’ said Peter.

‘So, if you know anyone who needs a ghillie suit you know where to send them,’ said Paul. ‘We’ve got 500 sets in all sizes so, unless we have a sudden rush on, it looks like I’m going to be buried in one when I pop me clogs.’

23. PROTECTION

PENELOPE and Spon were meeting at Penelope's rebuilt farm, Studworks. The two sat on a long mahogany Georgian settle pulled up to the kitchen table. The warmth of the adjacent Aga seemed to have no effect on Penelope despite her heavyweight tweed suit. Spon, on the other hand, felt as if he was melting. Perched uncomfortably on the raised edge of the settle, he felt a trickle of perspiration make its way down his back beneath an already soaked vintage Jermyn Street shirt.

'I'm amazed that you thought that the information would be forthcoming, Spon,' announced Penelope as she picked up the tea tray and moved towards the chintz haven of the drawing room. Spon scuttled along behind. He was about to respond when she cut him off.

'Henge knows that we know about his criminal activities. He's hardly going to send us the information we need to confirm our knowledge now, is he?'

Spon was just grateful to be in a cooler environment. 'I suppose not.' He placed himself carefully in a cane-backed bergère already over-populated with lively cushions and then leant forward to pour himself some tea. He was stopped in his tracks by Penelope's icy glare. No one else played 'mother' at Studworks when Penelope was in the house. He sat back and waited for the cup of hot, heady Darjeeling.

'Scone, Spon?' said Penelope offering him the cake stand. This did nothing to put him at his ease. His time at school had been difficult. He had been teased and bullied on account of his surname which, whilst as English as they come, sounded strange to his more conventionally named fellows.

'Thank you, Penelope,' he said.

'I went back to that restaurant the day after our meeting for a look-see,' said Penelope. 'The owner was out. I noticed that the men's loos were being redecorated. Just out of curiosity, I thought I'd check.'

'Check what?' said Spon.

'The loo.'

'For what?'.

'Just to see whether Henge was bonkers enough to even consider it.'

'Consider what?' said Spon.

'What do you think, Spon? The pas de deux from Swan Lake? Hamlet's second soliloquy? The Periclean Oration at Athens? No! I wanted to see whether he really was bonkers enough to re-enact 'the hit' from The Godfather. Do try and keep up, will you? And what do think I found?'

'A gun taped to the loo?' said Spon.

'Nothing that conclusive, I'm afraid, but worrying enough. I found clear evidence of sticky tape on the lower part of the toilet cistern. I can only conclude that Henge is every bit as psycho as we feared and that we had both better tread very carefully from now on. If we represent an existential threat to his operation, he's almost bound to want us dead.'

'Oh!' said Spon. Three years at Oxford's least-known college, his Law Society training and years of practice as a country solicitor had hardly prepared him for this.

'That is why I have enlisted the help of some old friends,' continued Penelope. 'Austin! Healey! You can come in now.'

Two enormous men entered the room. Their huge frames were adequately but not comfortably contained within suits of a dark material generously cut to allow for concealed weaponry.

'Good God!' stammered Spon.

'The British Security Services. Membership has its advantages, eh?' quipped Penelope without cracking her deadpan expression.

'Austin and Healey, here, have just returned from some horrible, sweaty, non-tourist destination where they have probably been 'offing a few'. They've been told to take some time off and have agreed to help me out with our little problem.'

'Oh really?' said Spon tremulously.

'Why yes!' said Penelope gazing directly at the solicitor. 'Henge has tried once. He'll almost certainly try again. We cannot rely on him being rankly incompetent a second time. Austin here is charged with the protection of your life, Spon, and Healey will be – how do our American cousins put it? – 'watching my back'. Frankly, I cannot think of anyone more suited to the task. Tea, Gentlemen?'

***

There had been a slight improvement in Walton's fortunes. This was surprising. Ieuan, in common with many psychopaths, was not only devoid of empathy for the misfortunes of others, he was also a card-carrying narcissist who couldn't even bear the presence of those who were ill or in any way damaged. As Walton underwent the painful process of having his foot and badly-twisted ankle removed from the u-bend of the restaurant toilet, all he could think of was the dangerous disadvantage this would put him in when dealing with the boss.

But his efficiency in setting up all those meetings, shoots and dinners with Ieuan's prospective investors was now beginning to pay off. Orders for the 'product' were coming in thick and fast accompanied by a huge influx of funds. Ieuan's greed overcame his natural propensity for violent bullying and paranoia. He even stopped off at Walton's office to see how he was recovering; hitherto unheard-of behaviour.

'You seem to have got all your ducks in a row with the investors, Walton. Nice work!' said Ieuan, his unnaturally white dentition gleaming through a shark-like grin.

Walton was a little taken aback by Ieuan's friendly manner. He nodded, half expecting some snide insinuation. But barbed comment came there none. Ieuan just stopped in front of the gold-framed mirror on the wall, admired himself for a couple of seconds, checked his teeth for rogue spinach from his breakfast of Eggs Benedict.

'I realise, Walton, that I may have been riding you a bit hard recently but I'm sure you appreciate that with all the pressure I've been under in recent weeks, it's only natural for a born-leader like myself to expect the best from his staff. I'm willing to overlook your recent mistakes and start afresh just as soon as you take care of that little matter which should have been resolved in the restaurant. You've done such a good job on the distribution side, it'd be just downright tragic if you weren't there at the Halfrod Hall event.'

'That's very good of you Ieuan,' said Walton. 'Leave it to me. I'll make sure everything is tidied up.'

'Take your time,' said Ieuan. 'That ankle looks mighty painful,' he said lapsing into mid-Atlantic. 'Take a load off ... By the end of the week would do,' he added as he headed towards the door.

'You've got them eating out of your hand, you genius,' thought Ieuan as he left Walton's office. 'Who says that Ieuan Henge isn't a people person?'

'What a king-sized jerk-stain!' thought Walton before turning his mind to the difficult task of remotely assassinating Penelope and Spon whilst recovering from a twisted ankle which was currently encased in what appeared to be a ski boot. He picked up the phone.

'Russlana? Can you find me Gregor's number, please.'

24. HALFROD HALL

TWO figures, deep in conversation, low light-levels and expensive claret were crammed into one of the smaller booths at Simpson's Tavern in The City.

'Look, Maurice. I really think it's time that we pulled the plug on Operation Wild Goose.' Maurice peered over the top of his half-moon glasses at his colleague and adopted a pained expression.

'You'll forgive me, Terry, but I really do wish that you would make up your mind about this whole bag of nonsense. First, you convince me that this 'VAT in the fields' ruse was the best way to keep what's-his-name out of the office and make sure he doesn't stick his nose into those more sensitive areas of the department's foreign travel expenses regime. Now you tell me that we have to bring him back. It's not like we've got an Empire anymore. We can't just send him off to Bongo Bongo Land and hope he contracts some lethal disease en route. Gone are the days when the sun never sets on the British Empire, Terry. Now it's all over in fifteen minutes, if you don't count Tristan de Cunha. Why is it now such a matter of life and death that we have to shut it down!'

Terry took a deep breath.

'The problem is that I have had half of the little elves and fairies from the Serious Narcotics Investigation Force crawling all over my office, assaulting my staff and sticking their pointy heads into matters that really shouldn't concern them. It's only a matter of time before they find out about the whole thing and we will then have rather a lot of explaining to do.'

'I heard it was the other way around,' smirked Maurice.

'What?' said Terry, disconcerted.

'I heard that it was your secretary who – oh, how do the unwashed put it? – 'stuck the boot in' first.'

'Who told you that?' said Terry. 'She was acting in self-defence! There she was doing her job when some burly brute of a police officer ...'

'Rimmer,' said Maurice, giggling. 'The report said that the sergeant who your secretary first decked and then trussed up like a chicken on her typing chair was called Detective Sergeant Rimmer.'

'That's as maybe, Maurice,' said Terry whose sang froid had now reached room temperature. 'But there won't be many laughs in the report which contains the reasons why the department decided to waste time and effort on quite an expensive little investigation into VAT fraud at country shows when there was absolutely no evidence to suggest that there was any. The more that idiot Figgis gets drawn into the drugs investigation, the greater the chance that this whole thing will be dragged outside the confines of the department and once it's out in the open, we can't control it.'

Even Maurice found it difficult to squeeze a laugh out of the prospect of a Cabinet Office investigation into departmental mismanagement.

'Perhaps you're right, Terry. But I think we'd be ill-advised to act precipitously. This would look suspicious in the eyes of the police. Is there a natural cycle to these shows?'

'Not that I can discern,' said Terry. 'However, in a couple of weeks there's an event at Halfrod Hall which is meant to be the high-point of this game fair season thingie.'

'Well then,' said Maurice. 'I'm sure that would be an appropriate point at which to curtail Operation Wild Goose, don't you?'

***

The lights stayed on late at Studworks.

Penelope and Spon honed their defence stratagem and

planned a crushing counter-attack ably assisted by Austin and Healey. The four gathered together in what Penelope called 'the boardroom' with its club chairs, hardwood bookshelves and capacious fireplace.

'From Healey's reports, it seems that all those ghastly, showy shooting days over at Raphe Episcopi Hall have now ended,' said Penelope. 'Daddy would be turning in his grave to think of this estate overrun with all those foreign johnnies.'

Spon nodded sagely whilst thinking that Sir Quentin would have no trouble at all with the 'foreign johnnies' if they had showered him with half the funds they appeared to be investing in Henge Enterprises.

'But to what end is all this activity? Have you found out anything from your investigations, Healey?' said Penelope.

Healey's nose had been broken more times than a politician's promise lending his voice that subdued tone so often heard in ex-boxers.

'Well. It looks like the financing stage of the operation is over. There don't appear to be any more plans to fly in these dodgy geezers from all over the world according to the guys I've spoken to on the estate. It seems that Henge and his crew have pretty much decamped and moved back to London.'

'But what are they up to? What's their next move?' asked Penelope drumming her fingers on the table. 'We need more information if we are to draw up a workable plan of action.'

'I was able to get alongside Henge's secretary, Russlana, at a bar. But I didn't get too much from her. She's sharp and I didn't want to stick around too long or it might arouse her suspicions,' added Healey.

'Well what did she say?'

'All the usual stuff about being terribly busy. Although I did catch something when she answered her phone. Something about 'Halfmad Hall', it sounded like.'

'You mean Halfrod Hall. That used to be Gewgaw's biggest show of the year. It's only a few weeks away.

Perhaps that's where they are planning their next move. If the financing phase of his operation is complete, he'll be keen to start realising his profits by selling and distributing his stock-pile of drugs. Perhaps he's planning to start the process there. That's where we need to hit them,' said Penelope decisively.

Austin had remained silent until now. He leant forward from his club chair.

'With respect,' he said. 'I think your biggest problem is not how to hit Henge at Halfrod Hall but staying alive until then.'

***

Pablo had spent a harrowing eight hours in the economy class of a tourist flight from Manchester to Mexico. Even with air-conditioning and a few cold beers, the additional three hours by road from the airport to El Cameleon's ranch had not been great but he was determined to put on a bold front. He hated these visits. He hated that he always felt tongue-tied and impotent in the presence of El Cameleon. He hated that residual fear that, for reasons unknown, the visit might be a one-way trip.

The limo drove past several fields of alien-looking mescal cactus before drawing up before a porch.

'Eh Pablo!' A thin reedy voice shouted. El Cameleon stepped out of the shade and walked down the steps of the enormous, single-storey ranch house towards the limousine and spread his cocktail-stick thin arms wide to encompass the girth of Pablo. 'Com es da? Joo look well! This Eenglish rain is doing you good, my friend.'

Half an hour later, El Cameleon and Pablo stood by the pool. They could not have been more dissimilar. Pablo was from real Mexican peasant stock, broad and thick set. His hands were used to manual work although in his case this wasn't exclusively confined to agriculture. The calluses on his right-hand thumb had been developed by his preferred method of removing his victims teeth with a set of mole grips. Recently, he had been touched almost to tears when El Cameleon had noticed this and had brought him a special set with rubberised handles. Pablo's moustache was thick and rarely trimmed in contrast to his shaven head with its multitude of tattoos. This was all part of gang culture but he never inquired as to the meaning of the blue marks. It was enough that he could show his compadres that, to him, the painful process of applying them was as nothing; a mere itch. This career gangster stood squarely by the sky-blue pool in his snake-skin boots, jeans and leather waistcoat.

But his body language told a different story. And that story was one of fear. Fear of the diminutive figure that was now before him. El Jefe. The Boss. El Cameleon.

Dressed in a suit so shiny and tight it might as well have been reptile skin, El Cameleon was on charm mode. His negligible stature had at first been a disadvantage in the early struggles to carve out his territory. But with his unparalleled powers of organisation, other gang leaders soon avoided any confrontation with the man they used to call 'Ojos Giratorios' or 'Old Swivel Eyes'.

His eyes – it was true – were El Cameleon's most noticeable feature and added credibility to his nickname. He could not only deceive like a chameleon but also look in two completely different directions at once. His strike when it came was lightning fast like the chameleon's tongue grabbing a passing fly. His thinning hair and pallid skin did as little to diminish his reptilian presence as the cold, dry smile which played upon his lips.

Pablo noted the bottle of expensive mescal sitting on the table.

'Joo must be tired, Pablo, after joo flight,' said El Cameleon. 'But I would appreciate joo update. Perhaps over a glass of mescal?'

'Joo're too kind, Jefe,' replied Pablo settling his aching back into one of the comfortable deck chairs.

'From joo time in England with Senor 'enge,' – not pronouncing the 'H' was a considerable physical effort – 'tell me what you think of heem and his operation. And Pablo, joo must speak honestly. Joo know I have no time for polite small-talk. Tell me what you feel, in joo *cojones*, about this gringo.'

'Well, Jefe. He is soft, like a woman. Ees miracle he can hold his operation together at all. He spends more time in the bathroom than a woman! All the guys who work for him. They, too, are soft, like women. Even the people they sell product too, they are all soft too, like ...'

'Yes, yes. Like women. I get the picture,' said El Cameleon topping up the mescal glasses. 'But who are the people who really run the show. Who should I be talking to if I wanted a piece of the action. Joo tell me who should I be talking to, Pablo?'

'There is one. He is a yankee gringo called Wal-ton. He is cunning and clever but he too is soft; soft like ...'

'Yes, yes, yes,' said El Cameleon. 'I know. Soft like a woman, eh Pablo?'

'You know heem?' asked Pablo, amazed.

'No, Pablo. I don't.' El Cameleon raised his hand to soothe his forehead.

He had forgotten just how 'one-track' conversations with Pablo could be and was now worried that his enforcer's intellectual powers – not that impressive to start with – might be showing signs of decline.

'This Wal-ton of whom joo speak, Pablo, is he the only one?'

'No, Jefe. There is another. A Russian woman called Russlana.'

'And would I be correct in guessing that she too is 'soft', as joo say, 'like a woman'.'

El Cameleon allowed a grin to spread across his features as he gently teased his enforcer. The effort was wasted.

'No, Jefe,' replied Pablo betraying no emotion at all. 'She is hard. Hard like a man!'

'So let's recap, Pablo,' said El Cameleon now concerned that his enforcer had developed gender issues whilst staying in Europe. 'All the men in 'enge Enterprises are soft 'like women' but the only woman in the organisation is 'ard 'like a man'. And, if we wanted to consider a takeover bid, we should really be talking to either the 'ard, man-like Russian woman called Russlana or the soft, woman-like yankee gringo called Wal-ton. Have I got it right so far?'

'Exactly, Jefe. Just as you say.' Pablo, now relaxed by the mescal, broke into some impromptu applause.

'But how would we be able to talk to these people without arousing the suspicions of Senor 'enge?'

'Ah well.' Pablo leant forward. 'The Eenglish have these outdoor events where everyone stands around in the rain and the cold without any good food or drink.'

'What?' said El Cameleon. 'Like that internment camp at Guadalajara?'

'Similar but people buy tickets for these events and come and go as they please,' said Pablo his eyes wide with amazement. 'They call them 'game fairs' and there are very many held all over the country.'

'So why should I bother with these events, Pablo. They sound so bad!'

'It is under the cover of these 'game fairs' that Senor 'enge wants to distribute the product to dealers. The biggest of these events will take place shortly, in just a few weeks. Everyone in 'enge's operation will be there and he hopes to sell the product at wholesale prices to only the largest dealers. It is here that you can meet with the man-like, Russian woman and the girlie, yankee gringo.'

'We must make arrangements. Buy tickets, if necessary,' said El Cameleon, fixing Pablo with one of his eyes. 'And the name of this event, Pablo. What is it called?'

Pablo emptied the remaining mescal into his mouth.

'It is called 'alfrod 'all.'

***

Croesus sat in his wheelchair. A nurse popped her head around the door.

'Everything alright, Mr Massey-Itch? Anything you need?'

A cup of refreshing peppermint tea would be wonderful, thought Croesus, but when he tried to tell the nurse this or anything else, all that came out of his mouth was 'Alan Titchmarsh'.

'Aah! Bless ... I don't think he's on the TV until this evening,' said the nurse. 'You do love your gardening shows, don't you, dear?'

'I'm sick, not three years old! And I bloody well hate Alan Titchmarsh and his sodding gardening programmes!' snapped Croesus.

'Well there's no need to be like that ... Oh!' replied the nurse. 'Mr. Massey-Itch! You can talk again! Just you wait there and let me go and get Dr. Subudar.'

'I do believe you're right,' said Croesus. 'Yes please, nurse. Do go and get Alan Titchmarsh. Oh dear ... Still I'm sure I can live with the occasional 'Alan Titchmarsh' creeping into the conversation. I'll wait here.'

Thrilled that he at least could communicate again, Croesus turned his wheelchair to the window returning his gaze to the outside world. He remembered how he had always loved this time of year and how he harboured a particular fondness for the gardens at Halfrod Hall. He would like to return there some day. Perhaps he'd ask Dr. Subudar if he could go to the game fair there. It must be some time soon.

***

In a caravan somewhere off the A12, Jayne said, 'Since they bumped off those Mancunians, the commercial side of Henge's distribution seems to have toned down a little.'

She was lying across the bed with her head on Peter's chest, puffing her e-cigarette.

'Well that's hardly surprising, is it?' said Peter shuffling the pillows behind his head. 'I mean not even drug dealers are stupid enough to go and buy drugs when they know the evening's finale comprises them and their dog being killed in the nastiest way imaginable by a bunch of Mexican gangsters and being buried in a childrens' sandpit.'

'No,' said Jayne. 'You're wrong. Bitter experience has taught me that most drug dealers are incapable of thinking that far ahead and that most have the same sense of self-preservation as a lemming.'

'So what's happening? There's no way that Henge can just sit on the drugs. He's got to move them on, hasn't he, or he's just a sitting target for a takeover bid by some other scum bag?' said Peter.

'True. But suppose he isn't selling to the little fish anymore. He might be biding his time until they can offer the drugs to buyers further up the food chain,' said Jayne, thinking aloud.

'But isn't that a much bigger risk, trying to sell large quantities of drugs at lots of events across the country. Doesn't it just multiply the chances of them getting caught?' said Peter.

'Well,' said Jayne. 'Perhaps that's why they have stopped selling at the last few shows. Perhaps they are waiting for a show of sufficient size so they can move the stuff on wholesale, all in one go.'

'Like the CLA?' said Peter animatedly.

'Don't be such a knob-head, Peter. I really do worry about the country if the job of collecting taxes is left to people like you,' said Jayne, teasing.

'The reptiles of the media are all over that show like a rash. It's just a townie event in the fields, in any case. If there was coke on the premises, the hoorays'd sniff it out in seconds. There's no way they could conceal it there. What's the biggest show Henge Enterprises operates?'

Jayne and Peter looked at each other: 'Halfrod Hall' they said together.

25. A DAMNED CLOSE-RUN THING

AT that weekend's show, Peter felt more isolated than ever. The truth was that, even despite their liaison, he felt professionally jealous of Jayne. He envied the ease with which she could get hold of her boss at any time to discuss her work. He coveted the resources she had at her disposal.

He, on the other hand, was left hanging on a line which was rarely answered. Even when it was, it was obviously a general office line; often on loudspeaker. The important matters that he wanted to report were now met with unconcealed hilarity and disdain by his erstwhile colleagues. The mobile number which Terry had given him had, after a few weeks, rung but remained unanswered. Then it went through stages of ringing and being answered by a recorded message asking him for a PIN with which he had never been issued. Now when he rang the number it was answered by a mini-cab firm in Hoxton.

Jayne seemed to have a good working relationship with her senior whom she referred to as 'Bellend'. Peter wasn't sure if this was her superior's actual name or just a macho, drugs squad-style nickname. Peter had no relationship with his colleagues at all.

He felt ground down and this manifested itself in new, problematic ways. He had become less than courteous with the buying public than he used to be. That morning, he had watched a thin, oddly-clad punter in his early thirties spend three-quarters of an hour putting on and taking off a cartridge pouch. He counted seventeen different attempts.

As the punter strapped the cartridge pouch about his waist for the eighteenth time, Peter could stand it no more.

'Are you going to buy that or are you just going to test it to destruction here on the stand?'

The punter had obviously been in a world of his own and, in a painfully delivered cut-glass accent replied, 'I have never been spoken to like that in all my years as a ...'

'Ladyboy?' chipped in Peter. The blood drained from the punter's face as he addressed the other customers.

'Frankly I find these goods rather shoddy,' he said in his bizarre brogue.

Peter couldn't stop himself.

'And it's only taken you forty-five minutes on a six-foot counter to work that out, has it?'

Before the astounded customer could respond, Peter pointed East and intoned, 'Fuck off. Now!'

Peter was surprised by the ripple of applause which came from the other customers who had been crowded off the stand by the punter's strange antics.

Peter wasn't proud of his behaviour but the pressure of his solitary mission made it difficult not to react to what he imagined were the inconsiderate actions of potential purchasers on the stand. At least he hadn't become as brazen as some on the shows. He knew that if he ever wanted fifteen minutes of entertainment, just drop the magic word, 'children' to another trader and stand back. It was as if he had lit the blue touch-paper on a particularly large, 'public display only' firework.

'Little fuckers. I hate them.'

'They should bar the little bastards ... One of 'em was sick over two hundred quid's worth of fudge. And the parent just grabbed the kid and ran!'

'Why can't they leave things alone ... fiddle, fiddle, bloody fiddle.'

'It's not a fancy dress game, it's a hat shop and it's my living ... now put it down and step away from the counter.'

This last description of an encounter with children was accompanied by a very convincing mime of the trader in question cocking a semi-automatic shotgun.

Peter remembered how shocked he had been when he first heard traders giving forth on the subject. But barely six months of watching stock being scratched or thrown into the mud by the little darlings had brought Peter to the view that other traders were right. He expressed to another trader the vaguely liberal viewpoint that perhaps the fault lay with the parents' permissive attitude to their kids who were just acting instinctively. This was immediately batted back, 'I used to let the dog do what he wanted but that all changed when we came back from the pub one Sunday and found my ninety-two-year-old father-in-law asleep on the floor by the Rayburn with the dog attempting to have sex with the bald patch on top of his head. It were a hell of mess. A quick kick up the charlies soon put things to rights.'

Peter still clung to the belief that it was the parents who were to blame but voiced it less often in trader company. He did find it amazing how visitors to the stall would treat his stock as a 'show and tell' opportunity for the vile spawn usually referred to as Tabitha or Jocelyn. Nowadays Peter didn't wait until sharp little nails had marked up an expensive gunslip before he brought matters to a close. The parents often took this badly: 'How dare this poor person prevent Tabitha and Jocelyn from exercising their lifelong entitlement to piss all over other people's property' seemed to be their attitude.

'Well!' said one outraged mother. 'I was going to buy my husband one of your gunslips for Christmas but with your attitude I don't think I'll bother!'

Peter heard himself say:

'Perhaps he'd like the one which he dropped into the mud when he was pissed on my stand last year and showing off to his friends or perhaps this one which your child has just scratched. Actually. Don't bother. I don't want a twat like him using my stuff. It's bad for business!'

The opening and closing of press studs had never bothered Peter in his life until now. These industrial closures made of brass or steel have a working life of several thousand cycles. Yet even adults seemed incapable of resisting the temptation to open and then close the press stud on a bullet pouch or a licence holder not once but up to thirty or forty times and then encourage their children to do the same. Polite advice like 'Yes, the press studs all work' would go unheeded as the temperature of the overworked press stud began to climb. More obvious comments such as 'Are you going to buy that or just undo and do up the press stud until it breaks?' were usually met with blank looks from the customer as if clueless of the nature of their offence. 'Don't do that, son. It'll be difficult to pick your nose with your hand in plaster' usually did the trick.

The afternoon at the show had included many such minor irritants. But even Peter had not been prepared for the finale of a well-dressed and well-spoken customer who wanted to buy a rifle slip. Business was slow and the customer seemed decisive so Peter thought nothing of knocking a tenner off the price to secure the sale. After a close examination of the rifle slip, the customer claimed that there were mud marks and that a further reduction of ten pounds might be in order. Peter obliged. It was only when the customer complained about the brassware not being shiny enough to justify the now heavily discounted price that Peter started to smell a rat. A further reduction of a fiver was made but Peter determined to go no lower. Finally, the customer put his hand in his pocket to withdraw what, at this price, Peter expected to be a handful of banknotes. Instead, he produced a Private Wealth Management credit card from Tarts Bank of Fleet Street.

'No,' said Peter. 'I'm sorry. The price is a good one and I'm not going to pay the cost of credit card transaction on top of it all.'

'But you have to,' said the customer, 'It's a contract.'

Peter's attitude hardened. 'The contract is still valid. It's the means of payment which is in question. And while we're at it, I would have thought that a man of your obvious resources ... what is it nowadays at Tarts Private Bank? A cool half a million in your account? ... might have the common sense to bring some notes to a game fair and pay in cash if you want to bargain like an unemployed

Scouser. I tell you what. I'll keep the slip. You keep your plastic. Cheapskate.'

At the close of the show, Peter, for the first time since he had started 'Operation Wild Goose', felt a bit depressed. Jayne was moving onto to another show that evening. He had elected to stay over. Unusually, Peter felt like he could do with a drink.

He arrived at the Kemsdale Outdoor stand. They too had opted to stay over. After he'd finished the last two litres of Abe's most recent cider delivery, Peter accepted a large glass of rum from Kemsdale's owner, Sean. It would be churlish not to accept. Three glasses later and Peter's mood was improving. At the suggestion of a man called Foul Weather Bob, Peter and Sean decided to try some different rum. The bottle was half empty but Bob said that he had bought it back from Fiji when he was visiting some of his relatives. From the initial taste, Peter suspected that the first half of the bottle had been used to fuel the flight. Anyway, like most ideas after a couple of large rums, this seemed like a really good one. Another half a bottle later, Peter struck upon another brilliant idea. He would go and share his newly acquired happiness with the German Shooting Team which he had met earlier in the day. They were staying in a nearby clubhouse.

Full of 'splash it all over', extra-proof, Fijian-rum confidence, Peter set off having collected a further gallon of Gray's cider from the van. Peter was determined to share this fine drink with the German visitors. Under normal circumstances, he would have followed the tarmac path to the German clubhouse but alcohol had conjured in him a new spirit of adventure.

'Tarmac paths are for losers,' he thought as he lurched into the undergrowth, determined to find his way 'cross-country'. It was already getting dark when he took his first glass of rum. Now, in the woods, it was pitch-black.

Within yards, Peter's hat fell victim to a low branch and was whipped from his head. As he knelt down to find it, his head churned with alcohol. He reached out with his hand but instead of finding his hat he found something evil-smelling and slimy. Standing up was not easy in these circumstances and after staggering forward, Peter now found that he had also lost his right shoe in the darkness. Whilst attempting to wipe whatever he had put his hand in, he lurched forward again ramming a twig into his unseeing left eye.

'Aaaargh!'

His cry went unheeded as all but the organisers had now left the show venue. Recoiling from the pain, he now found that his trousers had caught on a branch. Vigorous efforts to free them soon resulted in a large tear down the right leg revealing far too much thigh to be socially acceptable.

Peter's arrival on the footpath just outside the German Shooting Team's venue elicited a loud scream from a woman having 'a quiet fag' outside. Orientated at last, he staggered the remaining 100 feet and emerged into the light of German hospitality.

With badly soiled hand outstretched, a severely bruised and swollen left eye, a huge and unsightly hole in his trousers, and a missing shoe he resembled an Old Testament prophet; an Old Testament prophet that God really disliked.

With the surprise that that same God reserves exclusively for drunks, Peter looked at his dog-shit decorated jacket and his shoeless foot with his big toe protruding through the sock.

With the surprise that usually greets a nasty dose of the clap, the Germans gawped at this apparition before them and quickly gathered into a tight-knit defensive formation in the corner of the clubhouse awning.

Peter later admitted that it would have been better to have withdrawn at this point. But he decided to persevere and became most insistent that the Germans should try some real Devon cider, despite the fact that, during the course of its 'green lanes' journey, it had now acquired the look of frothy horse urine.

The Germans drank the cider with the same distaste usually reserved for historical discussions of the years

1933-1945. They drank it quickly, perhaps in the hope that once the cider was finished, Peter would leave. The abrupt shock of falling over backwards whilst seated indicated to even Peter's anaesthetised senses that the time had come to depart.

Staggering down the path towards his van, Peter felt a hand clamp down on his mouth stifling his shout of surprise.

'Eh? Not with the fast get-away this time, eh, Gringo?'

Juan had grown bitter with the memory of his humiliation in the Spend-Mo car park in Carlisle and had bided his time. Revenge is second nature to any Mexican but to Juan it was nearly a vocation. Weakened by the large quantity of alcohol he had consumed, Peter was no match for his assailant. Controlling Peter with a painful arm-lock, Juan guided him towards the darkness and privacy of the woods. Once there, one sharp blow from the handle of a heavy Bowie knife ended Peter's struggling.

When Peter came too, he found himself trussed up on the leaf litter. The intoxication of the rum had worn off. Peter couldn't work out whether it was the Fijian rum or the blow to his head that was the cause of his headache. Matters weren't improved by his assailant shining a torch directly into his eyes.

'So, Amigo,' said Juan with the false bonhommie so beloved of Mexican gangsters. 'We meet again.'

'Apparently so,' said Peter weakly. 'But what do you want?'

'I don't want anything from joo ...' said Juan coquettishly, '... apart from a few things. What joo say we start with your ears and move onto more interesting theengs?'

Peter saw the wide blade of the Bowie knife flash in the torch-light.

'But first joo tell me where your freend is. Joo know the one I mean. The fat one!'

Peter heard a strangely familiar sound; a sound he had heard before. The sound of an airborne Gaucho Brand Meat Pie.

The slightly misshapen tin struck Juan just above the

right eyebrow. He hit the ground like a sack of burrito flour, out cold.

'Right here, mate,' came Kev's laconic tones. 'I knew I'd find a use for that fucking thing eventually but I didn't think it'd be this soon.'

He paused.

'Oh mate! You haven't soiled yourself, have you? What's that smell?'

Peter – relieved at his rescue – said, 'Don't worry about that, Kev. That's the dog shit I rolled in earlier. I'll tell you later.'

26. CONVERGENCE

EL CAMELEON carefully negotiated the steps of his private jet onto the tarmac of Birmingham Airport. It was midday but his jet-lag and the surrounding light levels suggested to him a time closer to dusk. Still, he didn't care.

He was here to make money and, in his rigorously compartmentalised world, that objective was everything. Not even the delay in clearing customs diverted his attention. You didn't get to run one of the world's biggest drug cartels by caring about incompetent customs officials, the weather, the stock market or for people. 'Caring' didn't actually appear on El Cameleon's personal list of priorities. 'Caring' was a word he seldom heard, a bit like 'no' although it all depended on the context.

He rarely heard, 'No, you can't have that' or 'No, you can't do that.'

But he was more than familiar with, 'No, no! Please! I have a family.'

or

'No! Not that! Anything but that! Aaaaargh!'

or his personal favourite,

'Noooooooooo!'

Whilst dealing with his business competitors, El Cameleon liked to go about his bloody business less with a song in his heart and more with a high-pitched wail of pain in his ear.

Private jets were a necessity in his business for when he absolutely, definitely had to be somewhere. With the huge amounts of cash at his disposal, buying a private jet was one of the few forms of shopping available to him that he still enjoyed. His jets gave him a certain flexibility. Like Hitler, El Cameleon rejoiced in changing his schedules at the last minute, changing route details and even mode of transport. In a business sector not renowned for its pension arrangements, he put his longevity down to this ability to improvise.

'Yes, improvisation is the key,' he thought to himself as the limousine left the airport and made its way onto the motorway. His right eye swivelled towards the slumped figure of Pablo, twitching his way, like an over-sized family dog, through mescal-fuelled dreams of undoubted X-rated content.

'This is the trouble with most of my colleagues. They have no imagination. They cannot improvise. Uncertainty troubles them. They do not like change. I thrive on change ... Well, I suppose that's obvious ... that is why people call me El Cameleon ...'

He felt tired. In his heart of hearts, he really wanted to retire to Florida and live the good life ... well, the less bad life anyway ... but he couldn't share this with anyone. This would be seen as a sign of weakness and would shorten his life just as surely as that stuff 'cholesterol' which his heart specialist was always banging on about. If only he could delegate ... but to whom?

'Look at Pablo, Juan or Jesus,' thought El Cameleon to himself, licking his fingers and then wiping his eyes. 'All good men in their way but leadership is beyond them. They know how to do something, providing it is done the same way everytime. Look at the 'desayuno de perro' they made of killing those dealers from Manchester!'

He knew fruit-sellers in Guadalajara who would have made a better job of hiding the evidence. Still he could postpone any career-changing decisions until he was safely back home in Mexico. Perhaps he could come up with some unplanned business opportunities during the course of this trip which would engage his interest.

The aircraft landed. In minutes,El Cameleon and Pablo were comfortably installed in a Rolls Royce as it sped them towards their destination.

In the boot of the Rolls Royce, the tiny transponders hidden in El Cameleon's luggage by the customs officials mapped his progress towards Halfrod Hall.

***

'Are you out of your tiny little mind?'

Terry had never seen Maurice so agitated. This was the civil servant who had displayed nerves of steel as he progressed unsullied from one governmental disaster to the next as if he was coated with Teflon. All Terry had suggested was, in the interests of keeping their little mission to Halfrod Hall top secret, was that they go there by public transport and, to fit in with the other game fair visitors, that they should avoid hotel and B&B records by taking a tent and camping for the weekend.

Maurice's violent reaction to this suggestion confirmed to Terry that his colleague didn't share the fond memories he had of childhood camping trips.

'For God's sake! I'm 68, you know!' lied Maurice. 'Hardly the ideal age to take up a rucksack or whatever the bloody things are called. A bout of pneumonia could finish me off! When you said we had to go and sort this out by ourselves I didn't think we'd be living like a couple of truck-jumpers in Calais! Obviously I want to support you in this venture, Terry, but not to the extent of sharing a tent with you! Couldn't we borrow someone's caravan or one of those motorised caravans ...what do the Americans call them?'

'Recreational vehicle?' said Terry.

'Yes, yes ... Recreational vehicle ... RV's,' said Maurice as his blood pressure began its descent.

'Well, I suppose we could,' said Terry, 'but I'm afraid I don't know anyone who owns a caravan or a motorhome or an RV. We'd have to rent one under an assumed name ... for cash ... our cash.'

'Surely, you must know someone who owns one of

those things. You went to grammar school, after all. Isn't that what the middle classes are all about? Cheap holidays at home and so forth.'

Terry forgot just how hateful Maurice could be when he put his mind to it or when he was under pressure and let his patrician guard down.

'Sod that!' thought Terry as he pressed home his advantage, 'I'm afraid I can't lay my hands on that sort of cash at the moment. I still have school and university fees to pay and then there's Deirdre's treatment in Spain with Las Amicas Confundidas del Betty Ford. I'm afraid that you would have to fund the venture, Maurice.'

'If I do,' said Maurice grimly, 'there'll be no more talk of public transport or tents and the vehicle we rent will be suitably equipped for persons of our age and standing.'

'Agreed, Maurice. Agreed,' said Terry delighted with the knowledge that the paper trail followed by any subsequent investigation would lead directly to Maurice and not to him.

A couple of days later, Terry found a suitable vehicle. The Westingbourne Lazyboy was a battleship of a recreational vehicle. Brought over from the US to the UK on a whim by a newspaper magnate, it had remained garaged in South London for several years being carefully maintained and serviced by the magnate's staff.

The brilliantined stick-insect of an agent who was offering the vehicle gave Terry a short guided tour. Two bedrooms, both with ensuite bathrooms, a saloon measuring fifteen feet and galley of similar size were decked out in the gaudiest of American taste circa 1993 and propelled by nine litres of ecology-trashing diesel engine through the intercession of three axles and six wheels.

As Terry explored the luxury facilities, he could not help but notice the mirrored walls and chromium poles which rose from the centre of each saloon table ascending a full eight feet to the ceiling above. Before he had even considered the flat screen TV, the gaudy magnificence of the Art Deco cocktail cabinet and what appeared to be

CCTV in each room, his mind was made up. At seven thousand pounds for the weekend, he was convinced that it was a bargain and that its appearance would assuage all Maurice's doubts. A little on the expensive side, no doubt, but Maurice – with his house at Saint Jean Cap Ferrat, the boat in Puerto Banus and the small pile in the country – could certainly run to it and the little extra to pay for the four miles to the gallon fuel consumption.

'Let me get this clear in my mind, Terry,' said Maurice, removing his glasses and placing them on the mahogany club coffee table in front of him. 'Here we are trying to save our careers through what may prove to be desperate means and you are now suggesting that the inclusion of a 'ladyboy' in our team might improve our chances of success?'

'Lazyboy!' enunciated Terry in a stage whisper. 'Not "lady", "Lazy"!'

'I don't care if the transsexual in question has the work ethic of Martin Luther, I consider the whole thing ridiculous.'

His intransigence softened as he was introduced to the RV and visibly brightened as he started to discover and play with the facilities and explore the well-stocked cocktail cabinet.

On the Friday, while Terry piloted the Westingbourne Lazyboy to Halfrod Hall, Maurice sulked in the back, downing numerous brandy and sodas.

At Halfrod Hall, the general public had begun arriving on the Thursday night and set up their caravans, motor homes, trailers and tents for the weekend. Chief Inspector Bellend and Sergeant Rimmer had disguised themselves as members of the public although it became apparent at the outset that something had gone awry with Rimmer's research into what most people wore at game fairs.

In a sea of technical fabrics and camouflage clothing, the two policemen stood out like small islets of sartorial ineptitude in the badly-fitting tweeds which Rimmer had borrowed from his uncle and cousin. Bellend had never worn breeks before and had difficulty in keeping his socks in place even with the help of the brightly coloured garters provided. The CSI's jacket was clearly too small giving him the appearance of a man who was suspended by his shoulders. Sergeant Rimmer's trousers were too large by several sizes but he had managed to avert disaster by bringing along a set of braces. His Norfolk jacket was also an appalling fit. On the shoulders, it was fine but it was barely up to the job of encircling his girth.

The only other item which stood out in the sea of camo-clothing was a hundred yards away, standing by a Series 3 Landrover. It was Barry Parry clad in his day-glo orange safety camouflage.

Having collected the trailer tent from Godalming, they had driven, with what Rimmer thought was excessive care, to Halfrod Hall. A journey that would normally take three hours took five. Still, both men were grateful that they had managed to borrow the camping trailer as this would avoid them having to set up a tent, revealing their shortcomings and blowing their cover.

'Now, Rimmer,' said Bellend, 'pull that rope and the tent should just pop up.'

Rimmer pulled and nothing happened. Bellend examined the structure closely.

'Looks like we've got a bit of a rust problem here,' he said reaching for the mallet. A couple of smart blows seemed to do the trick.

'Try again, Rimmer.' The sergeant gave another heave on the rope and the structure swung upwards and outwards from the trailer. All looked well until a slight breeze hit it and the corner of the canvas disintegrated into dust.

'Looks like we've got a bit of a mouse problem as well,' said the Chief Inspector jauntily. 'Never mind, Rimmer. I'm sure you'll make do. Now, let's get my side sorted.'

The other side of the trailer tent was easy to erect. This was because the mice had chewed all around the edge of the covering canvas. The tent stood there for a moment but, with the next gentle gust, a satisfying ripping sound was heard, the canvas filled like a sail, detached itself from its frame and landed in a heap at the policemen's feet.

'You get on with this, Rimmer,' said Bellend. 'I think it's about time I reconnoitered the area. It's going to be a long weekend,' he muttered.

***

Back in Mayfair, Anwar Anbar was looking for his private secretary.

'Hamid, Hamid!'

After thirty seconds, a puffing sound was clearly audible as the overweight and flushed Hamid appeared in the tall doorway of Anwar's office. 'Yes, Sir.' he wheezed, 'what can I do for you?'

'Oh, nothing,' said Anwar. 'I just wanted to know where you were.'

'I was taking a toilet break, downstairs, Sir,' said Hamid bitterly.

'Oh well,' said Anwar nonchalantly surveying a letter. 'Never mind. Carry on. Carry on, Hamid.'

'I'm not sure I can!' thought Hamid. He turned to leave Anwar's office.

'Oh, just one thing,' said Anwar.

'His Excellency has decided against hiring the house for this 'game fair' weekend so please cancel the booking. He's decided that we will visit Halfrod Hall on the day by helicopter.'

Hamid remembered the hours it had taken him to persuade the owners of the country house in question to rent out the property for the weekend. Cancelling it would probably take just as long and would be infinitely more expensive.

***

Ieuan was in self-congratulatory mode. Despite the best efforts of Zog, the Assyrian God of Monumental Fuck-Ups, his master-plan was coming together nicely. His sociopathic side was in the habit of filtering out the contributions of others and serving up, on a gold platter, a version of events to delight the narcissistic side of his character. The best efforts of Russlana and Walton were consigned to the footnotes of a saga in which Ieuan and Ieuan alone was prime mover, heroic protagonist and eventual god-like victor.

Every hour Walton appeared with handfuls of messages confirming the attendance at Halfrod Hall of the biggest drug dealers in the country. Every hour Russlana reported the progress of the investors as they made their way towards the Halfrod Hall Game Fair & Country Show. During a normal working week, Ieuan might have reflected that these two loyal-ish retainers might deserve his thanks for arranging what would go down in criminal history as one of the greatest illicit drugs auctions of all time. But his ego was in overdrive. There was just no time for that sort of thing. Already his febrile mind was working out the details of which tweeds he would wear with what shoes and what accessories he should have about his person on the day.

'Yes,' he thought, 'yes. I'll use that long walking stick; the one made out of bog oak with the enormous silver acorn on the end of it. That'll be just right.'

He sent Walton off to inquire as to its whereabouts. Walton found Ieuan's valet, Portuguese Tony, polishing boots in the kitchen. Tony was dressed for the part with smart black trousers, waistcoat and starched white shirt protected from the flying Kiwi shoe polish by a yellow and black regency striped apron.

'Ieuan's looking for that bog oak walking stick again, Tony,' said Walton. 'Any idea where it is?'

'Oh no. He's not, is he?' said Tony. 'The one with that bloody acorn on it? It's more like a shepherd's crook. He just looks stupid wandering around with it. Like some Old Testament prophet who got lost. And that bloody silver acorn. It looks like a cock. Can't somebody tell him?'

'After you, Tony. Be my guest,' said Walton sarcastically.

Tony grimaced as he recalled the fate of his predecessor ... the one who had told Ieuan that when it came to shirts he had 'no taste'.

'Have a look in the umbrella stand, over there,' he said returning to the endless task of boot polishing.

27. ANOTHER COUPLE OF CLOSE-RUN THINGS

YOUNG Mr. Spon had enjoyed his time at Shrewsbury and even now, approaching old age, he took every opportunity to stop off at the borders market town and revisit his schoolboy haunts and the café where he and his select few school-friends had whiled away their free hours. He saw no reason to suspend this habit of a lifetime just because some psychotic criminal like Ieuan Henge had decided to put out a contract on him. Nor did he see why his newly-acquired bodyguard and chum, Austin, was all jittery about this digression from the direct route to Halfrod Hall.

''snot good,' said Austin, making the Spartans look chatty. 'You'll be out in the open. Too many ways to get to you.'

'Oh come, come, Austin,' said Spon, at his most avuncular, as they progressed at a snail's pace around the alleys and back streets. 'How could they know that we are here at all?'

Spon had never been the athletic type but he noticed that even these gentle peregrinations around the heart of the medieval town exhausted him more and more easily. The hunched and wheezing country solicitor motioned towards Francini's Café.

'Would you like a cup of tea and perhaps a teacake, Austin?'

'What's that?' came the brusque reply. The strapping six-footer wearing the badly-fitting suit was scanning every direction for signs of danger. Over the past couple of days, Spon had discovered that communication was easier if he just spoke 'squaddy'.

'Fancy a brew?'

Austin looked at Spon:

'Yeah. Go on then.'

The interior of the café was warm and steamy. Condensation trickled down the large misted window which looked out onto the street.

'Oh, excellent,' muttered Spon. 'It's hardly changed at all.'

He moved quickly across the café floor to his favourite corner table. He positioned himself on the bench behind it and allowed himself a smile and a sigh of satisfaction. Austin wedged himself between the opposite bench and the Formica-topped table. They just sat there for a good five minutes before the silence between them was broken.

'You bin 'ere before, then?' said Austin.

'Oh yes,' said Spon his smile widening. 'Many, many times. This was something of a sanctuary for me from school when the bullying became too much.'

'Oh yeah. Know what you mean,' said Austin nodding in agreement recalling his time at school. He remembered just how exhausting bullying other school kids could be.

Spon, by now, was in full 'All Our Yesterdays' mode.

'They were very kind to me here.' He leant forward confidentially and added under his breath, 'I think it's still run by the same family.'

'Just the job,' said Austin as his eyes roved around the other customers. 'Looks proper. D'ya mind if I grab some snap?'

'You have whatever you want,' said Spon pleased that his favourite café had met with Austin's approval.

They ordered and after a few minutes, two mugs of hot, sweet tea arrived, their steam adding to the general sauna effect of the café interior. Austin's sausage sandwich followed shortly afterwards. For the first time that day, the bodyguard concentrated on what was in front of him, not monitoring the horizon for potential threats.

'They still do a good sausage sandwich, I see,' said Spon.

'Want some?' said Austin pointing to his plate.

'Oh no, Austin. That's very kind of you but it would give me the most awful wind if I were even to try just a mouthful.'

Spon reached over to the plastic bottles next to the wall. 'Would you like tomato ketchup or some HP sauce with that?'

'You what?' said Austin.

'Red or brown?' said Spon waving the sauce bottles.

'Oh yeah. Brown, please,' said Austin leaning forward to take the bottle.

It was then that things became complicated. Everything happened so fast and blurred almost into one continuous action. It was as if the café window had shattered after he noticed that Austin had been hit.

'That's rather a lot of tomato sauce,' he thought as he watched the red liquid spread across the Formica tabletop. It was only when he noticed that Austin was holding the brown sauce bottle that the truth dawned upon him. Austin let out a long wheeze and slumped forward onto his sausage sandwich before regaining some of his composure. He reached across the table and pulled Spon sideways along the bench until he slid to the floor.

'Lie down!' groaned Austin. 'Lie down!'

In the chaos, Spon couldn't even tell if a second shot had been fired. He was more concerned with applying pressure to the bullet hole in Austin's arm which hadn't been there a moment earlier.

***

Across the street, in the second-floor flat, Mrs. Irene Edwards, two days short of her ninetieth birthday, was still trying new experiences. When she was eighty she had gone sky-diving. At eighty-five, she had held the record for the UK's oldest bungee jumper for a few weeks. She enjoyed these new experiences because she had been in control. Today she wasn't in control and this worried her. She was tied to one of her own kitchen chairs with a gag over her mouth.

When she had opened the door not fifteen minutes earlier, she had been expecting Niki, her community help, who usually called at about this time to help her bathe. For this reason, she did not expect to be confronted by a rotund, middle-aged man; a rotund, middle-aged man wearing a Tony Blair face mask and who reeked of stale alcohol.

'Yes?' was as far as she got before a large, sweaty hand was clamped over her mouth. As the stranger stepped over the threshold, he lifted Mrs. Edwards from her feet and manoeuvred her towards one of the kitchen chairs some feet behind her. The assault was firm but not violent so she decided to go with the flow. Mrs. Edwards had worked at a local school for thirty years, teaching Russian. This was handy. It enabled her to understand the seamless flow of grumbling which came from her assailant in a Siberian accent that she placed somewhere around Irkutsk.

'Go to Shrewsbury, Gregor'. 'Track old lawyer and bodyguard, Gregor'. 'Shoot old lawyer if opportunity presents itself, Gregor.' It's never 'Hello Gregor. Sorry to interrupt your weekend, Gregor. Sorry to ring you so late, Gregor. Sacha was saying that you've lost weight, Gregor. How's the wife and family, Gregor?' Not that that blood-sucking bitch would give two hoots about me or how I am getting on without her. Best thing you ever did, Gregor, leaving her.'

He broke off here to secure Mrs. Edwards to the chair with duct tape. In broken English he asked: 'Please, nice lady, put your foot against the chair leg, I don't want to hurt you but I will if you make trouble. Oh yes. Your friend Niki, she is okay. She is in the coal ... what is word? ... er ... Hitler had one ... ah yes ... bunker. Please remember because I won't have time to release you both after I have finished my work here. Agreed?'

Mrs. Edwards tried to reply in her best Russian but was prevented by the old and not very clean sock that the apparent hitman had used as a gag. She just nodded.

'Now,' continued Gregor, 'You are comfortable, yes?'

She nodded again. Gregor turned, adjusted his Tony Blair face mask, picked up his holdall and went up the stairs two at a time, his sprightliness belying his girth.

The next five minutes was a cacophony of heavy wooden furniture being dragged across the upstairs floor. In her frightened state, it crossed Mrs. Edwards' mind that she might be being burgled by an inept furniture thief.

'Well the joke's on him,' she thought. 'That chest of drawers had to be lifted in through the window by crane when I moved here in 1960.'

Still the longer she thought about it, the less compelling this explanation became. The silence upstairs now suggested that Gregor might be resting.

Then came the sound of footsteps moving across a de-carpeted floor. She heard a Russian expletive bellowed out and then heard Gregor coming down the stairs. She saw his feet on the landing and then heard more grumbling in Russian, 'Where is mask, Gregor? What have you done with mask?'

He retreated up the stairs before descending again wearing the Tony Blair mask. He entered the room and she could sense that he had been exerting himself and was nervous. Sweat darkened the shirt around his neck yet he remained polite and solicitous.

'Sometimes I wonder if I am in the wrong business!' He looked at Mrs. Edwards and threw up his arms in a gesture of hopelessness.

'Nice lady. Do you have a medium-sized Philips screw-driver, please?' he continued.

Mrs. Edwards was so taken in by his manner that she found herself nodding towards the kitchen cabinet.

'Over here?' asked Gregor.

Mrs. Edwards nodded her assent. He moved his hand down the front of the cabinet pausing over the drawers.

Am I getting warm?' he asked.

Mrs. Edwards nodded again.

'Right or ... or ...' his vocabulary eluded him for a moment, 'the other one?'

Mrs. Edwards nodded a final time.

'You are, what is word in English, ... a diamond geezer!' said Gregor grabbing the Philips screwdriver and returning upstairs.

Mrs. Edwards waited for what seemed like a long time but could only have been minutes. Then she heard a dull thud, as if someone had hit a muffled drum.

A howl of despair was followed by the hitman talking to himself again.

'Gregor. You are a great hairy baboon! A bungling idiot! How could you have missed?'

Sounds of furniture apparently being moved back to its original position were interspersed with the occasional sob from the incompetent hit-man and then more monologue.

'How to explain this to client. He won't be happy client. He won't pay me!'

He let out another sob as he thought of all this effort for no reward. Downstairs, Mrs. Edwards heard the monologue continue.

'Now, make sure you pack everything and don't leave anything behind ...especially bloody medium-sized Philips screwdriver. There we go. One buckle, two buckles ...all done.'

Mrs. Edwards heard Gregor's footsteps as he approached the stairs. He came down them two-at-a-time and made straight for the door. She heard the door open and then, rather worryingly, his footsteps returning, slowly. The Tony Blair face mask appeared framed in the kitchen doorway.

'I owe you for Philips screwdriver,' he said before turning on his heel and disappearing down the hallway and out of the door.

Mrs. Edwards wondered, 'I wonder how Niki is doing?'

***

'Spon, listen to me. You have to stay with Austin and the ambulance and give me a call when you get to the hospital. I shall meet you there.'

Penelope's words had a calming effect and, for the first time since the bungled attempt on his life, Spon felt his pulse-rate return to something approaching normal. He was strapped into a seat in the rear compartment of the ambulance. Next to him, on the stretcher, lay the heavily sedated form of Austin with his torso covered by a cellular blanket. His feet protruded from the end of the stretcher and bounced around as the ambulance attempted to negotiate the poor road surface.

'How are you feeling, old chap?' asked Spon being careful to pat the shoulder which wasn't in a sling.

'Muvver?' replied Austin weakly.

'Oh dear,' thought Spon. 'It's worse than it looks!'

After half an hour, he slid back the communications hatch and said to the crew, 'We seem to have been driving for an awfully long time. When will we get to the hospital?'

The paramedic in the passenger seat twisted round to explain.

'I'm afraid that we've had to divert to a hospital in Wales. There was some trouble at the Town Show in Shrewsbury and A&E were snowed under when we radioed in. It's the cheesemakers and bee-keepers ... again. They just can't leave it alone. Bloody nutters.'

'Where in Wales?'

'Wrexham, I think,' answered the paramedic looking at the map on his clipboard. 'Yes. Wrexham General.'

Spon picked up his mobile, donned his glasses, and dialled Penelope's number.

'Wrexham General,' he said curtly.

'Right-oh,' said Penelope. 'We'll come and find you there.'

***

Ryan was a competent hitman. He came highly recommended and Walton hired him without hesitation. Walton was impressed by his cool and distant demeanour.

Ryan had spent much of his early life in the army where his interest in explosives was soon noted. His aversion to soap, water and deodorants gave him the nickname 'Pem'. Ironically, he left the services a decade later with a clean record, an intimate knowledge of most things that go bang and no friends. Still, being a loner is an advantage if you are a hitman.

Research and planning were everything to Ryan. He was meticulous. He spent nearly a week hanging around near Studworks, finding out who worked there, getting close to the chauffeur in the local pub. He was delighted to discover that his target, Penelope, was truly a creature of habit. She never deviated from her chosen route or schedule without good cause and anyone who attempted to do this for her could expect a good tongue-lashing.

'And she's got a vicious tongue on her, too,' said Mike the chauffeur reaching for the fourth brandy at the end of a long evening in The Gravedigger's Arms. 'Now my mishsus has got a gob on her but, even when she's fired up, she's nothing compared to the bosh.'

'Really?' Ryan feigned interest. 'So, say she was going to that big game fair ... you know the one ... Hafron or something ...'

'Oh, you mean Halfrod Hall Game Fair,' blurted out Mike. 'I'm off there next week as it happens ... to that very show ... with the bosh.'

'Really?' repeated Ryan. 'So, I suppose you'd go on the A4 ...'

'No, you see,' interrupted Mike. 'You'd think that, wouldn't you? But no. The bosh always goes cross-country. It takes hours but she just doesn't care.'

Before the increasingly intoxicated chauffeur had reached the halfway point of his route map, Ryan knew exactly where he would position the roadside bomb. The junction he had in mind was perfect.

'Deserted country road,' he thought. 'Poor visibility in both directions so the target vehicle has to stop. Just pop the package 50 feet down the road to the right and catch the target just as it's accelerating. Perfect.'

***

'That was Spon,' said Penelope to Healey. 'They're taking Austin to Wrexham General. We should get there as quick as we can.'

She leant forward to speak to Mike the chauffeur.

'We're coming up to a junction in about a mile, Mike. I usually turn right. I want you to turn left so we can join the main road to Wrexham in a couple of miles.'

'Right-oh missus,' replied Mike.

The Bentley Mulsanne drew to a halt at the junction. Indicated left and pulled away silently.

One hundred yards away, a small bush became strangely agitated in the windless conditions. It began to shake, then to move about.

'Bollocks!' shouted the bush.

28. FANCY DRESS

THE Pemblington Guide to Country Houses of Britain read:

'Rumoured to be the furthest point south reached by the invading Jacobites in 1745. They obviously took one look at Halfrod Hall and turned tail… Get rid of the bars on the windows and the razor-wire pigeon deterrents and this place would look less like a secure hospital for the criminally insane and more like the Georgian country mansion that was originally intended.'

For the weekend of the Game Fair, the whole place was given a face-lift. The external grimness was countered with up-lighting. The setting was made more dramatic by the judicious installation of torches and braziers. The well-maintained interior decoration was the unique lasting testament to its designer, Charles Ignatius Adlestrope, a one-time student of Robert Adam. The reception rooms were lit by thirty magnificent chandeliers.

'Yes' thought Ieuan Henge as he made his way up the marble staircase to his rooms above. 'If this doesn't impress the hell out of the dealers then nothing will.'

As for the investors who were to attend that evening's fancy dress reception, he was not so sure. It may do the trick for El Cameleon and his peons from Mexico but the Amir could probably buy somewhere like this with his loose change. As he reached the landing where the staircase branched away to the right and left, he turned and looked back down the stairs. Within thirty seconds, Ieuan had convinced himself that the glittering scene below had all been of his own doing. He had willed it into existence. Weeks of preparation by Walton, often from a wheelchair; Russlana's methodical efficiency in arranging travel and accommodation for every guest; Portuguese Tony's meticulous preparation of menus, drinks and decoration were all subsumed by Ieuan's vaunting self-regard.

'Look on my works, ye mighty, and despair,' he thought to himself. 'Did I just make up those lines or have I heard them before? Who cares? They're mine now.' He headed off to his rooms wondering if he could fit in a 'victory shag' with Russlana before preparing for the evening's fancy dress reception.

'What have you got for me, Tony?' Ieuan shouted as he entered his dressing room.

'Captain Hook,' said Portuguese Tony.

'Pantomime?' said Ieuan. 'Men in tights and stuff? Although the pirate theme is quite appealing. Do I actually get a hook?'

Tony reached into a box and waved a shiny metal hook in the air by its convenient hand grip.

'Goody,' said Ieuan laconically. 'Well,' he added, sorting through the elaborate stage costume complete with periwig and moustache, 'At this stage, I suppose it'll have to do,' trying hard not to sound too impressed.

The one aspect of the reception which was worrying Walton was the security. Ieuan as usual had left contradictory orders. On the one hand he wanted every guest fully checked out as they entered. On the other, he didn't want any of the customers and especially the investors to be challenged. Someone would be bound to get the hump and kick off. Never a good idea when many of the guests would be armed. Ieuan's parting comment to Walton made security, in any meaningful sense, impossible.

As he left the meeting, he fixed Walton with one of his arrogant stares and said, slowly and clearly, 'And no fucking traders ... not a single one ... They are like cockroaches. If they smell free food and drink we'll be up to our tit-rings in 'em and the event will be ruined. Understand?'

Walton nodded. What could he do? He eventually took the view that having a few traders wandering about was better than a shoot-out and so, despite Ieuan's orders, he took the risk and told security to ease-off almost completely.

'So we just let 'em in even if they're behaving like cunts?' said Brad, the steroid-sculptured head of the security team, at the full dress-rehearsal team meeting.

'That's right,' said Walton patiently. 'Ieuan doesn't want any hold-ups or incidents while the guests are arriving. In any case, the whole thing would become a mess if we insisted on checking the identity of every guest.'

He was beginning to regret the decision to make the reception a fancy-dress event. He regretted even more letting Brad decide on the costumes for the whole security team. A few months after Christmas and here were two dozen burly security types dressed as Santa's elves.

'They were cheap and they had the right sizes in stock,' said Brad in his own defence.

'Yeah, it's not easy, you know ...' said the elf named Matt, 'finding stuff like fancy dress in the right size. There aren't many size 60 elves out there.'

'So what will my dogs do then?' said another elf called Ethan. 'I've got 'em all up here ready for a bit of one-on-one security work and you're now saying that they won't be deployed.'

'That's right,' said Walton maintaining his patience. 'Look, Ieuan just thought that the evening would go better if the guests remained unmolested by you elves and your dogs as they enter the event. After they've all gone in, everything goes back to normal with Team A patrolling the outside of the hall.

'Building,' repeated Brad pointing to Team A. Team A nodded their understanding.

'Team B'll do the grounds and gardens,' continued Walton only to be immediately cut short by Brad pointing at Team B and saying, 'Gardening, right?' Team B nodded their understanding.

'Nearly there,' thought Walton as he consulted his notes and continued.

'And that leaves Team C,' Brad stepped forward with his finger at the ready, 'patrolling the perimeter.'

'Team C,' echoed Brad. 'Rimming. OK?'

'What the hell are you going on about?' Walton's patience left the room. 'Rimming? What are you telling these people?'

'Don't worry,' said Brad. 'It's a technical term, just a shortened version of perimeter, innit.'

Exasperated, Walton left the Christmas elves to their preparations before getting ready for the evening. Mercifully, he was spared the indignity of fancy dress as he was 'staff'.

'Just a plain old tuxedo for you, Walton my boy,' he muttered to himself as he went through the tradesman's entrance into the cacophony of the kitchens.

***

'But Figgis has got to be here, Maurice. I've been around every square inch of this awful showground this afternoon and he's nowhere to be seen. If he's still on the trail of these drug dealers he's guaranteed to try and get into this reception at the Hall,' said Terry who was beginning to regret the whole venture to curtail Operation Wild Goose.

'Why haven't we been invited?' said Maurice childishly. Too many brandies had left him in a rather sore and grumpy mood. 'Didn't get where I am today, Terry, by gate-crashing house parties and I'm not particularly keen on starting now.'

'Don't worry, Maurice. We won't be alone. Every trader I have spoken to this afternoon will also be gate-crashing the event. The prospect of free food and drink is a magnet to these people. And they say that the security is going to be negligible,' said Terry.

'Alright, I suppose we can give it a go. But I have to say I'm not very impressed with this weekend so far, you know. It seems to be a complete botch-job and I have to say, Terry, that the finger of blame points pretty squarely at you,' said Maurice, pointing dramatically at Terry.

'Well, let's see about that after we've completed our work here, shall we, Maurice? After all, you haven't exactly worked your fingers to the bone so far, have you? Unless you count emptying brandy down your throat at a rate of knots,' replied Terry, bitterly. 'I mean, I don't mind sorting out the recreational vehicle and the supplies but I've even had to go and find costumes for this evening for us while you've been sitting here recovering from your excesses.'

Maurice heard a slight sob in Terry's voice and decided on a more conciliatory approach.

'Well,' he said, 'I suppose I have been a bit grumpy today. Let's do as you say and give this party a go this evening. But if we haven't found Figgis by ten o'clock, that's it. Agreed?'

Terry nodded.

'Now,' said Maurice surveying the two boxes which Terry had placed on the breakfast bar, 'Where on earth did you find fancy dress costumes at a Game Fair?'

***

In the half-light of dusk, Halfrod Hall took on a magical aura. The gloom accentuated the constant activity within the brilliantly-lit interior. The marquee in which the drugs auction was to take place glowed whilst hiding unsightly containers, portaloos and vehicles.

The chandeliers in the main rooms cast their light into the darkness as the doors and windows opened and closed with the passage of staff. Walton wanted to try and contain the partying to the nineteenth-century east-wing of the house. This would have the dual benefit of minimising damage and allowing the security elves to monitor access to the huge marquee at the appointed hour.

'It's nearly the size of the house!' said Jayne.

'What is?' said Peter. She handed him the binoculars. Parked barely three hundred yards from the hall, Jayne's food wagon made a particularly good observation platform.

'Good God! You're right', he said. 'Is the whole event going be held in that tent?'

'Oh no,' said Jayne. 'That's just for the drugs auction, I imagine. After all, there are a lot of drug dealers in the UK so you need a big enough space to house them all. You see those containers backed on to the marquee?'

'Hang on,' he said, waiting for the focus to adjust on the digital binoculars. He could see two rows of three containers arranged like a chevron with their open ends pointing towards each other. 'Yep. I see 'em,' he said.

'I reckon that's where the drugs are. Under guard at the moment but later this evening that place will be like a cash and carry.'

'Bloody hell!' said Peter. 'I had no idea of the scale of this thing. Surely every dealer in the country and his wife will be there.'

'Do you really think that most drug dealers marry?' said Jayne. 'Sometimes, I really worry about you.'

She took the binoculars and was about to continue her teasing when something caught her eye.

'Hello. Who have we got here, then?'

Two limousines drew up at the main entrance. Jayne could see Walton and his staff descend the steps and step forward to open the car door.

'That's something you don't see every day.'

'What is? What is?' said Peter. 'Let me see.'

'Hang on.' Jayne pushed away his hand. 'Just let me make sure. Oh yes. It's him. El Cameleon. One of the world's leading narco-criminals.'

Finally, Peter grabbed the binoculars. He saw the tiny, skinny frame of the Mexican drug lord in his trademark shiny suit standing at the entrance of Halfrod Hall. He looked like a child standing next to Walton and his staff. But Peter could see in their body language that El Cameleon was top dog.

'Look who's riding shotgun ... in the vintage Raybans and the other one with snake skin boots getting out of the second limo,' said Jayne.

Peter's heart sank as he saw Pablo and Juan. If he and Jayne were going to gate-crash this event, he would have to give them a wide berth or make sure that his fancy dress was bullet-proof, literally.

Minutes later, at the main entrance, Walton was again on hand to greet the Amir and a selection of his richly-attired wives who had just been shuttled from the heliport a few miles away. Anwar Anbar clucked around making sure that everything was in order.

'What a splendid welcoming pavilion, Mr. Walton,' said the Amir graciously sweeping forward in full Arab robes. 'I cannot wait to see the party at the house.'

Mr Anwar leant forward, 'I believe, Highness, that this is the house.'

'Oh,' replied the Amir undeterred. 'So the party will be just a small affair, then. Just a few friends of Ieuan's.'

'That's the idea, sir. Yes,' said Walton compliantly.

'How very ... what is your word in English? ... cozy. I always liked your fancy dress events. It means I don't have to change.'

Walton laughed politely but his attention was already diverted by two of his staff who were handling the Amir's luggage with the same level of skill that cattle handle glassware.

'Where the hell do we find these people? Did we even check if they have opposable thumbs?' he thought. He smiled at the Amir and got as far as, 'If you'd like to follow me, I'll show you to your rooms, Highness,' when he was interrupted by the security elf at the top of the entrance steps.

'You're a bit early mate, aren't you?' said the security elf to the Amir.

'I am sorry?' said the Amir. Anwar wheezed up the steps behind him.

'The party doesn't start until eight. Or have you come in fancy dress to save time?'

Walton hurriedly placed an arm around the shoulder of the over-sized elf, guided him away from the VIP and his party and stopped the potential protocol disaster in its tracks.

***

'It's just along here on the left. Here we go. In there,' pointed Croesus. Dr. Subudar slowed his Lexus to a snail's pace and gazed myopically through the windscreen. He was convinced that this whole adventure would end in tears but had no one to blame but himself. As a private consultant, he earned good money. Not as much as his senior colleague, Sir John Stiffener, but – there again – he wasn't the one who had to face the occasional malpractice suit. It hadn't been a good year and Croesus was most insistent that he be driven directly to this place. Once his offer of remuneration escalated to over five thousand pounds, Subudar found himself incapable of refusing.

The Lexus pulled to a halt in front of the ornamental wrought-iron gates of Halfrod Hall. A large man dressed as an elf stepped out of the shadows. As evenings go, this security elf was having a bad one. His first effort at keeping out 'undesirables' from the party had resulted in a shouting-at from that yank, Walton, and his demotion from 'house security' to 'gate security'. An obvious demotion, he wasn't looking forward to his break as all the other elves would take the piss out of him. More importantly, now that he was down at the gate, he wouldn't get a 'go' on the quad bikes. He was determined to take no risks with these new arrivals.

'Evening, Gents,' he said to Subudar as the window whirred open. 'Here for the party, are we?'

'Oh yes. Most certainly,' said Subudar in his best bedside-manner voice.

'And who have you come as, Sir?' he said addressing Croesus on the back seat, pencil and clipboard at the ready.

Croesus, still dressed in his hospital pyjamas and dressing gown, shuffled forward to the edge of the rear seat and spoke clearly and slowly as if addressing a spaniel, 'Alan Titchmarsh.'

Anxious not to create a second disturbance for the evening, he dutifully wrote down the name whilst commenting, 'Most amusing, Sir. And I think your get-up's very good n'all.'

He received a blank stare from Croesus for his trouble.

'Silly old sod!' muttered the elf to himself as he opened the gate.

'He doesn't look anything like Alan Titchmarsh.'

'What on earth is wrong with people nowadays?' thought Croesus, genuinely puzzled.

***

'And this is the best you could find, Terry?' said Maurice as he trudged sulkily through the darkness towards Halfrod Hall.

'Well given that we didn't know that the party was going to be fancy dress until six hours ago, I think I've done really rather well,' said Terry in an aggrieved tone.

'But could you have found something a little less earthy and little more dashing,' said Maurice.

'Not in your size, Maurice. Not in your size,' replied Terry, archly.

The darkness prevented Terry from seeing Maurice's face flush angrily like a vintage Armitage Shanks. Only a couple of hours before, Terry had returned to the RV, thrown two boxes onto the breakfast bar and removed the lid of the top one, with a flourish.

'What do you think, Maurice?' he said.

'What do I think of what?' replied Maurice as he surveyed the contents. 'Was whatever it is expensive?'

'I got them both for a hundred quid,' said Terry.

'For God's sake, man. One hundred quid for this old tat. It looks like a selection of off-cuts from a string factory ... or that squid-ink pasta that my good lady wife is always banging on about. Is it a costume? How do we wear it, Terry?'

'Yes. It is, Maurice. That's the beauty of it. It's entirely in keeping with the game fair theme but bizarre enough to pass as fancy dress. But the best thing about it is ... no one will be able to recognise us. They're ghillie suits!'

Maurice could dimly remember that one of his distant and ancient relatives had once worked as a ghillie on a royal estate north of the border but he certainly wasn't going to 'fess up' up to this in his current situation and was less than keen about clambering into the suit.

Terry held up the hooded top to reveal long strands of green and black camouflage material hanging from it.

'There's a mask as well,' he added, 'to ensure total anonymity.'

'Oh joy...,' sighed Maurice as he lifted the lid of the second box and sorted through the contents.

29. TRIFFIDS

ON the Pigeon Destroyer stand, Paul finished placing the last of his dead pigeons on the decoy cradle, connected the battery and checked that it worked. What a day it had been. He'd have normally finished setting up hours before but he hadn't allowed for the sudden demand for ghillie suits. He'd sold the first one at five-to-eight that morning and, after that, the sales had just kept on coming at five-minute intervals throughout the day. It was midday before he discovered the reason for this welcome and unexpected surge of business.

'But you don't go stalking, do you?' Paul had said to Ken as he bagged up two ghillie suits. 'No, but I don't need it for stalking. I need it for the fancy dress bash this evening at the Hall.' He'd been delighted that Paul had both his and Glenda's XXXL sizes in stock so it was an easy purchase.

He continued, 'After what they've charged me for these shows this year, too bloody right I'm gate-crashing their party! I'm going to do my best to eat and drink at least the cost of one pitch ... and don't think I can't do it!'

Paul nodded, sagely.

'Well if you know anyone else who's going and they need a disguise, point them in my direction.'

By the end of the day, Paul had nearly sold out of the suits and the knocking on his caravan door, much to Helen's annoyance, continued long after darkness fell.

***

In the brightly-lit kitchens of Halfrod Hall, staff were working at a frenetic pace in final preparation for the party. Walton was pink, sweaty and nervous and was being followed around by Pablo.

'Now isn't exactly a great time for me to chat unless, of course, your boss isn't happy with any of the arrangements,' he said. Looking over Pablo's shoulder, he saw two waiters weighed down with cases of Cristal champagne, collide. 'Hey, just look where you're going,' Walton bellowed. 'Those bottles are worth more than you are!'

'Do not worry, Wal-ton. El Cameleon is happy with his rooms but he said he really wants to see joo before the party starts,' insisted Pablo.

'The thing is, Pablo, Old Sport,' said Walton, 'There won't be any party unless I'm here to crack the whip, as you see. I mean look at these waiters. Half of them don't seem to have clothes that fit and a clumsier bunch it's difficult to imagine ... If it goes wrong, you know how forgiving Ieuan can be. He'll skin me alive.'

'I think that this is exactly what El Cameleon wants to discuss with joo.'

'Oh really?' said Walton sniffing an opportunity. 'Well, perhaps I can spare five minutes, after all.'

Another loud collision in the background.

'Now what? Have you people even done this sort of work before? Those canapés have to go into the guests not into the bin!'

***

A mobile communications unit was parked discreetly beyond the perimeter fence of Halfrod Hall. Inside, the SNIF team were hard at work.

'Bellend here. It's fine. We can hear you loud and clear. How's it going, over?' shouted the Chief Inspector into the microphone.

Luckily Rimmer had withdrawn to a quieter corner of the kitchens so that no one saw him wince with pain as he fumbled for his ear-piece to reduce the volume from 'ear-splitting' to 'acceptable'.

'I think the lads should have had some training before we sent them in here. None of them know what the hell they're doing.'

'Never mind the quality of the service, Rimmer. You only have to fake it for a couple of hours. Just keep an eye on Walton and the guests and make sure that when they withdraw for the auction you and your squad are in position.'

'Will do, sir. Rimmer, over and out.' He followed Walton and Pablo as they entered the hallway and went upstairs.

Pablo opened the door and Walton entered El Cameleon's rooms, gingerly. He wasn't doing anything wrong but he didn't want Ieuan finding out about any private discussions that might take place between him and the guests.

'Come in, come in, Wal-ton,' said El Cameleon, pouring a glass of mescal. 'Joo must sit down and make jooself comfortable. I know from what Pablo here tells me that joo have much to do this evening so I will – how do you Americans say it – 'chase to the cut'.'

'That's good of you,' said Walton as he watched his diminutive host glide across the room and nearly slither into an armchair. In the large armchair, El Cameleon looked child-like but his reason for wanting to talk with Walton was anything but innocent.

'Joo boss, Meester 'enge.' The effort of pronouncing the name made it look like El Cameleon had just swallowed a fly. 'He treats joo good?'

'Well, on the whole, yeah. I mean he is very demanding and he does load stuff onto me and he can be temperamental and ungrateful ... occasionally.'

Walton found these words flooding out of him in a nervous rush. It was as if El Cameleon had somehow hypnotised him into telling the truth. Walton suddenly felt very vulnerable.

'So, Pablo,' said El Cameleon. 'I don't know about joo but I am hearing the answer "No".'

‘Si, Jefe,’ replied Pablo as he poured himself a drink.

‘You see, Wal-ton. It is nice of your Meester ’enge to invite me to invest in his leetle concern here in Europe but I am not sure that I want to be a long-term investor. After all, why be content with the salsa when joo can have the whole burrito?’

‘I see,’ said Walton, shocked at both El Cameleon’s ambition and his apparent lack of care about who knew it. Walton knew he was in a bad place and he needed to get out.

‘Well, I do enjoy these little chats but as you know I have much to prepare for this evening’s ...’

El Cameleon waved a skinny arm as if dismissing a fly. ‘Sit down, sit down. Wal-ton.’ Out of the corner of his eye, Walton saw Pablo move silently towards the door to block any exit.

‘I can see my honesty shocks joo, no? But we talk here ‘off the record’ Eh? Eh?’ continued El Cameleon intent on cramming as much American slang into his monologue as possible. ‘Joo see, Wal-ton. I am in the ‘people business’.’

Walton knew of Pablo’s human trafficking operation into the US but wasn’t sure whether this was what El Cameleon was referring to.

‘Nothing happens in my world until I am fully prepared; until I have the right people in place. What we discuss this evening is like a dream. And I know that it will never become reality until I am fully prepared. But when I am fully prepared and ready to act then ...’

El Cameleon’s dramatic explanation was cut short by Pablo gently belching. El Cameleon cast his wayward eye in the direction of his henchman who blushed with shame.

‘... then I strike with all the speed of a Chameleon’s tongue! Actually, I get my nickname from this, joo know.’

‘Really?’ Walton was feeling a little more in control of matters and was starting to relax.

‘Joo see. I need people ... good people to run my operations. It’s true, I have good people like Pablo here. Where would I be without them? But they are more for, how joo say, 'persuasion'. I don't see Pablo here ever running a business, eh Pablo?'

'Si, Jefe,' said Pablo suddenly realising that Walton was going to be brought in over his head.

'With someone like joo, Wal-ton, running the business, I could sleep soundly knowing that my interests were being looked after. I make this offer to joo, Wal-ton, in good faith. All I ask is that you keep our talk secret and that you let me have your answer before I leave.'

Walton rose from his seat, head spinning and moved towards the door. Pablo fixed him with an oysterish eye and showed him out.

***

'Bloody hell!' bellowed Maurice. He was lying flat on his front having tripped over a tuft of tussock grass. His ghillie suit sucked up the cold, muddy ground water like an old floor mop. The distance between the game fair and the house had seemed just a few hundred yards when they started this jaunt but it seemed to go on for ever.

'Come on, Maurice,' said Terry brusquely. 'Do stop lying around. You nearly had me over, too.'

'How much bloody further?' snapped Maurice, wiping mud from his front.

'Just through this gate here and we are virtually there. If I'd known what a fuss you were going to make, I'd have left you back in the RV.'

They staggered the final few steps and leant against the gatepost.

'God, how do these people live like this?' said Terry catching his breath.

'I suppose they get used to it,' said Maurice. 'After all, after this little trek I now know why they are referred to as 'the great unwashed'. I mean look at me, Terry. I'm one of Her Majesty's most senior civil servants, at the height of my powers, and I'm now standing in a provincial field covered in mud and God knows what ... and for what? Just to save your skin! I meant what I said earlier. We have two hours. If we don't find that idiot Figgis by ten, we pack up and head back to civilisation.'

Terry snapped.

'Oh for God's sake, stop whingeing, will you, Maurice? That's all you've done all day. It's not going to help solve this problem. Just concentrate will you.' He waved his hand dismissively at Maurice and turned to mount the stile.

'Don't you dare wave me away!' said Maurice. 'How dare you! We may be in a field but I am still your superior, Terry, even if I am up to my tits in mud!'

As Terry turned to continue the angry spat, his gaze fell away from Maurice to the field beyond.

'My God!' he gasped. 'Look!'

Maurice turned. The light from the house shone out over the fields in illuminating beams. As far as the eye could see, there were ghillie suits moving towards the house. The camouflage effect gave the whole scene an unworldly even alien effect. Maurice's anger dissipated for a second.

'It's like some weird natural migration ... like the Day of the Triffids,' he muttered before switching back to whingeing mode. 'This really is the final straw, Terry. I don't mind fancy dress but it would be nice to stand out from the crowd. How the hell are we going to recognise Figgis – or each other for that matter – if we're all wearing ghillie suits?'

***

Many of the party guests had arrived early and Walton had had to deploy more staff at the main entrance to hand out gift bags to the investors and to guide the buyers.

Many of the buyers had chosen to ignore the fancy dress part of the invitation and had just turned up in their everyday work clothes ranging from skin-tight suits for those modelling themselves on the 'Lock, Stock and Two Smoking Barrels' type of East End villain through to urban drug vendors whose choice of attire often suggested a personal and cultural identity crisis. White Scousers turned up in baggy leisure suits with trousers at half-mast effecting the look of gangster/rappers. Black Brummies turned up in shiny colourful jackets which would not have looked out of place at an Indian wedding. Asian dealers turned up for the most part in sombre, smart suits suggesting that they were accountants who had lost their way. And indeed, many of them were and had.

As the queue at the entrance developed, one or two figures in ghillie suits were noticeable. After half an hour, the queue seemed to comprise mostly of people dressed in ghillie suits. It was obvious to Walton that these were the gate-crashers from the showground. But Ieuan had said that he didn't want any trouble, he wanted the evening to go smoothly, he wanted nothing to get in the way of the auction which was to begin at midnight.

***

On the far side of Halfrod Estate, the silence of the country lanes was broken by the roar of a powerful engine. Pheasants crouched motionless in ditches. Other hedgerow creatures retreated into their burrows to escape the glare of headlamps. Roosting birds gripped their twiggy perches a little tighter.

'You're quite sure you want to go ahead with this then, are you Penelope? Because you do know that what you are suggesting is entirely illegal on so many levels it's difficult to know where to begin,' said Spon from the passenger seat of Penelope's Bentley.

'It's now or never, Missus,' said Mike from behind the steering wheel, eyes fixed to the narrow lane ahead.

A grim-faced Penelope said, 'Let's do this thing and to Hell with the consequences!'

Two and a half tons of Bentley Mulsanne lurched to the right and crashed through the pair of ornamental wrought-iron gates without even slowing down. In the distance, the lights from Halfrod Hall pushed columns of light into the darkening evening sky.

30. ONE SERVANT, TWO MASTERS

PENELOPE, Spon and Healey made their entrance to Halfrod Hall with ease through the chaotic kitchens. Mike the chauffeur was left someway off to look after his badly dented Bentley.

On their approach to the house, Penelope briefed the others, 'We've just got one shot at this. We need to get in and get out without being spotted and we need to find Henge's laptop. That should contain all the evidence we need.'

Through the kitchens and along the service corridors they crept. Spon pushed the door to the main hallway open by a fraction of an inch. Through the gap he saw Henge dressed as a Pirate shouting to a larger man dressed as an elf. Not for a moment was he tempted to see the funny side of this. All he could do was wave and point, alerting the others to the closeness of their enemy. Penelope made for the back-stairs and they ascended quickly and silently to the guest rooms on the first floor.

Back in the party, all pretence at security had been abandoned and Brad, the security elf, and his colleagues just stood about looking uncomfortable. The security dogs were a lot happier. The appalling standards of service at the party ensured a steady flow of tasty morsels onto the floor. Most of the security staff were thankful that they didn't have to intervene. The crowd was made up of traders at various stages of intoxication and the country's more successful drug dealers who appeared to be no strangers to violence.

Many had not even bothered with the fancy-dress

theme giving the whole crowd the look of a theatre being emptied for a fire drill with gangsters and what appeared to be triffids mixing uncomfortably with pantomime, Disney and Star Wars characters. Male and female guests alike all adopted a swaggering and bluff attitude presumably to deter any staff from questioning their presence.

The serving staff were also feeling uncomfortable. The real waiters were doing their best to serve guests with some semblance of decorum. The policemen masquerading as waiters had no such illusions. One constable dressed in a dinner jacket two sizes too small for him, absent-mindedly handed a whole case of red wine to a ghillie-suited trader while he tried to follow a dealer into the meleé of the party.

This was immediately seen as a sign of weakness by other traders who surged forward and began relieving the staff of any food or drink they were carrying. Glenda was in the vanguard handing two trays of smoked salmon back to Ken in the crowd before acquiring two bottles of champagne and two of red. The real staff tried their best to ration the outgoing food and drink but, with years of pitch-fee abuse fresh in their minds, the traders were not to be denied. Some of the disguised policemen tried to protect what they saw as an essential part of their disguise. One unfortunate in a dinner jacket at least three sizes too small for him put up too much of a fight. Much to the amusement of the traders, the seams of his disguise gave way under the exertion. As the unfortunate officer struggled to regain his dignity he was hoisted shoulder-high and dumped unceremoniously into an ornamental pond outside.

Luckily, Walton had laid in quite a supply of drink and provisions so, even with traders consuming canapés by the tray load, the kitchens were able to keep up.

***

Maurice leant heavily on the bar and picked up another vodka martini from the tray before him. He was exhausted by the weight of the sodden, mud-spattered ghillie suit and it was all he could do to drag himself and it to the bar. Terry had remained silent since their argument in the field and once they had gained access to the party. He had disappeared into the crowd after hissing a simple order:

'Maurice. Do not call attention to yourself.'

Maurice turned to face the crowd with glass-in-hand trying to muster as much dignity as he could. Several party guests pointed and laughed at him.

'Damned impudence,' he slurred before noticing that his soiled ghillie suit had left a brown smear of mud all the way across the floor and up the front of the bar.

'Oh God, will this torture never end,' he thought. On a normal weekend, he would have been ensconced at some dinner party with his peers, the great and the good, sipping the finest wines and discussing important matters of state. What was he doing here? He finished his Martini and turned again to the bar for another. He tried to cover the brown mud smear he had left on the bar by standing in front of it. But every move he made caused the strings of his ghillie suit to swing against the brilliant white panel making the mess more extensive and more difficult to cover.

Terry found Maurice morose and morbidly drunk, more vodka martini than man. They had both removed their face masks as breathing and, in Maurice's case, drinking were otherwise nearly impossible.

'There you are,' slurred Maurice. 'Any luck? You've only got another hour you know.'

'Yes,' said Terry curtly. 'I see you've been working your fingers to the bone, as usual. Did you find Figgis or anything else useful at the bottom of that Martini pitcher, Maurice?'

'Well fuck you!' bellowed Maurice belligerently. The crowd around the bar instinctively shuffled away from him as one does from a retching child. Maurice turned again and grabbed another Martini from the tray. Terry continued his search.

***

As the party began to gather pace, the traders began to abandon any pretence they had made at keeping a low profile. Peter and Jayne had hung back from the group of traders making their way to the house so that when they arrived the event was in full swing.

The first person they bumped into was Kevin with a pint of red wine in one hand and tray of canapés in the other.

'It's my fifth!' he proudly announced before making off in the direction of the Jaegermeister stand in the corner.

Huge amounts of food and drink were on offer but it was the service which was truly noticeable. Some of the waiters, mostly the thin and foreign ones, performed their tasks well, moving effortlessly through the crowd dispensing food and drink to the guests. They had the added benefit of clothes which appeared to fit. The other waiters, usually larger and distinctly British-looking were truly awful at their job. Trays of food were dropped before reaching the table. Carrying more than two glasses seemed beyond some of them and holding a drinks' tray in the correct manner was rarely attempted and, if it was, always ended in disaster.

Out of the corner of her eye, Jayne saw a small black dog moving swiftly across the dance floor between the dancers' feet.

Peter made it through the crowd to the bar. Before he could remove his face mask to order a drink, a drunk to his right had grabbed him and started shouting at him.

'Your trouble, Terry,' sneered Maurice, 'is that the job has always been beyond your capa ... capabilly ... beyond you.'

Peter was about to shake off this annoyance when he recognised the face now glowing red beneath the ghillie suit hood like a ripe tomato nestling in foliage. Could it be? Maurice Grymm, the Permanent Secretary of Peter's department, not just here but obviously out of his mind on alcohol to boot.

'I told you, Terry. At ten o'clock, I'm off and let that annoying little tick, Figgis, do his worst.'

Peter huddled closer to the bar not knowing how to handle this case of mistaken identity. Perhaps silence was the best option. He pulled the ghillie suit mask back across his face.

'Go on then,' raged Maurice. 'Carry on sulking like the big girl's blouse that you are. No wonder Figgis worked out that you'd sent him on a wild goose chase to stop him from spoiling your little expenses scam! You are pathetic! And what's more, you don't know me at all! I am the boss of you so just pay bloody good attention. D'you hear?'

Maurice's tirade was interrupted by the arrival of another ghillie suit containing Terry. Peter retreated to the cover of the crowd.

'What is it about keeping a low profile you don't understand? And who are you yelling at?'

Maurice blinked like an owl.

'Well, actually I thought I was yelling at you,' said Maurice. 'After all, whoever it was was wearing one of these infernal ghillie suits or whatever they are called.'

'Please stop yelling at everyone in a ghillie suit or you'll damage yourself and make a bad situation even worse,' said Terry.

***

If Walton hadn't considered El Cameleon's job offer before the party had got going, he was certainly considering it now. The whole event was becoming a fiasco. His security policy had kept the peace at the entrance but he had no idea who was actually inside the party. Sure, the buyers were there in large numbers but there also appeared to be a whole load of freeloaders from the game fair behaving like complete oafs. The staff were appalling and seemed incapable of dispensing food and drink with the whole thing looking like some ghastly distribution from a truck in a refugee camp.

As he stood on the monumental staircase and surveyed the party below him, he thought, 'Perhaps a new job with El Cameleon might not be so bad after all.'

It was just half past ten and already civilisation seemed to be breaking down. He saw that the Martini bar had been decorated with a long smear of what he hoped was mud which carried on across the floor and ended at a motionless body in a ghillie suit over which other guests were carefully stepping. His attention was diverted by the sound of another tray of drinks hitting the floor and some over-sized idiot in an undersized suit attempting to clear up the mess. Giant elves stood impotently at all the doors unsure of why they were there. A loud voice started him from his reverie.

'Where's Walton?'

It was the voice of Ieuan but it came from the figure of Captain Hook.

'Where is he? Where's Walton?'

He repeated this, his voice cracking with rage. Walton from his vantage point on the stairs could not believe his eyes as two of the security elves closest to Ieuan started sniggering and one yelled, 'He's behind you! He's behind you!' in mock pantomime-style. Captain Hook approached the elves who, now realising their error, wilted in his presence. One pointed at Walton on the stairs.

Walton fled ignoring Ieuan's enraged cries behind him. Along the corridor he went, not sure how he would escape Ieuan's impending wrath. He took the first door on his right only to walk into the muzzle of a 9mm automatic held in Juan's bear-like paw.

'Ees okay, Juan,' said El Cameleon smiling. 'Ees Wal-Ton who I tell you about.'

Juan dropped the handgun back in its shoulder holster and stepped aside.

'So joo have decided, eh, Wal-ton?' continued El Cameleon.

'I have,' said Walton hurriedly. 'And it's a big 'yes' but with one condition.'

'Condition' was another of El Cameleon's least favourite words but he let it ride.

'And what is thees 'condition' joo want?' he said with the smile fading from his features.

'Er ...' stuttered Walton realising that the next few seconds might determine his fate. 'That our co-operation starts immediately and that you hide me from Ieuan who is coming up the stairs now. You can't miss him. He's dressed as Captain Hook.'

El Cameleon looked blankly at Juan who was opening the bathroom door for Walton.

'Captain who? Joo know this Captain, Juan?'

Juan shook his head.

'Eh, Juan. Have joo seen Pablo? Perhaps he can tell us.'

Before Juan could answer, the door crashed open and Ieuan lurched into the room. Juan fumbled for his gun but Ieuan was too fast for him. Captain Hook's right hand held the 9mm in its holster while his left arm pinned Juan to the wood-panelled wall by the throat with the metal hook dangerously close to his neck.

'Gentlemen, gentlemen,' soothed El Cameleon and then, with a look of delight, 'Ieuan 'enge! Ees that really joo in there? Ees very good. I hardly recognise joo, man!'

Ieuan, surprised at seeing his major investor, released Juan and turned to face El Cameleon. A thin, sycophantic smile stretched itself across his unnaturally white teeth.

'Hi, Felipe. We meet at last. It's really great to see you here, man. I've just got a bit of a thing going on here at the moment. I was looking for my man, Walton. You haven't seen him, have you?'

'Wal-ton? No, I do not theenk so,' said El Cameleon, hamming it up.

'Strange,' replied Ieuan casting his eyes around the room. 'I could have sworn I saw him come in here just a moment ago.'

El Cameleon clamped a thin frog's leg of an arm around Ieuan's shoulder and said amicably, 'Joo work too hard, my friend. You need to relax. Why don't joo and me have a mescal or two before we join the party, eh?'

***

Within minutes of his arrival at Halfrod Hall, the Patterdale terrier, Mackerel, had spotted his quarry for the evening. Following the crowd of traders across the field to the house, the small black dog had broken away from the main group and skirted the buildings until he found the entrance to the kitchens. He announced his presence on a couple of dustbins and a nearby Ford Fiesta before deciding to enter the building. Before he could get to the door, he was stopped in his tracks by a terrifying sound; a hiss so powerful it sounded like air escaping from a lorry tyre. The hackles immediately rose on the terrier's back and his body tensed as all of his instincts told him that he was in the presence of a formidable adversary. The sound was coming from above. Slowly, he looked up.

High up on the brick wall by the kitchen garden squatted the malevolent form of Suki, the seven-year-old Maine Coon house cat.

Mackerel relaxed a little. From his experience, he knew that he was a match for any cat. From this angle, the cat in question looked like a pushover; just another soft, puffy ball of piss and bad temper. It is impossible to say whether it was optimism, ignorance or myopia on the terrier's part which was responsible for this huge strategic error. It was probably a combination of all three.

Mackerel retreated a couple of feet to give himself room for manoeuvre in the coming struggle. Without taking her eyes off the canine interloper, Suki rose to her feet releasing her small Christmas tree of a fluffed tail, arched her back and let out another hiss of such violence that Mackerel felt a strange sensation. It was fear. Even at this distance, he could tell that this was no neighbourhood moggy or over-fed family pet. This cat was bigger than he was. Substantially bigger.

With eyes remaining fixed on the terrier, Suki moved slowly and deliberately along the wall, jumped down onto the top of a coal bunker and paused there to consider her next move.

Mackerel's pulse was racing. The noise from the busy kitchens provided the only background to the thudding of blood in his ears. Before he had a chance to formulate a plan, the cat again took the initiative.

With a feral snarl, Suki jumped down from the coal-bunker. Mackerel realised that his earlier estimate of the cat had been overly optimistic. This cat was nearly twice his size with teeth, claws and attitude to match. The combatants circled each other like wild west gunfighters, looking for any sign of fear or weakness that could be exploited. Both crouched down, every nerve, muscle and sinew tensed for the fray when the crash of a dustbin lid falling to the ground suddenly broke the tension and both cat and dog bolted in opposite directions taking the 'flight' rather than the damaging 'fight' option.

31. PARTY PEOPLE

CROESUS and Dr. Subudar had been circulating but Croesus's wheelchair and his 'Alan Titchmarsh-ing' had made progress difficult. Subudar had spotted a discreet lift positioned to the right of the main staircase.

The lift descended to the kitchen level and the doors opened onto a storage area. Subudar and Croesus were as surprised to see the group of heavily-armed policemen as the policemen were to see an old bloke in a wheelchair and, judging from the stethoscope around his neck, what appeared to be his doctor. Surprise gave way to confusion as the figure in the wheelchair waved and said, 'Alan Titchmarsh!' before the doors closed and the lift took off for the upper floors.

The policemen all looked at the team leader who growled. 'Come on you lot. Concentrate!'

On the first floor, the doors opened and Subudar and Croesus carefully manoeuvred the wheelchair out of the lift and along the sumptuously-carpeted corridor. As they turned a corner, they could hear voices behind a door. Not strident, aggressive voices, but voices whispering.

Croesus motioned towards the door. He wanted to enter but Subudar was not so sure. In moments of high tension he could still remember the excellent advice he received at medical school all those years ago. At this moment, foremost in his mind was the caveat, 'Never follow directions given by an individual who has recently suffered brain trauma.'

To him it seemed a sound piece of advice, like 'never search for a petrol leak with a match' or 'never parachute into an area which you have recently carpet-bombed'. Croesus, however, was most insistent and he was, after all, paying the bills. Taking a deep breath, Subudar watched Croesus turn the door handle before propelling his charge into the room beyond.

Subudar had never been that close to the business end of a .455 Webley service revolver. Croesus could not remember whether he had ever had a 9mm automatic pointed at his head before but he suspected not. Fear gave way to relief when he saw that the Webley was in the secure grip of his sister Penelope and that the 9mm belonged to someone who was obviously one of her strange 'intelligence friends'. On the chaise, in the middle of the room, sat Spon poring over a computer.

'Croesus,' barked Penelope. 'What the hell are you doing here?'

'I wanted to come and see how the old place was getting along.'

'Oh!' she said. 'Thank God! You can talk again. We don't have to put up with that 'Alan Titchmarsh' nonsense any longer.'

'Alan Titchmarsh,' said Croesus.

'Yes,' said Penelope. 'That's what I said. Alan Titchmarsh.'

'I am sorry,' said Subudar, 'but he still has the occasional relapse.'

'Ah yes,' said Croesus. 'Doctor Subudar. This is my sister Penelope and, Penelope, this is my consultant neurologist, Alan Titchmarsh.'

They were interrupted by Spon.

'It seems that our Mr. Henge has been foolish enough to leave his laptop unattended. Let's just take the computer with us and we can then dismantle his criminal empire at our leisure.'

'Let's do it,' said Penelope. 'Do not dally! Now we can get out of here.'

Healey raised a finger to his lips. Someone was approaching down the corridor but it sounded like he had gone into another room. Spon gathered up the computer and hard drives, deposited them into a hold-all and attempted, with difficulty to lift it. Penelope looked at the sad scene and motioned for Healey to pick up the hold all. As he stepped forward, a panel in the wall slid open. Walton stepped smartly into the room, bringing down the handle of his automatic sharply onto the back of Healey's head.

The intelligence officer slumped to the floor. Walton stepped forward and quickly relieved Penelope of her revolver saying as he did so, 'What do we have here? Quite the little thieves bazaar, don't we.'

'You mean 'isn't it',' said Penelope.

'Look Lady. I'm the one with the gun and the computer so frankly I don't give a fifty-cent blow job about your English syntax and grammar.'

'Evidently. I suppose you're going to hand us over to that blond-haired loony tune, Henge,' said Penelope.

Before Walton could answer, the wood-panelled door flew open and Ieuan entered the room. He had swapped his metal hook for the altogether more useful Uzi machine pistol.

'Aha!' said Ieuan triumphantly levelling the Uzi at Walton.

'Oho!' he added, surprised by the other occupants of the room. Walton appeared to be the person least pleased to see him.

'Alan Titchmarsh!' said Croesus pointing at Ieuan.

'What do we have here?' said Ieuan.

'What's with the Uzi, Ieuan? I was just on my way to get you,' said Walton.

'Oh really?' said Ieuan, wavering.

'I've just spent the last hour tracking these idiots. They were just about to steal your laptop when I stopped them! I was just on my way to find you,' said Walton raising the holdall full of computers.

'Actually, Sport,' said Ieuan dropping the barrel of the Uzi to the floor, 'this might be a convenient way of getting rid of all of my problems in one go. But it'll have to wait until after the auction. Nothing must be allowed to get in the way of that.'

He pressed the machine pistol into Walton's hands fixing him with an unblinking stare.

'Your party organisation's pretty crap. Let's see if you can keep these idiots under guard for the next couple of hours without fucking it up. There'll be time to consider your future tomorrow. Now, I've got to go. I've got a fortune to make!'

So saying he turned, pausing for a millisecond to admire himself in the cheval mirror, and left the room.

'I bet you're looking forward to that little chat ...' said Penelope.

'Don't you ever shut up?' responded Walton but Penelope was on a roll.

'He doesn't like your parties. He's started pointing guns in your direction and now he wants to discuss your future. Mmm... As you Americans say, looks like your 'ass' is toast. Although how you make toast from a beast of burden has always been a mystery to me.'

Walton had no intention of waiting around for that particular conversation with Ieuan. He was more interested in finding El Cameleon. If he was lucky, he could leave it to the diminutive Mexican drug lord to remove Ieuan, clearing the way for him to step into his previous employer's shoes.

'Just for once, Penny,' said Walton, enjoying Penelope's grimace, 'You've got it right. Ieuan's history. The future's burrito-shaped and I've just got me a super-size helping.'

He crossed quickly to the door in the panelled wall, sliding it closed. He then made for the door, levelled the Uzi at his prisoners but then thought better of it. He left pulling the door closed behind him and locking it.

'He's locked us in,' said Spon, his voice hitting the octave.

'In the circumstances', said Penelope, 'I think we should be grateful for how things have turned out. It's just a shame we don't have that laptop.'

***

Terry had finally found Peter.

'Figgis! Is that you?' he bellowed over the music.

He poked the ghillie-suited figure in front of him. The figure lifted its mask and replied:

'Sorry, no,' said Jayne being careful not to take her eyes off Sergeant Rimmer who, positioned across the room, was in touch with the SNIF command vehicle.

'But if you are looking for Peter Figgis, he's here.'

She tapped another plant-like figure on the shoulder and yelled into his ear, 'There's a bloke here who wants a word with you.'

Peter squinted at Terry. He'd never really imagined seeing his principal dressed as a vegetable and so it took a couple of seconds for the penny to drop.

'Oh! Hi Terry!' was the best he could come up with.

'Don't you 'Hi Terry' me with all the trouble you've caused. This operation is terminated. Operation Wild Goose is now officially concluded. I want you out of that ridiculous suit, out of this ridiculous party and out of my department at the earliest possible opportunity.'

'Oh, don't be like that, Terry. Loosen up a bit. It's a party! Enjoy yourself! Didn't I see Maurice here earlier?'

'Oh God!' said Terry. 'Yes, you probably did. Do you know where he is now?'

Peter glanced in the direction of an unconscious figure draped over an ornamental fountain. His trousers had been drawn down and a plastic daffodil inserted into an orifice not originally designed for the job.'

As they both gazed at the debauched sight, Peter added, 'Makes you proud to be Welsh, doesn't it?'

Terry shook his head.

'Still the traders from Caerphilly didn't get hold of him before he'd spilled the beans to me about Operation Wild Goose. Your little diversionary tactic to keep me occupied whilst you got rid of the evidence of the huge amounts of money wasted on departmental jollies. Well, looks like your little plan hasn't worked out.'

'Oh, I don't know about that,' responded Terry. 'We've

been destroying the files you left in your office since the day you departed. Can't imagine there's much left by now.'

'Oh, those? Didn't I mention? They were just the leftovers from the old investigation. I scanned the files for the foreign trips so I could work on them at home. I can't recall how many digital copies there are. It's so easy nowadays,' said Peter.

Terry felt faint, 'Well you've really done it, this time. You realise that copying official documents is a sacking offence.'

'Sorry, Terry,' said Peter. 'You've mistaken me for someone who gives a shit.'

They were interrupted by Jayne.

'Both of you. Shut up. Something's happening.'

The music stopped abruptly and the lights were turned up. Without his periwig and tricorn hat, Ieuan was instantly recognisable with his closely-cropped platinum hair. He walked quickly down the side of the main hall. He stepped around a ghillie suit-clad figure which lay unmoving across his path as one would around a small crocodile and made his way up to the platform which housed the DJ and all his works. The platform backed into a large bay window, the view through mostly taken up by the brightly-lit marquee gently billowing in the night breeze. Having completed a complicated gangster-style hand-shake with the DJ, Ieuan took up his position behind the microphone and drew in a long deep, breath.

A hush fell over the crowd of drug dealers, gangsters, investors and traders as they waited to hear Ieuan speak.

'Friends, honoured guests, gate-crashers ...'

Beneath stairs, Rimmer and his officers were ready to burst into the party and bring the evening's things to a shuddering halt.

Outside, in SNIF's mobile communications unit, Chief Inspector Bellend was waiting for the word.

In the main hall, Jayne had been watching and reporting back to her superior the activities of the last half hour. The previously unemployed security elves had spent much of the time moving through the crowd. Some guests had been issued with some sort of ticket which gained them entrance into the huge well-lit marquee behind Halfrod Hall. Those who could not produce the ticket were left to their own devices finishing the food and drink from the party.

'I think we're nearly there,' she said to Bellend on the headset concealed within her ghillie suit head-dress.' Just a couple more seconds ...'

The end of her sentence was lost in what sounded like a huge explosion. Bellend and his colleagues piled out of the back of the van. There was another blast. Their faces were illuminated by a series of loud combustions and fingers of fire reaching up into the night sky. And another explosion. Every officer present felt the blast wave even at this considerable distance closely followed by another blast.

'Christ!' said Bellend before he was cut short by another huge combustion. 'How many's that?'

He lip-read a constable's attempt to answer 'Five' before his voice was again overwhelmed by another massive explosion.

'Get onto Central and get the emergency services here right away,' he shouted, ears ringing.

'I want everything that's available. Fire, ambulance, army, the AA and …' he hesitated, '… even Her Majesty's Bloody Department for Tax & Sodding Revenue Affairs as I have a sneaking suspicion that they are somehow involved in this twenty-four carat cock-up.'

32. FETCH!

THIRTY minutes earlier, Pablo had found himself wandering about in the dark behind the giant marquee. In front of him stood two lines of containers in a chevron formation. He walked slowly around and between them.

He needed to be alone. He needed time to think. Where had he gone wrong with his life? He'd worked for El Cameleon since the early years when the boss had simply been known as Felipe. Everyone knew Felipe. He was the only drug-lord in the region who weighed less than one hundred and twenty pounds and his taste in suits meant that he was probably the only drug-lord who didn't rely on satellites to be clearly visible from space. Still he wouldn't have survived long without Pablo and his gang providing protection and enforcement services. And now, Felipe was going to bring in this gringo Walton and make him second-in-command.

The final metal container loomed out of the darkness. Another hundred yards and he found the scaffolding which was prepared for the firework display which was to bring the event to a close after the auction.

'I ask joo,' he muttered to himself, 'Would Felipe have survived to become El Cameleon had it not been for me or Juan or Jesus and all those guys who are now dead?'

He stumbled back across the field in the dark to the container. He sat down on the step. Just inside, there was a large Maglite torch. He switched it on and shone it into the gloomy, dank interior of the container. The pyrotechnics guys had come well prepared. The container was full of rockets, catherine-wheels and crackers with lots of spares. He rummaged around in the first crate and picked out a bag of sparklers. He let it fall back into the crate, unimpressed. But then he noticed a small box.

'Thees is more like it, Amigo,' he muttered.

Pablo had fond childhood memories of bangers. It was the closest he could get to the sound of gunfire when he was five. At seven, his predilection for torture and cruelty began to develop when he started taping bangers to a range of household pets and marvelling at the bloodthirsty results. By the age of ten, he had extended this activity to a money-earning exercise by threatening to shove lighted bangers down the trousers of his schoolmates unless they handed over their lunch money.

'Ah. Memories,' he crooned.

A noise in the undergrowth made him switch off the light and reach for the gun in his pocket. He stopped breathing and listened. Nothing. He relaxed again.

'Problem ees, Pablo, The Boss. He may not be very strong but he is very clever. Joo would not be able to trick him even if joo wanted to.'

On the whole, he decided, his position as an important member of El Cameleon's cartel was as good a place to be as any, even if it did mean the occasional public humiliation. Just kill who needs to be killed, do as you are told and take the money. No, not a bad situation at all. Much better than the poor gringo, Walton.

''enge rides him like a burro,' Pablo thought. 'At least El Cameleon uses the whip only when absolutely necessary.'

He took a banger from the box and lit it immediately chucking it into the long grass behind the trailer just to test how long the fuse would burn for.

'Bang!' Ten seconds. Quite long, he thought.

The short, sharp explosion not only lifted his spirits but also frightened whatever it was that had been moving about in the dark only moments before. He squinted into the gloom and saw a small black dog watching him from a safe distance.

Pablo picked up a stick and chucked it down a few feet in front of him. After the cat incident earlier in the evening, Mackerel had also been wandering around aimlessly and was happy to pass the time playing 'fetch' with this solitary human. He retrieved the stick and dropped it by Pablo's boot.

'Joo're a good dog, aren't you,' said Pablo encouragingly and tossed the stick again saying 'Fetch!' as he did so.

Again, Mackerel brought it back and dropped it on the ground. Pablo threw the stick further this time. Mackerel broke into a trot to retrieve it and even looked eager to continue the game. This was what Pablo had been waiting for. Too many years going about his violent business meant that his innate cruelty just couldn't help rising to the surface to spoil even this innocent entertainment.

Mackerel retrieved the stick and dropped it at Pablo's feet but this time the dog noticed that Pablo was preparing to throw a different stick, one which had something sparkly at one end. Even if he had doubts about this, the Patterdale could not resist the urge to fetch this new object. As the banger described an arc through the dark and landed just beyond the end of the container, Mackerel shot after it. As he picked up the banger, being careful to avoid the hot end, his canine senses told him that he was in danger. He looked up just in time to see Suki trying to sneak past the end of the container. Without hesitation, Mackerel took off in pursuit.

Pablo rubbed his hands with diabolical glee waiting for the explosion and demise of the small black dog. But it was not to be. In the time it took the banger's fuse to expire, Pablo experienced the following.

Anticipation gave way to surprise as he saw a large cat sprint for cover into the container full of fireworks. Surprise immediately gave way to anxiety as he saw the small black dog follow the cat with an unexploded banger still held firmly in its jaws. Anxiety gave way to horror as Pablo realised the likely outcome of this series of events. He sprinted away from the container as fast as he could.

Seconds earlier, in the gloomy interior of the firework container, Mackerel rushed in to find Suki cornered and preparing for a life-and-death struggle. He dropped the banger which rolled beneath a large pallet of pyrotechnics and made a lunge for the cat. His senses reeled as the bear-like paw of the Maine Coon complete with five razor-like claws slashed him across the face. One claw became lodged in the corner of his nostril. Mackerel recoiled in pain and confusion and took to his heels, howling. His nose hurt so much he barely noticed the fat, panting Mexican gangster he overtook.

Suki's victory although complete, was short-lived.

From some distance away Pablo heard the initial explosion of the banger followed directly by an apocalyptic combustion heralded by what appeared to be a flaming cat being shot into the lower reaches of the stratosphere. The forty-foot container acted like a medieval cannon, directing a shaft of fire across the aisle into the open doors of the container opposite, which set off a chain reaction as the cocaine and other narcotics ignited.

The explosion of the third container rendered the marquee and its contents a blasted wreck. The shaft of fire from the final container punched its way through the bay window into the interior of Halfrod Hall. After six deafening explosions all that remained were six twisted hulks of containers illuminated by their own fires.

Pablo hardly had time to survey his handiwork before his sense of duty returned. 'El Jefe!' he thought. 'I must save El Jefe!'

El Cameleon was in the main entrance hall, just on his way into the marquee when Walton found him. His first attempt at updating his new boss on the situation with Ieuan was lost in the roar of the first explosion.

Walton tried a second time but his words were redacted by the explosion of the second container.

After that, Walton gave up. Both he and El Cameleon were too disorientated by the noise and flames for any normal conversation. Everything became a blur. Their ears were ringing. Guests were rushing to exit the building. Traders were stocking up on food and drink before rushing to exit the building. The sudden arrival of armed police on the scene brought them to their senses. In the smoke and mayhem, Walton noticed Pablo entering through the gap which had once been occupied by the bay window. Despite his girth, the Mexican gangster could run like the wind. He covered the length of what had been the main hall like an Olympic sprinter. 'Jefe!' he shouted as he made directly for El Cameleon who was brushing the dust from his suit. Almost without slowing down, he grabbed the diminutive figure of El Cameleon and tucked him beneath his arm as one would a gun case and continued on his way exiting via the gap which had recently been filled by the marquee.

'Oh well,' thought Walton. 'Better follow their excellent example.' Dropping the Uzi, he ran after Pablo as quickly as the holdall of computers would allow.

***

In a limousine on the M25, the events of the early evening were being analysed.

'I don't think we have missed much by leaving early,' said the Amir.

'But please enlighten me, Excellency,' said Anwar. 'The man with the flower in his bottom in the fountain, was this another strange English tradition?'

'None of which I am aware, Anwar,' replied the Amir graciously. 'It is true. The English are a strange people. It is hard to understand a culture that allows alcohol, bacon sandwiches, women drivers and voting.'

He let out a long sigh.

'I weary of Mr. Henge and his associates. They are not nice people. After this evening's auction I shall not be investing in such ventures again, Anwar.'

'I will make a note, Excellency,' said Anwar dutifully.

His mind raced. Anwar had wanted to stay until the end. Alcohol, semi-naked women, canapés with forbidden food stuffs and strangely clad men being used as flower vases. If such debauchery took place early in the evening at these parties, there must be many fat ladies all singing very loudly by the end of the party. He was truly sorry to have missed that.

'I am finding the very fat ladies most appealing ...' he muttered to himself as he made a note in his diary.

33. THE MORNING AFTER THE NIGHT BEFORE

THE next morning, Chief Inspector Bellend paced through the smoking wreckage of what had been the southern elevation of Halfrod Hall. He had hardly slept. Since the first explosion at around midnight, he had struggled to piece together an explanation for the night's events. On several occasions he thought he had succeeded only to have his hopes dashed by some inconvenient piece of evidence or eyewitness account.

Halfrod Hall had been reduced to a war zone. 'Just for once,' he thought, 'they can't blame this on SNIF's armed response.'

His original plan was to contain and hold the party-goers and go through identities and details, methodically weeding out the known drug felons for further processing. The plan was blown to bits by the first explosion with most of the drug dealers who, fearing the worst, burst from every door and window of the Hall putting as much distance between themselves and the action as possible.

'It must have been one of Henge's competitors that blew up that first container,' said Sergeant Rimmer.

'Care to volunteer any names, Sergeant?' said Bellend bitterly.

Answer came there none.

'And what about the party-goers? Who did you manage to catch?' continued Bellend.

'Well, in the lads' defence, Sir, it wasn't an easy job. Most of the guests were heavily camouflaged.'

In fact, it had been impossible. He himself had attempted to follow a group heavily laden with what looked like trays of food as they made their way back to the game fair site. As soon as they lay down and stopped moving, they were invisible in the dark.

'So who did we nick, Sergeant?'

'Er, well, there's a couple of them in the van who refuse to give their names but they don't seem to be your usual villains. Off their heads on drugs if you ask me, Sir,' said Rimmer.

'All right, we'll start with them.'

The back door of the police van opened to reveal two men clad in ghillie suits.

'And about time, too!' said the older of the two. 'I demand to speak to your commanding officer.'

'I'm in charge here,' said Bellend. 'Who are you?'

'I'm Maurice Grymm, principal secretary at Her Majesty's Department of Revenue and Tax Affairs. And this is ...'

'Course you are, Sir,' said Rimmer, smirking. 'See what I mean, Sir. La-la Land, both of 'em, if you ask me.'

The other figure kept his face covered and muttered 'shut up' to his companion.

'And who do we have here?' continued Bellend. 'Hang on a minute. Sergeant take that mask away from his face.'

Bellend squinted at the face before the penny dropped.

'Fancy seeing you here, Mr Dudley-Vaughan. What a surprise. Doing a little fieldwork are you?'

Terry groaned.

'I trust you've left your secretary back at the office this time. Just as well, really. Rimmer here's armed and wouldn't hesitate to use his weapon in self-defence.'

Rimmer blushed angrily.

'Now look, Chief Inspector. I was only here backing up our incompetent field operative, Figgis. You can ask him, if you like. He'll back me up.'

'Oh, I will, Mr Dudley-Vaughan. I will,' replied Bellend.

Maurice seemed unphased by the situation and was in full whingeing mode.

'Look here, whatever your name is, I don't care if you and Terry here are old muckers from down the lodge or whatever. I'll have you know that I have been held in this van for several hours in quite some discomfort. My arse feels like a .416 bullet wound and I need urgent medical attention.'

Sergeant Rimmer slammed the van door.

'Has DS Harvey come up with anything?' asked Bellend.

But he knew that even Jayne had been concentrating on Henge when the first explosion took place. She had been as surprised as the rest of them.

'What about the 'wild card'?'

By way of response, Rimmer pointed to Jayne and Peter who were picking their way through the wreckage in the cold morning light.

'How are things, Harvey?' asked her superior officer. 'You didn't get hurt, did you?'

'No, Sir,' said Jayne. 'We were lucky. The blast missed us. Were there many casualties?'

'Mostly wounds from flying glass,' said Rimmer. 'Amazingly, we haven't had one confirmed fatality yet. Although there's still a few to be accounted for.'

'Who's this?' said Bellend, turning to Peter.

'Oh. This is special investigator Figgis from the Tax & Revenue,' said Jayne before Peter could speak. 'He's been a great help.'

'That's not what I've heard. Did you know that your Mr Dudley-Vaughan was here?'

'Yes,' said Peter. 'I saw him here last night and … Maurice Grymm, I think.'

'Step this way, if you would, Mr Figgis.'

The two policemen guided him to the rear of the police van. Rimmer opened the doors.

'Ah Figgis. Thank God! Please tell Chief Inspector Bellend here that I was here yesterday evening to support you in your mission.'

Even though Peter could clearly remember Terry's stream of threats from the previous evening he still felt a residual loyalty to his superior.

'Is this right, Figgis?'

Before he could answer, a figure appeared from the far side of the van. The figure seemed strangely familiar but Peter had difficulty in placing the smartly-suited individual who was now having a quiet word with Bellend. A card was flashed and then replaced in an inside pocket.

Bellend motioned to Rimmer who stepped forward, 'Right, you two. Out. This gentleman and his friends want a word with you.'

'Is he a doctor?' asked Maurice as he limped down from the van.

A plain clothes policeman with a severe military hair-cut applied handcuffs to them both.

'Is that strictly necessary?' said Peter to Bellend.

'On matters of security, I'm afraid it is,' replied Bellend.

'No need to worry about Mr Dudley-Vaughan and Mr Grymm,' said the smartly suited man. 'They have an appointment with the Cabinet Secretary who will be asking them a lot of impertinent questions about their international travel expenses thanks to those files you collated, Peter. But before that there's the matter of employing attractive female Russian spies as research assistants.'

'Oh God!' moaned Terry.

'In short, Mr Dudley-Vaughan, your department tea-lady, Mrs. Krasnogorsk, has coughed and you are … how do Russian speakers put it? ... up to your *siski* in the *derrmo*.'

Suddenly, the penny dropped. Gone was the beard, long hair, the Somerset accent, the wellies and the camo clothing but Peter now definitely recognised his former teacher.

'Abe?' said Peter. 'Is that you?'

'I'm afraid it is, Peter. I hope all of that bollocks that Nigel and I taught you back in Ealing didn't get you into too much trouble. You see the whole thing was dumped on us at rather short notice so I'm afraid that you were given the edited highlights from the Bare Girls' Christmas Survival Guide and Roy More's Road Kill For Special Occasions.'

Peter was speechless, 'You mean it was all made up!'

'Yeah,' said Abe. 'All apart from the cider, anyway. Neither Nigel nor I have ever spent more than a weekend outside London. Nigel can't because of all his allergies. And I choose not to because I like my creature comforts.'

'So the carp bed?'

'Yep. Never slept on one of those. And certainly not in the back of a van.'

'And the rabbit?'

'Only the second time I'd ever done it. Nasty, eh?'

'Market frame?'

'New to me. That's why I told you to do it. Not because you needed the practice, I just didn't know how to?'

'Bloody Hell!' said Peter, exasperated.

A constable arrived holding an evidence bag.

'What do we have here?' asked Bellend.

The bag contained a shiny gold object about half-an-inch long.

'Is it a filling?' asked Rimmer.

'No. Too symmetrical,' said Bellend.

'Looks like a cufflink,' said Peter.

'It's got some initials engraved on it,' said Jayne peering into the bag. 'There's an "I" and then it's an "H".'

Their deliberations were interrupted by Maurice.

'For God's sake! Do you people have any form of social life at all? It's plainly an 'albert' belonging to someone whose initials are "IH".'

Jayne smiled. Bellend, Rimmer and Peter chorused 'Albert?'

'Yes,' said Maurice. 'To put through a hole in your todger!'

'But how do you go to the loo?' asked Rimmer.

'Not that hole. You idiot,' said Maurice. 'You have to get another one done using a surgical punch.'

The full awfulness of what was being suggested now dawned upon Sergeant Rimmer. As the blood drained from his face and his knees buckled Bellend shouted, 'Catch him, somebody!'

Maurice was undeterred, 'Now I've helped you with your enquiries, please can you get me a doctor!'

He and Terry were led off.

'So, we have to assume that this small and unpleasant nugget is all that is left of our criminal mastermind and wannabe drugs lord, Ieuan Henge,' said Bellend.

'It's possible,' said Jayne. 'He must have taken the full blast of that final explosion when it came through the bay window. Strange that this is the only thing left though.'

***

Penelope, Spon and the heavily-bandaged Healey sat on the bench by the kitchen garden wall. Doctor Subudar stood next to Croesus's wheelchair.

'Well, at least we're in the clear,' said Croesus. 'No one could possibly imagine us having anything to do with all this. We were locked in that room all the time.'

'Daddy would have been heart-broken to see Halfrod Hall in this state,' said Penelope. 'It's going to cost a fortune to put it back together again.'

'I shouldn't concern yourself about that,' said Spon soothingly. 'Even in the darkest hour, there's always insurance.'

'At least we have got control of the business again,' said Croesus conveniently glossing over his part in the chaos of the preceding months.

Penelope was about to say something but Spon patted her hand gently. She remained silent. Unexpectedly, Spon then held her hand. He expected to be rebuffed but was pleasantly surprised by Penelope's acquiescence.

'Yes,' said Croesus. 'I think that's the last we'll see of … oh, what's his name ... you know.' He was tired after the exertions of the previous night and struggled to remember.

'Alan Titchmarsh?' suggested Healey.

'Yes, that's the one,' said Croesus. 'Ieuan ... Ieuan Henge.'

34. POSTSCRIPT

HIGH up in the control tower of Birmingham Airport, an air traffic controller was shouting into his headset, 'What are you doing, you bloody idiot? AV 270 you are not cleared for take-off ... Stop your run and return to ...'

But it was too late. The private jet was already halfway down the runway and heading towards take-off speed. To say that the atmosphere in the cockpit was tense would be an understatement.

Nelson, the Brazilian pilot, hated these ad hoc, unauthorised take-offs. It was the one thing about being a drug lord's private pilot that he had never got used to. As the plane banked sharply, the tail section of a Boeing 747 filled the cockpit windshield. 'Close,' he thought, 'but we've had closer.' He exhaled and, as the jet gained altitude, he started to relax by thinking about the huge amount of American dollars he was paid each month by El Cameleon and the good things that this amount of money allowed him to introduce into his life. The beachfront property, the fast cars and – Ay, ay, ay – the *chicas*.

Back in the leather upholstery and hardwood furniture of the passenger compartment, the atmosphere was also tense.

'So you mean, Wal-ton,' said El Cameleon, 'that was it ... total? 'enge had put all his 'eggs' – how you say? – 'in one basket'.'

'Eggs,' repeated Pablo chuckling.

'That's pretty much the long and short of it,' said Walton. 'His entire stockpile of product was held in those five containers and the whole lot went up in smoke.'

El Cameleon licked his fingers and rubbed his eyes. It had been an exhausting twenty-four hours and he was still trying to wrap his sleep-deprived head around the night's events. On the positive side of things, he had seen with his own eyes the size of the market for his 'products' here in the UK. He had also won over the gringo, Wal-ton. On the negative side, he had lost money on the trip, he had lost the stockpile of drugs he was looking forward to inheriting from Ieuan Henge and he had spent far too long tucked beneath Pablo's warm, sweaty armpit. He sniffed his jacket sleeve. 'I will have to burn this.' He made a mental note.

'So, Wal-ton. You see my problem. I bring you in to run the European distribution of my operation but then – 'Bang!' – I have no product to distribute.'

'Bang,' chuckled Pablo.

'So.' El Cameleon brought both eyes to bear upon Walton, who found the experience unnerving. 'What you do for me now, Wal-ton?'

'Jefe,' said Walton. 'Have you heard of designer drugs or legal highs? This is what young people in Europe and the States are now turning to. They consider our type of product to be outdated, unfashionable. Designer drugs are a lot easier to manufacture and are often entirely legal.'

Pablo snorted his disbelief but El Cameleon silenced him with a raised hand. The combination of words like 'fashion', 'designer' and 'drugs' appealed to him.

'Tell me more, Wal-ton.'

Walton was flying by the seat of his pants and he knew it. Still, it was better than flying outside the plane half-way across the Atlantic. Hell, he was always at his best when the pressure was on.

***

'This man's backside is more glass than arse,' said Sir John Stiffener as he surveyed the set of buttocks on the operating table in front of him. 'I'm not sure whether we should operate on it or glue coloured paper around it and make a kaleidoscope.'

Since his suspension from the private clinic, pending an investigation into the Croesus Massey-Itch case, Sir John had been keeping his hand in at the local accident and emergency department. He was on good form. The 'blood and guts' of A&E was more to his liking than the ego massage and bedside manner of private practice.

'Who is he, Subudar?'

'Not Subudar, Sir John. My name is Chowdry.'

'Of course, of course,' said Sir John apologetically, as he picked up a shiny set of pincers and started removing the bloody shards.

'Unknown, apparently,' said Dr. Chowdry. 'The rather striking woman who brought him in was not in much better a state. They both looked like they'd been in some sort of crash or fire. She waited to be seen for the first two hours in A&E but obviously gave up in and wandered off leaving him face down on the floor.'

'Whoever it is, he's had a lot of expensive American dental work done and there's some scarring around the hairline that suggests some cosmetic work as well. I've never seen hair like this either. It's almost white. He isn't an albino, is he?' said the anaesthetist.

The surgical team stopped and stared at the anaesthetist in appalled silence.

'Oh let's just drop everything and check, shall we?' said Doctor Chowdry sarcastically. 'Look, Whiffy. Why don't you just concentrate on keeping the patient alive and unconscious. We'll deal with the surgical stuff.'

Sir John, Chowdry and the theatre nurse all turned back to the buttocks.

'Bloody cheek,' said Sir John.

'Oh, sorry Sir John.' said the nurse. 'I thought we'd cleaned him up rather well.'

'No, not these.' replied Sir John. 'Aneasthetists! Always sticking their bloody noses in.'

The anaesthetist adopted a hounded expression behind his mask.

'I heard a good joke, last week,' said the theatre nurse.

'Oh, go on, then,' said Doctor Chowdry.

'There was this advert, right?' she said eagerly, 'in the back of The Lancet. It read: 'To A Good Home, Grey's Anatomy, latest edition. No longer needed. Anaesthetist knows it all!'

Once the laughter had died down, Sir John removed the last of the fragments of glass and dropped them into the stainless-steel kidney dish.

'Well it looks like our boy here was lucky. The damage appears to be mostly superficial but that bit there looks like it's seen better days. His days as a swimwear model are well and truly over. I just wish I could be as positive about the hole in the end of his todger. It's a hell of a mess. Looks like he caught it on a fishhook or something. Well, even if we can't put it back together again, at least we can introduce him to an oboist to show him how to finger it.'

***

'No one wants you.'

Reginald Trimly-Smugg peered over his bifocals at Peter. He rose from behind the teak monstrosity of Terry's modernist, Danish desk.

'You're damaged goods, old boy. Regardless of what your new pals have promised you, no one will let you through the door of their department. You're a whistle-blower. And what's more, you're an efficient whistle-blower. Frankly speaking, I don't know which is worse.'

Peter let out a long relaxing sigh. He smiled. It really didn't matter. He was in love.

Reginald Trimly-Smugg had been brought in to run the department while Terry was on 'gardening leave' – with full pay and pension rights, of course. Reginald was another Cromwell Club member. If the club had a committee for pettifogging time-servers, he would have been its chairman. If there was a sub-committee for clumsiness, he'd be chairman of that, too.

The news of Maurice and Terry's suspension pending inquiry had spread through the club like bird flu. The full details had been suitably redacted by the investigation team. Any reference to Mrs Krasnogorsk and the talented and flexible Irina, was removed from the official statement. If two high-flyers like Maurice and Terry could be brought down by a mere executive officer then all of their expectations about job security, pension and perks were proved worthless. There was a genuine sense of panic in Cromwell's saloons and smoking rooms.

'Did he really ask for these ghastly paintings?' said Reginald staring in disgusted incomprehension at the painting of Theseus and the Minotaur.

'Ah yes,' said Peter wisely. 'Krapp-Innit.'

'Well. It's not very good but I wouldn't put it quite so bluntly.'

Peter let it go. He was letting everything go. Nothing mattered today because he was in love.

Reginald continued thinking aloud, 'The best we could offer you is a posting overseas. Nothing too menial, you know. You might even get a hat with a dead chicken on it. But, as you know, our choices have diminished in recent years.'

He sauntered over to the drinks' cabinet and scrutinised the items therein eventually lifting up a decanter by its stopper to examine the contents.

'It'd be something on Saint Vargas or Pitcairn Island or some such rock. I'd like to be able to suggest the Caribbean but I'm afraid those postings are quite popular. Can't imagine why.'

The decanter separated from its stopper and fell to the floor with a satisfying crash.

'Drat!' said Reginald. 'Still, I'm sure that Office Supplies will be able to rustle up another.'

'Unlikely,' chipped in Peter, savouring the moment. 'It was part of a set by Lalique made in the twenties. One of Terry's favourite pieces.'

'Are you sure?' asked Reginald nervously.

Peter wasn't but thought 'What the hell. Let him sweat'. He didn't care because he was in love with Jayne Harvey.

'I mean to say,' said Reginald taking a seat on the sofa across from Peter. 'Have you given this matter any thought? What do you see yourself doing? Do you think you can ever fit back into departmental life?'

'To tell you the truth, Reginald.' His superior winced at the informality. 'I'm not sure that I want a future back here.'

'Really?' said Reginald who couldn't believe his luck. 'You mean you actually want to leave the Department. Well, it could make things much easier for us all.'

'Yes,' said Peter decisively. 'Looking back on the experience, I've enjoyed my time on the game fairs and I am thinking about staying on.'

'You mean spend your time travelling around the country and living in vans and so forth? Sounds ghastly. I mean, I was told that Nigel Grind used to send you the stuff you sold. So what are you going to do about stock? What are you going to sell?'

Peter shook his head. 'You see, Reginald. I don't want to sell anything. I'm going to be offering a service. I noticed that many of the businesses at the shows could actually benefit from being VAT registered. That way they could claim back quite a lot each quarter. It's just that no-one's shown them how to do it.'

Reginald was incredulous. 'You mean you're going to help the ... the taxpayers? But that's downright dishonest. You'll be a pariah. You'll never work any department again.'

'Sounds pretty much like the situation I'm in already,' said Peter with a smile.

He didn't care because he was in love with Jayne Harvey and Jayne Harvey was in love with him and together they were going to resign from their old jobs, buy a Land Rover and a caravan and start a new life.

ABOUT THE AUTHOR

Philip Moss was born in 1958 and was educated at Berkhamsted, University College at Buckingham and The Shakespeare Institute at Birmingham University.

He worked as a freelance journalist and speech writer before joining the Conservative Research Department in 1983. He worked as a corporate lobbyist from 1985 to 1990 when he joined Nimbus Records subsequently representing the company in the Far East. From 1995, he ran his own China-based technology agency returning to the UK in 2002 when he started making and selling leather goods for the game and country show circuit.

He published his first freelance article at the age of fourteen and has rarely left the keyboard unbothered since, writing on subjects including cider; local history, vegetables, wine, digital technology, politics, cars, comedy, classical music, restaurants, books, the country show circuit and terriers.

Flogging The Field is the first of three volumes based on game fair life.

Philip is divorced and lives in the UK. He has a son and daughter.

www.ingramcontent.com/pod-product-compliance
Lightning Source LLC
Chambersburg PA
CBHW022124050726
47590CB00002B/397

9781527250154